Plan B

OTHER NORTON BOOKS
BY LESTER R. BROWN

Earth Policy Institute® is a nonprofit environmental research organization providing a vision of an eco-economy and a roadmap on how to get from here to there. It seeks to reach a global constituency through the media and the Internet. Its primary publications are *Eco-Economy: Building an Economy for the Earth*, *The Earth Policy Reader*, and a series of four-page Eco-Economy Updates that assess progress in building an eco-economy. All of these can be downloaded at no charge from the EPI Web site.

Web site: <www.earth-policy.org>

PLAN B

Rescuing a Planet under Stress and a Civilization in Trouble

Lester R. Brown

EARTH POLICY INSTITUTE

W · W · NORTON & COMPANY

NEW YORK   LONDON

The EARTH POLICY INSTITUTE trademark is registered in the U.S. Patent and Trademark Office.

The views expressed are those of the author and do not necessarily represent those of the Earth Policy Institute; of its directors, officers, or staff; or of any funders.

Composition by Elizabeth Doherty; manufacturing by the Maple-Vail Book Manufacturing Group.

ISBN 0-393-05859-x (cloth) 0-393-32523-7 (pbk)

W. W. Norton & Company, Inc., 500 Fifth Avenue,
New York, N.Y. 10110
www.wwnorton.com

W. W. Norton & Company, Ltd., Castle House, 75/76 Wells Street,
London W1T 3QT

1 2 3 4 5 6 7 8 9 0

❸ This book is printed on recycled paper.

To Orville L. Freeman
1918–2003

Orville Freeman was one of the most remarkable public servants of the last century. A World War II veteran and three-term governor of the State of Minnesota, he placed John F. Kennedy's name in nomination for the presidency at the Democratic National Convention in Los Angeles in 1960. This chapter of Freeman's life is described in detail in Rodney Leonard's engaging new book, *Freeman: The Governor Years, 1955–1960*.

As Secretary of Agriculture from 1961 to 1969, Freeman was one of three Kennedy cabinet members, along with Dean Rusk and Stewart Udall, to serve throughout the eight years of the Kennedy-Johnson administration. After leaving the Department, he was for many years the CEO of Business International.

My relationship with Orville Freeman goes back to the U.S. Department of Agriculture, where I served as his advisor on international agricultural policy and later as Administrator of the Department's technical assistance agency, known then as the International Agricultural Development Service. Our official relationship quickly turned into a close personal one, as he became not only a mentor, but a friend.

One of the highlights of our years of working together came in 1965, when we negotiated the reform of agricultural policy in India following a short harvest induced by a monsoon failure. This reform revitalized the country's agriculture, enabling India to double its wheat harvest in seven years, going from being the world's largest wheat importer to being self-sufficient in wheat.

Thus when I founded the Worldwatch Institute in early 1974, it was natural to turn to Orville Freeman to chair the Board of Directors. It could not have been a better choice. During our 21 years as Chairman and CEO we had a close and extraordinarily productive relationship.

Orville Freeman was a football player, playing backup quarterback on the University of Minnesota's national championship team; a Marine who won the Purple Heart for heroism when leading his unit onto the beach at Bougainville Island; and a lawyer. He had the dual distinction of being the youngest governor in Minnesota's history, at age 36, and then the youngest U.S. Secretary of Agriculture, at age 42. On February 20, 2003, the world lost a great public servant and I lost a lifelong friend.

ACKNOWLEDGMENTS

Writing a book of this scope requires a lot of help from other people. First among these is Reah Janise Kauffman, our indefatigable Vice President, who so ably manages the Institute, allowing me to concentrate my energies on research. She coordinates our worldwide network of publishers and marketing of publications. In doing this and in negotiating speaking fees and bulk sales of our books, she has helped boost our earned income to where it now covers half of our budget. And as if this were not enough, she reviewed the manuscript several times, aiding in its evolution.

Janet Larsen, who anchors our research program, has provided invaluable support. I rely heavily on her for research help, assistance in the analysis, and judgment on how to present information. In research and writing, she is my alter ego and my best critic. Viviana Jimenez has been enormously helpful with research, working tirelessly to gather needed information while also providing administrative support.

Millicent Johnson, our Director of Publications Sales, uses her knowledge of customer services to manage our publications department, running the gamut from book procurement to order fulfillment. She also serves as our office quartermaster and assists with bookkeeping.

We'd like to especially thank the United Nations Population Fund for its generous support of *Plan B*. We are also indebted to the Carolyn, Geraldine R. Dodge, Farview, Richard and Rhoda Goldman, William and Flora Hewlett, Shenandoah, Summit, and Turner Foundations and to the Educational Fund of America. Their support enables us to provide and disseminate the vision of an eco-economy.

Earth Policy is also supported by individual donors, including the late Robert Wallace and his wife Raisa Scriabine, Junko Edahiro, and David and Katherine Moore (in memory of their daughter Kate). We are inspired by the generosity of other donors, including Douglas and Deborah Baker, David Blittersdorf, Nancy Loomis Eric, Maureen Hinkle, James McManis, Scott and Hella McVay, Paul Myers and Welthy Soni, Peter Seidel, and Marion Weber.

I am indebted to more than a dozen reviewers of the manuscript, including Board members Judy Gradwohl and William Mansfield. Toby Clark brought his decades of experience as an environmental analyst and administrator to bear on the manuscript, providing both the broad structural suggestions and detailed commentary that money cannot buy. Readers are indebted to him for raising the book to a higher level.

Peter Goldmark, for many years publisher of the *International Herald Tribune*, was extraordinarily helpful in identifying the principal strengths and the weaknesses of the manuscript. Ellen Goldensohn, until recently editor of *Natural History*, provided useful feedback on overall structure. Douglas and Deborah Baker both reviewed the manuscript, helping me to think through some of the more complex technical issues.

Maureen Kuwano Hinkle drew on her 26 years of experience working on agricultural issues with the Environmental Defense Fund and the Audubon Society to review several drafts of the book as it evolved. She provided valuable comments and encouragement all along the way.

Vlatka Landay, who volunteered to do research on the World War II mobilization, also reviewed the manuscript twice, providing feedback and encouragement. Jean Miller, who helped to expand our international press database as a volunteer, also reviewed the manuscript, offering specific suggestions for improving the structure.

My thanks also to individuals who were particularly helpful in providing specific information: Claudine Aholou, L. H. Allen, Jr., Adam Gromis, Ed Mongan, Erich Pica, Reto A. Ruedy, Pedro A. Sanchez, and John E. Sheehy.

As authors know, finding an engaging title can be trying. This one was made easy. When I was describing the book concept to Catherine Cameron, Executive Director of the Wallace Global Fund, she said, "It sounds like Plan B to me." Thanks, Catherine.

We are supported by a network of dedicated publishers for our books and Eco-Economy Updates in some 19 languages—Arabic, Catalan, Chinese, Czech, English, French, Indonesian, Italian, Japanese, Korean, Persian, Polish, Portuguese (in Brazil), Romanian, Russian, Spanish, Swedish, Turkish, and Ukrainian. There are three editions in English (U.S.A./Canada, U.K./Commonwealth, and India), two in Chinese (mainland and Taiwan), and two in Spanish (Spain and Latin America).

These translations are often the work of environmentally committed individuals. In Iran, for example, Hamid Taravati and his wife Farzaneh Bahar, both medical doctors, are concerned not only about the health of their patients but also that of the earth. Our collaboration began 14 years ago at Worldwatch, when Hamid began publishing *State of the World* in Iran. Farzaneh's translation of *Full House* won the Ministry of Culture's award for the best translation of a foreign book.

In China, Lin Zixin, with whom I've worked for nearly 20 years, was responsible for publishing *Eco-Economy*, personally leading the team of translators. I am also grateful to him for arranging a trip to Inner Mongolia and Gansu provinces that helped me better understand the pressures on the land in China's northwest.

In Japan, Soki Oda, who started World Watch Japan nearly 20 years ago, leads our publication efforts. He is already hard at work planning the outreach effort for the release of the Japanese edition of *Plan B*. Junko Edahiro, my interpreter in Japan, has also been extraordinarily helpful. In addition to organizing Japan for Sustainability, she has put together several highly successful fundraisers in Japan for the Earth Policy Institute.

Gianfranco Bologna, with whom I've worked for nearly 25 years, arranges for the publishing of our books in Italian. As head of World Wildlife Fund Italy, he is uniquely positioned to assist us in this effort.

In Brazil, Eduardo Athayde is responsible for translating our books into Portuguese, where he has done an excellent job of organizing fast-paced promotional tours in that country's major cities.

And in Romania, President Ion Iliescu, who started publishing our books some 16 years ago when he headed Editura Tehnica, personally assumes responsibility for getting our books out quickly in Romanian.

A small organization like EPI relies on the goodwill and dedication of many people. A growing number of individuals and organizations are posting our Eco-Economy Updates on their web sites. We are grateful to all, and I especially thank the individuals or groups who translate and post them, including Leif Ohlsson

(Swedish), Li Kangmin (Chinese), Gianfranco Bologna (Italian), Soki Oda (Japanese), Eduardo Athayde (Portuguese), Joseph Robertson (Spanish), Jacques Bougie (French), and Pacific Currents (Russian distributed through its listserv).

This book would not be complete were it not for the editing of Linda Starke, a veteran editor of my books. Linda's sure-fire editing, insight, and environmental knowledge sharpened the book in many ways. Thanks also to Liz Doherty, who responded to our needs for a quick design and layout even though she was starting a new full-time job, and to Ritch Pope, who prepared a useful index.

And finally, saving the best for last, my thanks to the team at W.W. Norton & Company: Amy Cherry, our editor; Lucinda Bartley, her assistant; Andrew Marasia and Anna Oler, who put the book on a fast-track production schedule; Ingsu Liu, Art Director for the book jacket; Bill Rusin, Marketing Director; and Drake McFeely, President, with special thanks for his support. It is a delight to work with such a talented team.

Lester Brown

CONTENTS

PREFACE

Two years ago I wrote a book entitled *Eco-Economy: Building an Economy for the Earth*, which argued that the environment was not part of the economy, as many corporate planners and economists believe, but instead that the economy was part of the environment. If we accept this latter view, I wrote, it follows that the economy must be designed so that it is compatible with the ecosystem of which it is a part.

Eco-Economy described this environmentally compatible economy, noting that we now have the technologies to build it. Almost everything we need to do to build this new economy, I noted, is now being done by one or more countries in the world.

Plan B not only argues further for the restructuring of the economy, it points out why this needs to be done at wartime speed. Time is running out. Whereas historically we lived off the interest generated by the earth's natural capital assets, we are now consuming those assets themselves. We have built an environmental bubble economy, one where economic output is artificially inflated by overconsumption of the earth's natural assets. The challenge today is to deflate the bubble before it bursts.

The most vulnerable economic sector may be food,

where the bubble is most obvious. The overpumping of an aquifer to expand food production in the short run almost guarantees a drop in production in the long run. Although grain production has declined in some smaller countries, it is now declining in China. Over the last five years, China's grain harvest has dropped from 390 million to 340 million tons—a drop equal to the grain harvest of Canada.

Thus far China has been covering its shortfall by drawing down stocks, but it can do so for only another year or two. When China enters the world grain market for massive imports, it will put heavy pressure on exportable grain supplies. We will not have to read about this in the newspapers. We will see the effects at the supermarket checkout counter. Rising food prices may be the first global economic indicator to signal serious trouble between us, now 6.2 billion, and the earth's ecosystem.

The scope of *Plan B* has been limited so that it will be short enough to be read by busy people. There is, for example, no chapter on biological diversity. Yet the principal policy recommendations—stabilizing population and stabilizing climate—are central to protecting the diversity of life. The traditional approach of protecting biological diversity by fencing off land as parks or preserves, as valuable as that is, is not enough. If we cannot stabilize population and if we cannot stabilize climate, there is not an ecosystem on earth we can save.

Nor do I deal with water pollution in any detail. I have concentrated on the emergence of water scarcity as a defining issue of this new century. To the extent that water pollution is reducing the usable supply of water, it is further exacerbating emerging scarcity.

And I have not included environmental education. My good friend Ray Anderson, CEO of Interface, urged that I promote environmental education, especially in business schools. Ray is right. We desperately need to produce a generation of environmentally literate business and financial leaders for tomorrow, but it is my hope that today's business leaders will hear the call to greatness outlined in *Plan B* and respond to it.

And finally, my apologies for using material that I published earlier in articles, Eco-Economy Updates, and even in my last two books. I think it was Ken Galbraith who said, "Self-plagiarism is an indulgence of authors that publishers ought not to tolerate."

It is time to redefine security. Ironically, on September 11, 2001, I was in New York to give a luncheon talk on *Eco-Economy* to the science and environment staff of the *New York Times*. Needless to say, that talk was never delivered. The shift in attention from environmental issues to terrorism that began on that fateful date continues to this day.

The basic point of *Plan B* is that our principal threats are now more environmental than military. Terrorists are a threat. But the destruction wrought by terrorists is likely to be small compared with the worldwide suffering if the environmental bubble economy collapses.

And, finally, I do not have the credentials for writing this book. Nor do I know anyone who does. But someone had to give it a try.

Lester R. Brown

Earth Policy Institute
1350 Connecticut Ave., NW, Suite 403
Washington, DC 20036

Phone: (202) 496-9290
Fax: (202) 496-9325
E-mail: epi@earth-policy.org
Web site: www.earth-policy.org

May 2003

Plan B

1

A Planet under Stress

As world population has doubled and as the global economy has expanded sevenfold over the last half-century, our claims on the earth have become excessive. We are asking more of the earth than it can give on an ongoing basis, creating a bubble economy.

We are cutting trees faster than they can regenerate, overgrazing rangelands and converting them into deserts, overpumping aquifers, and draining rivers dry. On our cropland, soil erosion exceeds new soil formation, slowly depriving the soil of its inherent fertility. We are taking fish from the ocean faster than they can reproduce.

We are releasing carbon dioxide (CO_2) into the atmosphere faster than nature can absorb it, creating a greenhouse effect. As atmospheric CO_2 levels rise, so does the earth's temperature. Habitat destruction and climate change are destroying plant and animal species far faster than new species can evolve, launching the first mass extinction since the one that eradicated the dinosaurs 65 million years ago.

Throughout history, humans have lived on the earth's sustainable yield—the interest from its natural endowment. But now we are consuming the endowment itself. In ecology, as in economics, we can consume principal along with interest in the short run, but in the long run it leads to bankruptcy.

In 2002, a team of scientists led by Mathis Wacker-nagel, an analyst at Redefining Progress, concluded that humanity's collective demands first surpassed the earth's regenerative capacity around 1980. Their study, published by the U.S. National Academy of Sciences, estimated that our demands in 1999 exceeded that capacity by 20 percent. We are satisfying our excessive demands by consuming the earth's natural assets, in effect creating a global bubble economy.[1]

Bubble economies are not new. American investors got an up-close view of this when the bubble in high-tech stocks burst in 2000 and the NASDAQ, an indicator of the value of these stocks, declined by some 75 percent. Japan had a similar experience in 1989 when the real estate bubble burst, depreciating stock and real estate assets by 60 percent. The bad-debt fallout and other effects of this collapse have left the once-dynamic Japanese economy dead in the water ever since.[2]

The bursting of these two bubbles affected primarily people living in the United States and Japan, but the global bubble economy that is based on the overconsumption of the earth's natural capital assets will affect the entire world. When the food bubble economy, inflated by the overpumping of aquifers, bursts, it will raise food prices worldwide. The challenge for our generation is to deflate the economic bubble before it bursts.

Unfortunately, since September 11, 2001, political leaders, diplomats, and the media worldwide have been preoccupied with terrorism and, more recently, the invasion of Iraq. Terrorism is certainly a matter of concern, but if it diverts us from the environmental trends that are undermining our future until it is too late to reverse them, Osama Bin Laden and his followers will have achieved their goal of bringing down western civilization in a way they could not have imagined.

In February 2003, U.N. demographers made an announcement that was in some ways more shocking than the September 11th attack: the worldwide rise in life expectancy has been dramatically reversed for a large segment of humanity—the 700 million people living in sub-Saharan Africa. The HIV epidemic has reduced life expectancy among this region's people from 62 to 47 years. The epidemic may soon claim more lives than all the wars of the twentieth century. If this teaches us anything, it is the high cost of neglecting newly emerging threats.[3]

The HIV epidemic is not the only emerging mega-threat. Numerous countries are feeding their growing populations by overpumping their aquifers—a measure that virtually guarantees a future drop in food production when the aquifers are depleted. In effect, these countries are creating a food bubble economy—one where food production is artificially inflated by the unsustainable use of groundwater.

Another mega-threat—climate change—is not getting the attention it deserves from most governments, particularly that of the United States, the country responsible for one fourth of all carbon emissions. Washington wants to wait until all the evidence on climate change is in, by which time it will be too late to prevent a wholesale warming of the planet. Just as governments in Africa watched HIV infection rates rise and did little about it, the United States is watching atmospheric CO_2 levels rise and doing little to check the increase.[4]

Other mega-threats being neglected include eroding soils and expanding deserts, which are threatening the livelihood and food supply of hundreds of millions of the world's people. These issues do not even appear on the radar screen of many national governments.

Thus far, most of the environmental damage has been local: the death of the Aral Sea, the burning rainforests of Indonesia, the collapse of the Canadian cod fishery, the melting of the glaciers that supply Andean cities with water, the dust bowl forming in northwestern China, and the depletion of the U.S. Great Plains aquifer. But as these local environmental events expand and multiply, they will progressively weaken the global economy, bringing closer the day when the economic bubble will burst.[5]

Ecological Bills Coming Due

Humanity's demands on the earth have multiplied over the last half-century as our numbers have increased and our incomes have risen. World population grew from 2.5 billion in 1950 to 6.1 billion in 2000. The growth during those 50 years exceeded that during the 4 million years since we emerged as a distinct species.[6]

Incomes have risen even faster than population. Income per person worldwide nearly tripled from 1950 to 2000. Growth in population and the rise in incomes together expanded global economic output from just under $7 trillion (in 2001 dollars) of goods and services in 1950 to $46 trillion in 2000, a gain of nearly sevenfold.[7]

Population growth and rising incomes together have tripled world grain demand over the last half-century, pushing it from 640 million tons in 1950 to 1,855 million tons in 2000. To satisfy this swelling demand, farmers have plowed land that was highly erodible—land that was too dry or too steeply sloping to sustain cultivation. Each year billions of tons of topsoil are being blown away in dust storms or washed away in rainstorms, leaving farmers to try to feed some 70 million additional people, but with less topsoil than the year before.[8]

Demand for water also tripled as agricultural, industrial, and residential uses climbed, outstripping the sustainable supply in many countries. As a result, water tables are falling and wells are going dry. Rivers are also being drained dry, to the detriment of wildlife and ecosystems.[9]

Fossil fuel use quadrupled, setting in motion a rise in carbon emissions that is overwhelming nature's capacity to fix carbon dioxide. As a result of this carbon-fixing deficit, atmospheric CO_2 concentrations climbed from 316 parts per million (ppm) in 1959, when official measurement began, to 369 ppm in 2000.[10]

The sector of the economy that seems likely to unravel first is food. Eroding soils, deteriorating rangelands, collapsing fisheries, falling water tables, and rising temperatures are converging to make it more difficult to expand food production fast enough to keep up with demand. In 2002, the world grain harvest of 1,807 million tons fell short of world grain consumption by 100 million tons, or 5 percent. This shortfall, the largest on record, marked the third consecutive year of grain deficits, dropping stocks to the lowest level in a generation.[11]

Now the question is, Can the world's farmers bounce back and expand production enough to fill the 100-million-ton shortfall, provide for the more than 70 million people added each year, and rebuild stocks to a more secure level? In the past, farmers responded to short supplies and higher grain prices by planting more land and using more irrigation water and fertilizer. Now it is doubtful that farmers can fill this gap without further depleting aquifers and jeopardizing future harvests.[12]

In 1996, at the World Food Summit in Rome, hosted by the U.N. Food and Agriculture Organization (FAO), 185 countries plus the European Community agreed to reduce hunger by half by 2015. Using 1990–92 as a base, governments set the goal of cutting the number of people who were hungry—860 million—by roughly 20 million per year. It was an exciting and worthy goal, one that later became one of the U.N. Millennium Development Goals.[13]

But in its late 2002 review of food security, the United Nations issued a discouraging report: "This year we must report that progress has virtually ground to a halt. Our latest estimates, based on data from the years 1998–2000, put the number of undernourished people in the world at 840 million…a decrease of barely 2.5 million per year over the eight years since 1990–92."[14]

Since 1998–2000, world grain production per person has fallen 5 percent, suggesting that the ranks of the hungry are now expanding. As noted earlier, life expectancy is plummeting in sub-Saharan Africa. If the number of hungry people worldwide is also increasing, then two key social indicators are showing widespread deterioration in the human condition.[15]

Farmers Facing Two New Challenges

As we exceed the earth's natural capacities, we create new problems. For example, farmers are now facing two new challenges: rising temperatures and falling water tables. Farmers currently on the land may face higher temperatures than any generation since agriculture began 11,000 years ago. They are also the first to face widespread aquifer depletion and the resulting loss of irrigation water.

The global average temperature has risen in each of the last three decades. The 16 warmest years since record-keeping began in 1880 have all occurred since 1980. With the three warmest years on record—1998, 2001, and 2002—coming in the last five years, crops are facing heat stresses that are without precedent.[16]

Higher temperatures reduce crop yields through their effect on photosynthesis, moisture balance, and fertilization. As the temperature rises above 34 degrees Celsius (94 degrees Fahrenheit), photosynthesis slows, dropping to zero for many crops when it reaches 37 degrees Celsius (100 degrees Fahrenheit). When temperatures in the U.S. Corn Belt are 37 degrees or higher, corn plants suffer from thermal shock and dehydration. They are in effect on sick leave. Each such day shrinks the harvest.[17]

In addition to decreasing photosynthesis and dehydrating plants, high temperatures also impede the fertilization needed for seed formation. Researchers at the International Rice Research Institute in the Philippines and at the U.S. Department of Agriculture have together developed a rule of thumb that each 1-degree-Celsius rise in temperature above the optimum during the growing season reduces grain yields by 10 percent.[18]

These recent research findings indicate that if the temperature rises to the lower end of the range projected by the Intergovernmental Panel on Climate Change, grain harvests in tropical regions could be reduced by an average of 5 percent by 2020 and 11 percent by 2050. At the upper end of the range, harvests could drop 11 percent by 2020 and 46 percent by 2050. Avoiding these declines will be difficult unless scientists can develop crop strains that are not vulnerable to thermal stress.[19]

The second challenge facing farmers, falling water tables, is also recent. With traditional animal- or human-powered water-lifting devices it was almost impossible historically to deplete aquifers. With the worldwide spread of powerful diesel and electric pumps during the last half-century, however, overpumping has become commonplace.

As the world demand for water has climbed, water tables have fallen in scores of countries, including China, India, and the United States, which together produce nearly half of the world's grain. Water tables are falling throughout the northern half of China. As the water table falls, springs and rivers go dry, lakes disappear, and wells dry up. Northern China is literally drying out. Water tables under the North China Plain, which accounts for a fourth or more of China's grain harvest, are falling at an accelerating rate.[20]

In India, water tables are also falling. As India's farmers try to feed an additional 16 million people each year, nearly the population equivalent of another Australia, they are pumping more and more water. This is dropping water tables in states that together contain a majority of India's 1 billion people.[21]

In the United States, the third major grain producer, water tables are falling under the southern Great Plains and in California, the country's fruit and vegetable basket. As California's population expands from 26 million to a projected 40 million by 2030, expanding urban water demands will siphon water from agriculture.[22]

Scores of other countries are also overpumping their aquifers, setting the stage for dramatic future cutbacks in water supplies. The more populous among these are Pakistan, Iran, and Mexico. Overpumping creates an illusion of food security that is dangerously deceptive because it enables farmers to support a growing population with a practice that virtually ensures a future drop in food production.

The water demand growth curve over the last half-century looks like the population growth curve, except that it climbs more steeply. While world population growth was doubling, the use of water was tripling. Once the growing demand for water rises above the sustainable yield of an aquifer, the gap between the two widens further each year. As this happens, the water table starts to fall. The first year after the sustainable yield is surpassed, the water table falls very little, with the drop often being scarcely perceptible. Each year thereafter, however, the annual drop is larger than the year before.

In addition to falling exponentially, water tables are also falling simultaneously in many countries. This means that cutbacks in grain harvests will occur in many countries at more or less the same time. And they will occur at a time when the world's population is growing by more than 70 million a year.[23]

These, then, are the two new challenges facing the world's farmers: rising temperatures and falling water tables. Either one by itself could make it difficult to keep up with the growth in demand. The two together provide an early test of whether our modern civilization can cope with the forces that threaten to undermine it.

Ecological Meltdown in China

In the deteriorating relationship between the global economy and the earth's ecosystem, food is the most vulnerable economic sector, but geographically it is China that is on the leading edge. A human population of 1.3 billion and their 400 million cattle, sheep, and goats are weighing heavily on the land. Huge flocks of sheep and goats in the northwest are stripping the land of its protective vegetation, creating a dust bowl on a scale not seen before. Northwestern China is on the verge of a massive ecological meltdown.[24]

Since 1980, the Chinese economy has expanded more than fourfold. Incomes have also expanded by nearly fourfold, lifting more people out of poverty faster than at any time in history. Like many other countries, China is exceeding the carrying capacity of its ecosystem—overplowing its land, overgrazing its rangelands, overcutting its forests, and overpumping its aquifers. In its determined effort to be self-sufficient in grain, it cultivated highly erodible land in the arid northern and western provinces, land that is vulnerable to wind erosion.[25]

While overplowing is now being partly remedied by

paying farmers to plant their grainland in trees, overgrazing is destroying vegetation and increasing wind erosion. China's cattle, sheep, and goat population more than tripled from 1950 to 2002. The United States, a country with comparable grazing capacity, has 97 million cattle, while China has 106 million. For sheep and goats, the figures are 8 million versus 298 million. Concentrated in the western and northern provinces, sheep and goats are destroying the land's protective vegetation. The wind then does the rest, removing the soil and converting productive rangeland into desert.[26]

China is now at war. It is not invading armies that are claiming its territory, but expanding deserts. Old deserts are advancing and new ones are forming, like guerrilla forces striking unexpectedly, forcing Beijing to fight on several fronts. And worse, the growing deserts are gaining momentum, occupying an ever-larger piece of China's territory each year.

China's expanding ecological deficits are converging to create a dust bowl of historic dimensions. With little vegetation remaining in parts of northern and western China, the strong winds of late winter and early spring can remove literally millions of tons of topsoil in a single day—soil that can take centuries to replace.

For the outside world, it is these storms that draw attention to the dust bowl forming in China. On April 12, 2002, for instance, South Korea was engulfed by a huge dust storm from China that left residents of Seoul literally gasping for breath. Schools were closed, airline flights were cancelled, and clinics were overrun with patients having difficulty breathing. Retail sales fell. Koreans have come to dread the arrival of what they now call "the fifth season"—the dust storms of late winter and early spring. Japan also suffers from dust storms originating in China. Although not as directly exposed as Koreans are, the

Japanese complain about the dust and the brown rain that streaks their windshields and windows.[27]

Each year, residents of eastern Chinese cities such as Beijing and Tianjin hunker down as the dust storms begin. Along with the difficulty in breathing and the dust that stings the eyes, there is the constant effort to keep dust out of homes and to clean doorways and sidewalks of dust and sand. Farmers and herders, whose livelihoods are blowing away, are paying an even heavier price.

Desert expansion has accelerated with each successive decade since 1950. China's Environmental Protection Agency reports that the Gobi Desert expanded by 52,400 square kilometers (20,240 square miles) from 1994 to 1999, an area half the size of Pennsylvania. With the advancing Gobi now within 150 miles of Beijing, China's leaders are beginning to sense the gravity of the situation.[28]

The fallout from the dust storms is social as well as economic. Millions of rural Chinese may be uprooted and forced to migrate eastward as the deserts claim their land. Desertification is already driving villagers from their homes in Gansu, Inner Mongolia (Nei Monggol), and Ningxia provinces. A preliminary Asian Development Bank assessment of desertification in Gansu Province reports that 4,000 villages risk being overrun by drifting sands.[29]

The U.S. Dust Bowl of the 1930s forced some 2.5 million "Okies" and other refugees to leave the land, many of them heading west from Oklahoma, Texas, and Kansas to California. But the dust bowl forming in China is much larger, and during the 1930s the U.S. population was only 150 million—compared with 1.3 billion in China today. Whereas the U.S. migration was measured in the millions, China's may measure in the tens of millions. And as a U.S. embassy report entitled *The Grapes of Wrath in Inner Mongolia* noted, "unfortunately, China's twenty-first century 'Okies' have no California to escape to—at least not in China."[30]

Food: A National Security Issue

The ecological deficits just described are converging on the farm sector, making it more difficult to sustain rapid growth in world food output. No one knows when the growth in food production will fall behind that of demand, driving up prices, but it may be much closer than we think. The triggering events that will precipitate future food shortages are likely to be spreading water shortages interacting with crop-withering heat waves in key food-producing regions. The economic indicator most likely to signal serious trouble in the deteriorating relationship between the global economy and the earth's ecosystem is grain prices.

Food is fast becoming a national security issue as growth in the world harvest slows and as falling water tables and rising temperatures hint at future shortages. More than 100 countries import part of the wheat they consume. Some 40 import rice. While some countries are only marginally dependent on imports, others could not survive without them. Iran and Egypt, for example, rely on imports for 40 percent of their grain supply. For Algeria, Japan, South Korea, and Taiwan, among others, it is 70 percent or more. For Israel and Yemen, over 90 percent. Just six countries—the United States, Canada, France, Australia, Argentina, and Thailand—supply 90 percent of grain exports. The United States alone controls close to half of world grain exports, a larger share than Saudi Arabia does of oil.[31]

Thus far the countries that import heavily are small and middle-sized ones. But now China, the world's most populous country, is likely to soon turn to world markets in a major way. When the former Soviet Union unexpectedly turned to the world market in 1972 for roughly a tenth of its grain supply, following a weather-reduced harvest, world wheat prices climbed from $1.90 to $4.89 a bushel. Bread prices soon rose too.[32]

If China depletes its grain reserves and turns to the world grain market to cover its shortfall, now 40 million tons per year, it could destabilize world grain markets overnight. Turning to the world market means turning to the United States, presenting a potentially delicate geopolitical situation in which 1.3 billion Chinese consumers with a $100-billion trade surplus with the United States will be competing with American consumers for U.S. grain. If this leads to rising food prices in the United States, how will the government respond? In times past, it could have restricted exports, even imposing an export embargo, as it did with soybeans to Japan in 1974. But today the United States has a stake in a politically stable China. With an economy growing at 7–8 percent a year, China is the engine that is powering not only the Asian economy but, to some degree, the world economy.[33]

For China, becoming dependent on other countries for food would end its history of food self-sufficiency, leaving it vulnerable to world market uncertainties. For Americans, rising food prices would be the first indication that the world has changed fundamentally and that they are being directly affected by the growing grain deficit in China. If it seems likely that rising food prices are being driven in part by crop-withering temperature rises, pressure will mount for the United States to reduce oil and coal use.

For the world's poor—the millions living in cities on $1 per day or less and already spending 70 percent of their income on food—rising grain prices would be life-threatening. A doubling of world grain prices today could impoverish more people in a shorter period of time than any event in history. With desperate people holding their governments responsible, such a price rise could also destabilize governments of low-income, grain-importing countries.[34]

When I projected in 1995 in *Who Will Feed China?* that China would one day turn abroad for part of its grain, the U.S. National Intelligence Council, the umbrella over all the U.S. intelligence agencies, launched the most detailed assessment of China's food prospect ever undertaken. The council was concerned precisely because such a move by China could drive up world grain prices and destabilize governments in developing countries. An interdisciplinary team led by Michael McElroy, Chairman of Harvard's Department of Earth and Planetary Sciences, conducted this extraordinarily ambitious study. Relying on an interdisciplinary approach and a vast array of resources, including 35 years of CIA satellite data on land use and the Sandia National Laboratories to model the water supply-demand balance of every river basin in China, the team concluded in its "most likely" scenario that China would one day have to import massive quantities of grain.[35]

The team then decided that the world would not have any difficulty in supplying grain on such a vast scale. The shortcoming of this conclusion, in my opinion, was that it relied too heavily on extrapolating late twentieth-century grain production trends into the twenty-first century, failing to take into account emerging constraints on harvests, such as aquifer depletion and rising temperatures.

When grain prices began to climb in 1972–74, it did not take long for a politics of food scarcity to emerge. Pressure from within grain-exporting countries to restrict exports in order to check the rise in domestic food prices was common.[36]

More recently, the Canadian Wheat Board, which handles the nation's wheat exports, announced in early September 2002 that it had no more to sell. This abrupt withdrawal from the market—even before that year's drought-reduced harvest was complete—illustrates the kind of action that exporters can take when confronted with scarcity. Instead of letting the world market allocate scarce supplies of high-quality wheat, the Board decided that it would protect domestic supplies, then sell only to traditional clients, leaving other importers to fend for themselves. In late October, Australia—also experiencing a severe drought—announced that it would ration wheat and barley exports among its best customers, excluding all other potential buyers.[37]

Historically, the world had two food reserves: the global carryover stocks of grain and the cropland idled under the U.S. farm program to limit production. The latter could be brought into production within a year. Since the U.S. land set-aside program ended in 1996, however, the world has had only carryover stocks as a reserve.[38]

Food security has changed in other ways. Traditionally it was largely an agricultural matter. But now it is something that our entire society is responsible for. National population and energy policies may have a greater effect on food security than agricultural policies do. With most of the 3 billion people to be added to world population by 2050 being born in countries already facing water shortages, childbearing decisions may have a greater effect on food security than crop planting decisions. Achieving an acceptable balance between food and people today depends on family planners and farmers working together.[39]

Climate change is the wild card in the food security deck. It is perhaps a measure of the complexity of our time that decisions made in the Ministry of Energy may have a greater effect on future food security than those made in the Ministry of Agriculture. The effect of population and energy policies on food security differ in one important respect: population stability can be achieved by a country acting unilaterally. Climate stability cannot.

The Case for Plan B

Thus far, this chapter has focused primarily on how environmental changes can affect the food prospect, but there could be other wake-up calls, including more destructive storms or deadly heat waves.

Unless we quickly reverse the damaging trends that we have set in motion, they will generate vast numbers of environmental refugees—people abandoning depleted aquifers and exhausted soils and those fleeing advancing deserts and rising seas. In a world where civilization is being squeezed between expanding deserts from the interior of continents and rising seas on the periphery, refugees are likely to number not in the millions but in the tens of millions. Already we see refugees from drifting sand in Nigeria, Iran, and China.[40]

We are now looking at the potential wholesale evacuation of cities as aquifers are depleted and wells go dry. Sana'a, the capital of Yemen, and Quetta, the capital of Pakistan's Baluchistan province, may become the early ghost towns of the twenty-first century.[41]

A reversal of the basic trends of social progress of the last half-century has long seemed unthinkable. Progress appeared inevitable. But now we are seeing reversals. As noted earlier, the number of hungry may be increasing for the first time since the war-torn decade of the 1940s. And a rise in life expectancy—a seminal measure of economic and social progress—has been interrupted in sub-Saharan Africa as a result of the HIV epidemic. As millions of able-bodied adults die, families are often left with no one to work in the fields. The disease and spreading hunger are both weakening immune systems and reinforcing each other, something epidemiologists had not reckoned on.

The failure of governments to deal with falling water tables and the depletion of aquifers in the Indian subcontinent could be as disruptive for the 1.3 billion living there as the HIV epidemic is for the people in sub-Saharan Africa. With business as usual, life expectancy could soon begin to fall in India and Pakistan as water shortages translate into food shortages, deepening hunger among the poor.[42]

The world is moving into uncharted territory as human demands override the sustainable yield of natural systems. The risk is that people will lose confidence in the capacity of their governments to cope with such problems, leading to social breakdown. The shift to anarchy is already evident in countries such as Somalia, Afghanistan, and the Democratic Republic of the Congo.

Business as usual—Plan A—is clearly not working. The stakes are high, and time is not on our side. Part I details the mounting evidence that our modern civilization is in trouble. The good news, as outlined in Part II of this book, is that there are solutions to the problems we are facing. The bad news is that if we continue to rely on timid, incremental responses, our bubble economy will continue to grow until eventually it bursts. This book argues for a new approach—for Plan B—an urgent reordering of priorities, a restructuring of the global economy in order to prevent that from happening.

I

A CIVILIZATION IN TROUBLE

2

Emerging Water Shortages

The world is incurring a vast water deficit—one that is largely invisible, historically recent, and growing fast. Because the impending water crunch usually takes the form of aquifer overpumping and falling water tables, it is often not apparent. Unlike burning forests or invading sand dunes, falling water tables cannot be readily photographed. They are often discovered only when wells go dry.

Newspapers carry frequent accounts of rivers failing to reach the sea, or lakes disappearing, or wells going dry, but these stories typically describe local situations. It is not until we begin to compile the numerous national studies—such as a 748-page analysis of the water situation in China, a World Bank study of the water situation in Yemen, or a detailed U.S. Department of Agriculture (USDA) assessment of the irrigation prospect in the western United States—that the extent of emerging water shortages worldwide can be grasped.[1]

The world water deficit is recent—a product of the tripling of water demand over the last half-century and the worldwide spread of powerful diesel and electrically driven pumps. The drilling of millions of wells has pushed water withdrawals beyond the recharge of many aquifers. The failure of governments to limit pumping to the sustainable yield of aquifers means that water tables are now falling in scores of countries. The mining of groundwater is quite literally undermining the future of some countries.[2]

Rivers running dry are far more visible. Among the rivers that now fail to reach the sea all or part of the time are the Colorado, the major river in the southwestern United States; the Yellow River, the cradle of Chinese civilization; and the Amu Darya, one of the two rivers that feed the Aral Sea in Central Asia. Other major rivers that have been reduced to a trickle when they reach the sea include the Nile, the Indus, and the Ganges.[3]

Water shortages are generating conflicts between upstream and downstream claimants, both within and among countries. For the Yellow River, the competition is between impoverished upstream provinces and more prosperous coastal provinces. For the Nile, competition is among countries, principally Egypt, the Sudan, and Ethiopia, where much of the Nile's flow originates.[4]

Water scarcity, once a local issue, is now crossing international boundaries via the international grain trade. Countries that are pressing against the limits of their water supply typically satisfy the growing need of cities and industry by diverting irrigation water from agriculture, then importing grain to offset the loss of productive capacity. Because it takes 1,000 tons of water (1,000 cubic meters) to produce 1 ton of grain, importing grain is the most efficient way to import water. Countries are now satisfying their growing demand for water by tapping international grain markets. As water shortages intensify, so too will the competition for grain in these markets. In a sense, to trade in grain futures is to trade in water futures.[5]

The link between water and food is a strong one. Our

individual daily water requirements for drinking average 4 liters per day, while the water required to produce our food each day totals at least 2,000 liters—500 times as much. In affluent societies, where grain is consumed in the form of livestock products, water consumed as food can easily reach 4,000 liters daily.[6]

Worldwide, 70 percent of all the water diverted from rivers or pumped from underground is used for irrigation. Twenty percent is used by industry and 10 percent for residential purposes. With the demand for water growing steadily in all three sectors, competition is intensifying. In this struggle for water, farmers almost always lose to cities and industry.[7]

Falling Water Tables

Scores of countries are overpumping aquifers as they struggle to satisfy their growing water needs, including each of the big three grain-producing countries—China, India, and the United States. Their populations, along with those of other countries where overpumping will measurably reduce the food supply when aquifers are depleted, exceed 3 billion people, or half the world total. (See Table 2–1.)[8]

As noted in Chapter 1, falling water tables are already affecting harvests in some countries, including China, the world's largest grain producer. A little-noticed groundwater survey released in Beijing in August 2001 revealed that the water table under the North China Plain, which produces over half of China's wheat and a third of its corn, is falling faster than earlier reported. Overpumping has largely depleted the shallow aquifer, reducing the amount of water that can be pumped from it to the annual recharge from precipitation. This is forcing well drillers to turn to the region's deep aquifer, which, unfortunately, is not replenishable.[9]

Table 2–1. *Countries with Extensive Overpumping of Aquifers in 2002*

Country	Population
	(million)
China	1,295
India	1,050
United States	291
Pakistan	150
Mexico	102
Iran	68
South Korea	47
Morocco	30
Saudi Arabia	24
Yemen	19
Syria	17
Tunisia	10
Israel	6
Jordan	5
Total	3,114

Source: See endnote 8.

The survey, conducted by the Geological Environmental Monitoring Institute (GEMI) in Beijing, reported that under Hebei Province in the heart of the North China Plain, the average level of the deep aquifer dropped 2.9 meters (nearly 10 feet) in 2000. Around some cities in the province, it fell by 6 meters. He Qingcheng, head of the GEMI groundwater monitoring team, notes that as the deep aquifer under the North China Plain is depleted, the region is losing its last water reserve—its only safety cushion.[10]

His concerns are mirrored in a World Bank report:

"Anecdotal evidence suggests that deep wells [drilled] around Beijing now have to reach 1,000 meters [more than half a mile] to tap fresh water, adding dramatically to the cost of supply." In unusually strong language for a Bank report, it foresees "catastrophic consequences for future generations" unless water use and supply can quickly be brought back into balance.[11]

The U.S. embassy in Beijing reports that wheat farmers in some areas are now pumping from a depth of 300 meters, or nearly 1,000 feet. Pumping water from this far down translates into exorbitant costs and reduced profit margins that often force farmers to abandon irrigation and return to less productive dryland farming.[12]

Falling water tables, combined with reduced government grain support prices and the loss of farm labor in provinces that are rapidly industrializing, are shrinking China's grain harvest. The wheat crop, grown mostly in arid northern China, is particularly vulnerable to water shortages. After peaking at 123 million tons in 1997, the wheat harvest has fallen in five of the last six years, coming in at 87 million tons in 2003, a drop of nearly 30 percent.[13]

The U.S. embassy in Beijing also reports that the recent decline in rice production is partly the result of water shortages. After peaking at 140 million tons in 1997, the harvest has dropped in each of the five years since then, falling to an estimated 121 million tons in 2003. Only corn, China's third major grain, has thus far avoided a decline. This is because corn prices are stronger and because the corn crop is not as dependent on irrigation water as wheat and rice are.[14]

Overall, China's grain production has fallen from its historical peak of 392 million tons in 1998 to an estimated 338 million tons in 2003. (See Figure 2–1). For perspective, this drop of over 50 million tons is equal to the Canadian grain harvest. Thus far, China has covered the

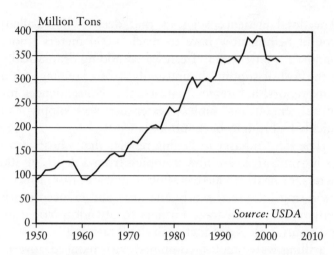

Figure 2–1. *Total Grain Production in China, 1950–2003*

fall in production by drawing down its once vast stocks, but it can only do that for one or two more years. Then it will have to turn to the world market for imports. When it does so, we likely will see the effects in higher food prices at the supermarket checkout counter.[15]

A World Bank study indicates that China is overpumping three river basins in the north by 37 billion tons—the Hai, which flows through Beijing and Tianjin; the Yellow; and the Huai, the next river south of the Yellow. At 1,000 tons of water per ton of grain, this would produce 37 million tons of grain, enough to feed 111 million Chinese.[16]

The other country with extensive overpumping is India, which is depleting aquifers in Punjab (the country's breadbasket), Haryana, Gujarat, Rajasthan, Andhra Pradesh, and Tamil Nadu. The International Water Management Institute estimates that aquifer depletion could eventually reduce India's grain harvest by one fourth.[17]

The latest data indicate that under Punjab and Haryana, water tables are falling by up to a meter a year.

Data for monitored wells in northern Gujarat suggest that the water table has fallen from a depth of 15 meters to 400 meters over the last three decades. At this point, the harvests of wheat and rice, India's principal food grains, are still increasing. But within the next few years, the loss of irrigation water could override technological progress and start shrinking the harvest, as it is already doing in China.[18]

In the United States, the USDA reports that in parts of Texas, Oklahoma, and Kansas—three leading grain-producing states—the underground water table has dropped by more than 30 meters (100 feet). As a result, wells have gone dry on thousands of farms in the southern Great Plains.[19]

Irrigated land accounts for about four fifths of the grain harvest in China and close to three fifths in India, but only one fifth in the United States. Of the leading grain producers, only China is currently experiencing a substantial decline in production. Even with a worldwide grain crunch and climbing grain prices providing an incentive to boost production, it would be difficult for China to regain earlier grain production levels given the loss of irrigation water. India can probably still expand its harvest somewhat before water shortages overwhelm the gains in production from advances in technology. For the United States, the ongoing irrigation water loss from aquifer depletion and diversion to cities does not appear to be large enough to reduce the grain harvest, but it will slow its growth.[20]

Pakistan, a country with 150 million people and growing by 4 million per year, is also overpumping its aquifers. In the Pakistani part of the fertile Punjab plain, the drop in water tables appears to be similar to that in India. Observation wells near the twin cities of Islamabad and Rawalpindi show a fall in the water table from 1982 to 2000 ranging from 1 to nearly 2 meters a year.[21]

In the province of Baluchistan, a more arid region, water tables around the provincial capital of Quetta are falling by 3.5 meters per year. Richard Garstang, a water expert with the World Wildlife Fund and a participant in a study of Pakistan's water situation, says that "within 15 years Quetta will run out of water if the current consumption rate continues."[22]

Future irrigation water cutbacks as a result of aquifer depletion will undoubtedly reduce Pakistan's grain harvest. In Pakistan, as in India, the harvest of wheat—the principal food staple—is continuing to grow, but more slowly.

Water shortages are common in Middle Eastern countries. Iran, a country of 68 million people, is overpumping its aquifers by an average of 5 billion tons per year, enough to produce one third of its annual grain harvest. Under the small but agriculturally rich Chenaran Plain in northeastern Iran, the water table was falling by 2.8 meters a year in the late 1990s. But, in 2001, the cumulative effect of a three-year drought and the new wells being drilled both for irrigation and to supply the nearby city of Mashad dropped the aquifer by an extraordinary 8 meters. Villages in eastern Iran are being abandoned as wells go dry, generating a flow of "water refugees."[23]

Saudi Arabia, a country of 24 million people, is as water-poor as it is oil-rich. It has tried to develop an extensive irrigated agriculture based largely on deep fossil aquifers. After several years of using oil money to support the price of wheat at five times the world market level to encourage farmers to develop an irrigated agriculture based on deep pumping, the government was forced to face fiscal reality and cut back on the program. Craig Smith writes in the *New York Times*, "From the air, the circular wheat fields of this arid land's breadbasket look like forest green poker chips strewn across the brown desert. But they are outnumbered by the ghostly silhouettes of fields left to fade back into the sand, places where the kingdom's gamble on agriculture has sucked precious aquifers dry." In some areas, farmers are now pumping water from 4,000-foot-deep wells—in other words, from nearly four fifths of a mile down.[24]

A 1984 Saudi national survey reports fossil water reserves at 462 billion tons. Half of that, Smith reports, has probably disappeared by now. This suggests that irrigated agriculture could last for another decade or so and then will largely disappear, limited to the small area that can be irrigated with water from the shallow aquifers that are replenished by the kingdom's sparse rainfall. The lush fields of thirsty alfalfa, grown to feed a recently created modern dairy industry, will also become history.[25]

In Yemen, a country of 19 million, the water table under most of the country is falling by roughly 2 meters a year as water use far exceeds the sustainable yield of aquifers. In the Sana'a basin in western Yemen, the estimated annual water extraction of 224 million tons exceeds the annual recharge of 42 million tons by a factor of five, dropping the water table by 6 meters per year. Projections by the World Bank indicate the Sana'a basin, home of the national capital and 2 million people, will be pumped dry by 2010. In the search for water, the Yemeni government has drilled test wells in the basin that are 2 kilometers (1.2 miles) deep—depths normally associated with the oil industry—but they have failed to find water. Yemen must soon decide whether to bring water to Sana'a, possibly by pipeline from coastal desalting plants, if it can afford it, or to relocate the capital. Either alternative will be costly and potentially traumatic.[26]

With its population growing at a near-record 3.5 percent a year and with water tables falling everywhere, Yemen is fast becoming a hydrological basket case. Aside from the effect of overpumping on the capital, World

Bank official Christopher Ward observes that "ground-water is being mined at such a rate that parts of the rural economy could disappear within a generation."[27]

Israel, a pioneer in raising irrigation water productivity, is depleting its two principal aquifers—the coastal aquifer and the mountain aquifer that it shares with the Palestinians. Conflicts between Israelis and Palestinians over the allocation of water in the latter are ongoing. Because of severe water shortages, Israel recently discontinued the irrigation of wheat.[28]

In Mexico—home to a population of 102 million that is projected to reach 140 million by 2050—the demand for water is outstripping supply. Mexico City's water problems are legendary. Rural areas are also suffering. For example, in the agricultural state of Guanajuato, the water table is falling by 2 meters or more a year. At the national level, 51 percent of all the water extracted from underground is coming from aquifers that are being overpumped.[29]

There are two types of aquifers: replenishable and nonreplenishable (fossil) aquifers. Most of the aquifers in India and the shallow aquifer under the North China Plain are replenishable. When a replenishable aquifer is depleted, the maximum rate of pumping is necessarily reduced to the rate of recharge.

For fossil aquifers, such as the vast Ogallala under the Great Plains of the United States, the deep aquifer under the North China Plain, or the aquifer under Saudi Arabia, depletion brings pumping to an end. Farmers who lose their irrigation water have the option of returning to lower-yield dryland farming if rainfall permits. In desert situations, however, such as the southwestern United States or the Middle East, the loss of irrigation water means the end of agriculture.

The overpumping of aquifers is occurring in many countries more or less simultaneously. This means that

the depletion of aquifers and the resulting harvest cutbacks will come in many countries at roughly the same
time. And the accelerating depletion of aquifers means
this day may come sooner than expected, creating a
potentially unmanageable situation of food scarcity.

Rivers Running Dry

As the world's demand for water has tripled over the last
half-century and as the demand for hydroelectric power
has grown even faster, dams and diversions of river water
have drained many rivers dry. As water tables have fallen,
the springs that feed rivers have gone dry, leading to the
disappearance of some rivers.

As noted earlier, the Colorado, the major river in the
southwestern United States, now rarely makes it to the
sea. With the states of Colorado, Utah, Arizona, Nevada,
and, most important, California, depending heavily on
the Colorado's water, the river is simply drained dry
before it reaches the Gulf of California. This excessive
demand for water destroys the river's ecosystem, including, of course, its fisheries.[30]

Dams on rivers are built for irrigation, to generate
electricity, and to supply water to cities and industry.
Since 1950, the number of large dams, those over 15
meters high, has increased from 5,000 to 40,000. Each
dam deprives a river of some of its flow. Engineers like to
say that dams built to generate electricity do not take
water from the river, only its energy, but this is not entirely true since reservoirs increase evaporation. The annual
loss of water in arid or semiarid regions, where evaporation rates are high, is typically equal to 10 percent of the
reservoir's storage capacity.[31]

The loss of river flow can affect the health of estuar-
ies and of inland lakes and seas. The Helmand River,
which originates in the mountains of eastern

Afghanistan, flows westward across the country and into Iran, where it empties into Lake Hamoun. When the Taliban built a new dam on the Helmand during the late 1990s, in violation of a water-sharing agreement between the two countries, they effectively removed all the remaining water. As a result, Lake Hamoun, which once covered 4,000 square kilometers, is now a dry lakebed. The abandoned fishing villages on its shores are being covered by sand dunes coming from the lakebed itself.[32]

A similar situation exists with the Aral Sea. The Amu Darya—which, along with the Syr Darya, feeds the Aral Sea—is now drained dry by Uzbek and Turkmen cotton farmers upstream. With the flow of the Amu Darya now cut off, only the diminished flow of the Syr Darya keeps the Aral Sea from disappearing entirely.[33]

Over the last few decades, the Aral Sea has shrunk some 58 percent in area and has lost 83 percent of its volume of water. The loss of freshwater recharge and the sea's shrinkage have led to a dramatic rise in salt levels and the demise of its rich fisheries. In addition to sandstorms, the region also now suffers from salt storms, which arise from the exposed seabed.[34]

China's Yellow River, which flows some 4,000 kilometers through five provinces before it reaches the Yellow Sea, has been under mounting pressure for several decades. It first ran dry in 1972, and since 1985 it has failed to reach the sea for part of almost every year.[35]

The Nile, the site of another ancient civilization, now barely makes it to the sea. Sandra Postel, in *Pillar of Sand*, notes that before the Aswan Dam was built some 32 billion cubic meters of water reached the Mediterranean each year. After the dam was built, however, and irrigation and other demands on the river increased, the Nile's discharge declined to less than 2 billion cubic meters.[36]

Pakistan, like Egypt, is essentially a river-based civilization. The Indus not only provides surface water, it also recharges aquifers that supply the thousands of irrigation wells that now dot the Pakistani countryside. But it, too, is starting to run dry in its lower reaches.[37]

In Southeast Asia, the flow of the Mekong is being reduced by the dams being built on its upper reaches by the Chinese. The downstream countries, including Cambodia, Laos, Thailand, and Viet Nam—countries with 160 million people—complain about the reduced flow of the Mekong, but this has done little to curb China's efforts to exploit the power and the water in the river.[38]

A similar situation exists with the Tigris and Euphrates rivers, which originate in Turkey and flow into Syria and Iraq en route to the Persian Gulf. This river system, the site of Sumer and other early civilizations, is being used at near capacity. Large dams erected in Turkey and Iraq have reduced water flow to the once "fertile crescent," helping to destroy more than 90 percent of the formerly vast wetlands that enriched the delta region.[39]

Many of the river systems just discussed are described by hydrologists as "closed basins"—that is, virtually all the water in the basin is being used. If one party gets more water, other parties will get less. In most cases, this means that as urban and industrial needs rise, there is less available for irrigation.

Farmers Losing to Cities
In the competition for water among agriculture, cities, and industry, the economics of water use do not favor farmers, simply because it takes so much water to produce food. For example, while it takes 1,000 tons of water to grow a ton of wheat, it takes only 14 tons to make a ton of steel. In China, where water scarcity is a national security issue, 1,000 tons of water can be used either to produce 1 ton of wheat worth, at most, $200, or to

expand industrial output by $14,000—70 times as much. In a country preoccupied with expanding the economy and creating jobs, the policy decision to make agriculture the residual claimant comes as no surprise.[40]

Many of the world's largest cities are located in closed basins. Cities in these watersheds, such as Mexico City, Los Angeles, Cairo, and Beijing, can increase their water consumption only by importing water from other basins or taking it from agriculture.

In a world of water scarcity, literally hundreds of cities are now taking water from agriculture. Among the U.S. cities that are likely to satisfy future growth in water demands by taking irrigation water from farmers are San Diego, Los Angeles, Las Vegas, Denver, and El Paso. A USDA study of 11 western states for 1996 and 1997 found that during these two years, annual sales of water rights averaged 1.65 billion tons or roughly 1 percent of the underground water used for irrigation nationwide.[41]

When the federal government reduced the flow of Colorado River water into California by 765 million tons on January 1, 2003, in accordance with a longstanding agreement that allocated the river's water among several states, it immediately set off a flurry of urban water purchases from farmers in California, including a 120-million-ton water purchase from the Sacramento Valley Irrigation District by San Diego's Municipal Water District. This purchase meant that farmers would idle riceland, reducing rice production by an estimated 120,000 tons or 3 percent of U.S. consumption.[42]

Literally hundreds of cities in other countries are meeting their growing water needs by taking some of the water that farmers count on. In western Turkey, for example, Ismir now relies heavily on well fields from the neighboring agricultural district of Manisa.[43]

Although reliable projections of rural-urban transfers

do not yet exist for many countries, World Bank calculations for South Korea, a relatively well watered country, indicate that growth in residential and industrial water use there could reduce the supply available for agriculture from 13 billion tons at present to 7 billion tons in 2025.[44]

Between 2000 and 2010, the World Bank projects that China's urban water demand will increase from 50 billion cubic meters (50 billion tons) to 80 billion, a growth of 60 percent as the country's population is projected to grow by 90 million. Industrial water demand, meanwhile, will go from 127 billion cubic meters to 206 billion, up 62 percent. Several hundred cities are looking to the countryside to satisfy their future water needs. In the region around Beijing, this shift has been under way since 1994, when farmers were banned from the reservoirs that supplied the city.[45]

As China attempts to accelerate the economic development of the upper Yellow River basin, emerging industries upstream get priority in the use of water. And as more water is used upstream, less reaches farmers downstream. In most recent years, the Yellow River not only has failed to reach the sea for part of the year, but sometimes it has failed to reach Shandong, the last province that it flows through en route to the sea.[46]

Farmers in Shandong have traditionally received roughly half of their irrigation water from the Yellow River and half from wells. Now they are losing water from both sources as the downstream river flow shrinks and as overpumping depletes local aquifers. Losses of irrigation water in a province that produces a fifth of China's corn and a seventh of its wheat help explain why China's grain production is declining. As a supplier of grain, Shandong is more important to China than Iowa and Kansas together are to the United States.[47]

Although there is no worldwide monitoring system for the diversion of irrigation water to cities and industry,

the trend is clear. Slowly but surely cities are siphoning
water from agriculture even as the world's farmers try to
feed 70 million more people each year.[48]

Scarcity Crossing National Borders

Historically water scarcity was a local issue. It was up to
national governments to balance the supply of and
demand for water. Now this is changing as scarcity cross-
es national boundaries via the international grain trade.
One of the consequences of economic globalization is that
water scarcity anywhere can affect people everywhere.

The Middle East and North Africa—from Morocco
in the west through Iran in the east—has emerged as the
world's fastest-growing grain import market. Virtually
every country in the region is pressing against the limits
of its water supply. In this situation, the growing demand
for water in cities and industry can be satisfied only by
taking irrigation water from agriculture.

Iran and Egypt, each with some 70 million people,
have become leading importers of wheat, in recent years
vying with Japan—traditionally the leading wheat
importer—for the top spot. Both countries now import
40 percent of their total grain supply.[49]

Algeria, with 31 million people, imports some 75 percent of its grain, which means that the water used to produce the imported grain exceeds water consumption
from domestic sources. Because of its heavy dependence
on imports, Algeria is particularly vulnerable to disrup-
tions, such as grain export embargoes.[50]

It is often said that future wars in the Middle East will
more likely be fought over water than over oil, but the
competition for water is taking place in world grain markets. It is the countries that are financially the strongest,
not necessarily those that are militarily the strongest, that
are likely to fare best in this competition.

If we want to know where grain import needs will be concentrated tomorrow, we should look at where water deficits are developing today. Thus far, the countries importing a large share of their grain have been small or medium-sized nations. Now for the first time we are looking at fast-growing water deficits in both China and India, each with more than a billion people. As of 2002, both countries have small exportable grain surpluses, but in both cases they are based on overpumping aquifers.[51]

This situation is not likely to last much longer. Each year the gap between water consumption and the sustainable water supply widens. Each year the drop in water tables is greater than the year before. Both aquifer depletion and the diversion of water to cities will contribute to the growing irrigation water deficit and hence to a growing grain deficit in these countries.

After China and India, there is a second tier of smaller countries with large water deficits—Algeria, Egypt, Iran, Mexico, and Pakistan. Four of these already import a large share of their grain. Only Pakistan remains self-sufficient. But with a population expanding by 4 million a year, it will also likely soon turn to the world market for grain.[52]

When will the population giants turn to the world market for a large share of their grain? No one knows for sure. The diversion of water to cities, a gradual process, is likely to continue expanding for the indefinite future, given projected urbanization trends. The final depletion of aquifers could be abrupt and less predictable simply because we do not know how much water remains in many aquifers.

A Food Bubble Economy

As noted earlier, overpumping is a way of satisfying growing food demand that virtually guarantees a future drop in food production when aquifers are depleted.

Many countries are in essence creating a "food bubble economy"—one in which food production is artificially inflated by the unsustainable use of water. When a stock bubble bursts, the stocks eventually regain their value. But when a food bubble bursts, production may not regain earlier levels. With aquifer depletion, either the rate of pumping is reduced to the level of recharge, if it is a replenishable aquifer, or pumping ceases entirely, if it is a fossil aquifer.

This consequence of excessive reliance on underground water was not obvious when farmers began pumping on a large scale a few decades ago. The great advantage of pumping groundwater is that farmers can apply the water to crops precisely when it is needed, whereas surface water is released for everyone at once, whether or not that is the best time for individual farmers. Groundwater, in contrast, is also available throughout the year, including during the dry season, enabling farmers to double crop their land.

The superior productivity of pump irrigation water over surface water is evident from data collected from farms in India. Yields of foodgrains in Punjab for land irrigated from wells was 5.5 tons per hectare, while yields on land irrigated with water from canals averaged 3.2 tons per hectare. Similar data for the southern state of Andhra Pradesh also showed a strong advantage going to pumped irrigation, with foodgrain yields averaging 5.7 tons per hectare compared with 3.4 tons on land irrigated with canal water.[53]

The high productivity of irrigation based on groundwater means that the food production losses will be that much greater when the groundwater runs out. For India, where roughly half the irrigated land is watered with underground water, production losses could be steep. In the Pakistani Punjab, overpumping may be less damaging than in India partly because Pakistan depends so heavily on surface water from the Indus River.[54]

In the United States, 37 percent of all irrigation water comes from underground; 63 percent comes from surface sources. Yet three of the top grain-producing states— Texas, Kansas, and Nebraska—each get 70–90 percent of their irrigation water from the Ogallala aquifer, which is essentially a fossil aquifer with little recharge.[55]

At what point does water scarcity translate into food scarcity? In which countries will the loss of irrigation water from aquifer depletion translate into an absolute decline in grain production? David Seckler and his colleagues at the International Water Management Institute summarize this issue well: "Many of the most populous countries of the world—China, India, Pakistan, Mexico, and nearly all the countries of the Middle East and North Africa—have literally been having a free ride over the past two or three decades by depleting their groundwater resources. The penalty of mismanagement of this valuable resource is now coming due and it is no exaggeration to say that the results could be catastrophic for these countries and, given their importance, for the world as a whole."[56]

Since irrigation water played such a central role in the tripling of the world grain harvest from 1950 to 2000, it comes as no surprise that water losses will shrink harvests. Outstanding among the countries that are living in a food bubble economy are China and India, which together contain 38 percent of the world's people. Less populous countries in a similar position are Pakistan, Mexico, and Saudi Arabia. The question for each of these countries, and for the entire world, is not whether the bubble will burst, but when.[57]

3

Eroding Soils and Shrinking Cropland

In 1938 and 1939, Walter Lowdermilk, a senior official in the Soil Conservation Service of the U.S. Department of Agriculture (USDA), traveled abroad to look at lands that had been cultivated for hundreds and even thousands of years, seeking to learn how these older civilizations had coped with soil erosion. He found that some had managed their land well, maintaining its fertility over long stretches of history. Others had failed to do so and left only remnants of their illustrious pasts.[1]

In a section of the report of his travels entitled "The Hundred Dead Cities," he described a site in northern Syria, near Aleppo, where ancient buildings were still standing in stark isolated relief, but they were on bare rock. During the seventh century, the thriving region had been invaded, initially by a Persian army and later by nomads out of the Arabian Desert. In the process, soil and water conservation practices used for centuries were abandoned. Lowdermilk noted, "Here erosion had done its worst....if the soils had remained, even though the cities were destroyed and the populations dispersed, the area might be re-peopled again and the cities rebuilt, but now that the soils are gone, all is gone."[2]

Now fast forward to a trip in 2002 by a U.N. team to

assess the food situation in Lesotho, a tiny country imbedded within South Africa. Their finding was straightforward: "Agriculture in Lesotho faces a catastrophic future; crop production is declining and could cease altogether over large tracts of the country if steps are not taken to reverse soil erosion, degradation, and the decline in soil fertility." Michael Grunwald, writing in the *Washington Post*, reports that nearly half of the children under five in Lesotho are stunted physically. "Many," he says, "are too weak to walk to school."[3]

Whether the land is in northern Syria, Lesotho, or elsewhere, the health of people living on it cannot be separated from the health of the land itself. A large share of the world's 840 million hungry live on land where the soils are worn thin by erosion.[4]

Soil Erosion: Wind and Water

The thin layer of topsoil that covers much of the earth's land surface is the foundation of civilization. Today perhaps a third or more of that foundation, the world's cropland, is losing topsoil through erosion faster than new soil is forming, thereby reducing the land's inherent productivity. Where losses are heavy, productive land turns into wasteland or desert.[5]

Some early civilizations, such as that of the Mayans in the lowlands of what is now Guatemala, which flourished from the sixth century B.C. to the ninth century A.D., may well have declined because soil erosion undermined the food supply.[6]

Over long periods of geological time, new soil formation exceeded soil erosion, forming a fertile layer of topsoil over much of the earth. But in recent decades, soil erosion has accelerated, often outpacing the creation of new soil. This loss of soil can be seen in the dust bowls that form as wind erosion soars out of control. Among those that stand out are the U.S. Dust Bowl in the Great Plains during the 1930s, the Soviet dust bowl in the Virgin Lands in the 1960s, the huge dust bowl that is forming in northwest China, and the dust storms that come out of Africa, crossing the Atlantic with the prevailing winds. Each of these is associated with a well-developed pattern of agricultural expansion onto marginal land followed by retrenchment as the soil begins to disappear.[7]

The erosion of soil can be seen in the silting of reservoirs and from the air in muddy, silt-laden rivers flowing into the sea. Pakistan's two large reservoirs, Mangla and Tarbela, which store Indus River water for that country's vast irrigation network, are losing roughly 1 percent of their storage capacity each year as they slowly fill with silt from their deforested watersheds. And Pakistan is not alone. In varying degrees, reservoirs are plagued with siltation spurred by deforestation and farming, yielding a lose-lose situation where the loss of soil also reduces the supply of irrigation water.[8]

As soils erode, land productivity falls. An analysis of several studies on the effect of soil erosion on crop yields in the United States concluded that for each 1 inch of topsoil lost, wheat and corn yields declined by 6 percent. A 1982 USDA Natural Resource Inventory, which measured the loss of topsoil from U.S. cropland at 3.1 billion tons per year, found that excess erosion was concentrated on a small share of the land. It set the stage for the landmark 1985 Conservation Reserve Program.[9]

Ethiopia, a mountainous country with highly erodible soils on steeply sloping land, is losing an estimated 1 billion tons of topsoil a year. This is one reason why Ethiopia always seems to be on the verge of famine, never able to accumulate enough grain reserves to provide a meaningful measure of food security.[10]

India is thought to be losing 4.7 billion tons of topsoil a

year, mostly through water erosion. Its monsoonal climate, with the concentration of rainfall during a few months of the year, leaves its exposed soils vulnerable to erosion.[11]

In neighboring Nepal, a government report estimated annual soil nutrient loss from erosion at 1.3 million tons—on top of the 500,000 tons of soil nutrients removed through harvesting of crops. Of this total loss of 1.8 million tons, only 300,000 tons are being replaced through the use of organic and mineral fertilizers.[12]

In China, plowing excesses became common in several provinces as agriculture was pushed northward into the pastoral zone between 1987 and 1996. In Inner Mongolia (Nei Monggol), for example, the cultivated area increased by 1.1 million hectares, or 22 percent, during this period. Other provinces that expanded their cultivated area by 3 percent or more during this nine-year span include Heilongjiang, Hunan, Tibet (Xizang), Qinghai, and Xinjiang. Severe wind erosion of soil on this newly plowed land made it clear that the only sustainable use of much of it was grazing. As a result, Chinese agriculture is now engaged in a strategic withdrawal in these provinces, pulling back to only the land that will sustain crop production.[13]

Since the health of people is closely related to the health of the soil on which they depend, most hunger is found in the mountains and the hills and on semiarid farmlands with marginal rainfall. Little hunger is found on well-watered agricultural plains. In the absence of conservation practices, marginal soils tend to marginalize the people who depend on them. Richard Bilsborrow, an economist/demographer at the University of North Carolina, notes: "Three quarters of the poorest 20 percent in Latin America live on marginal lands. Fifty-seven percent of Asia's poor and 51 percent of Africa's also inhabit marginal lands. Not just the lack of land, but also its *quality*, contributes to world poverty."[14]

Advancing Deserts

Desertification, the process of converting productive land to wasteland through overuse and mismanagement, is unfortunately all too common. Anything that removes protective grass or trees leaves the land vulnerable to wind and to water erosion and the loss of topsoil.

In the early stages of desertification, the finer particles of soil are removed by the wind, creating dust storms. Once the fine particles are removed, then the coarser particles—the sand—are also carried by the wind. Sand storms are capable of destroying vegetation and of disrupting transportation by blocking highways and railroads with drifting sand. A scientific paper analyzing a particularly severe dust and sand storm in May 1993 in Gansu Province in China's northwest reported that it reduced visibility to zero and described the daytime sky as "dark as a winter night." The storm killed 49 people, destroyed 170,000 hectares (450,000 acres) of standing crops, damaged 40,000 trees, and killed 6,700 cattle and sheep. Forty-two trains were cancelled, delayed, or simply parked to wait until the storm passed and the tracks were cleared of drifting sand.[15]

Large-scale desertification is concentrated in Asia and Africa—two regions that together contain nearly 4 billion of the world's 6.2 billion people. The demands of growing human and livestock populations are simply exceeding the land's carrying capacity.[16]

On the northern edge of the Sahara, Algeria is facing the desertification of its cropland. In December 2000, agriculture ministry officials announced a four-year plan to halt the advancing desert by converting the southernmost 20 percent of Algeria's grainland into fruit and olive orchards, vineyards, and other permanent crops. The government hopes that this barrier of vegetation will halt the northward movement of the Sahara and save the country's fertile northern region.[17]

To the south, Nigeria—Africa's most populous country—is fighting a losing battle with the advancing desert. Each year, it loses 351,000 hectares (877,000 acres) of land to desertification. Affecting each of the 10 northern states, desertification has emerged as Nigeria's leading environmental problem.[18]

In East Africa, Kenya is being squeezed by spreading deserts, and desertification affects up to a third of the country's 32 million people. As elsewhere, the unholy triumvirate of overgrazing, overplowing, and overcutting of trees are all contributing to the loss of productive land.[19]

Iran is also losing its battle with the desert. Mohammad Jarian, who heads Iran's Anti-Desertification Organization, reported in 2002 that sand storms had buried 124 villages in the southeastern province of Sistan-Baluchistan, leading to their abandonment. Drifting sands had covered grazing areas, starving livestock and depriving villagers of their livelihood.[20]

Neighboring Afghanistan is faced with a similar situation. The Registan Desert is migrating westward, encroaching on agricultural areas. A U.N. Environment Programme (UNEP) team reports that "up to 100 villages have been submerged by windblown dust and sand." In the country's northwest, sand dunes are moving onto agricultural land in the upper reaches of the Amu Darya basin, their path cleared by the loss of stabilizing vegetation from firewood gathering and overgrazing. The UNEP team observed sand dunes 15 meters high blocking roads, forcing residents to establish new routes.[21]

China is being affected more by desertification than any other major country. For the outside world, the evidence of this is often seen in the dust storms in late winter and early spring, as described in Chapter 1. These storms, which regularly reach the Korean peninsula and Japan, sometimes even cross the Pacific, depositing dust in the western United States.[22]

Overgrazing is the principal culprit. After the 1978 economic reforms, when China shifted to a market economy, the government lost control of livestock numbers. As a result, the livestock population soared. The 106 million cattle and 298 million sheep and goats that now range across the land are simply denuding the western and northern part of the country, a vast grazing commons.[23]

A report by a U.S. embassy official in May 2001 after a visit to Xilingol Prefecture in Inner Mongolia notes that official data classify 97 percent of the prefecture as grassland, but that a simple visual survey indicates that a third of the terrain appears to be desert. The report describes the livestock population in the prefecture climbing from 2 million as recently as 1977 to 18 million in 2000. A Chinese scientist doing grassland research in the prefecture says that if recent desertification trends continue, Xilingol will be uninhabitable in 15 years.[24]

A recent U.S. Embassy report entitled "Desert Mergers and Acquisitions" says satellite monitoring shows two deserts in north-central China expanding and merging to form a single, larger desert overlapping Inner Mongolia and Gansu provinces. To the west in Xinjiang Province, two even larger deserts—the Taklimakan and Kumtag—are also heading for a merger. Highways in this area are regularly inundated by sand dunes.[25]

The overgrazing, overplowing, and overcutting that are driving the desertification process are intensifying as the growth in human and livestock numbers continues. Stopping the desertification process from claiming ever more productive land may now rest on stopping the growth in human numbers and in the livestock on which they depend.

Crops and Cars Compete for Land

In addition to the losses to degradation, prime cropland is also being paved over. As the new century begins, the competition between cars and crops for land is intensifying. The addition of 12 million cars each year consumes, in new roads, highways, and parking lots, roughly 1 million hectares of land—enough to feed 9 million people if it were all cropland. Since the world's people are concentrated in the agriculturally productive regions, a disproportionate share of the land paved for cars is cropland.[26]

Millions of hectares of cropland in the industrial world have been paved over for roads and parking lots. Each U.S. car, for example, requires on average 0.07 hectares (0.18 acres) of paved land for roads and parking space. Thus for every five cars added to the U.S. fleet, an area the size of a football field is covered with asphalt. More often than not, it is cropland that is paved simply because the flat, well-drained soils that are well suited for farming are also ideal for building roads.[27]

The United States, with its 214 million motor vehicles, has paved 6.3 million kilometers (3.9 million miles) of roads, enough to circle the earth at the equator 157 times. In addition to roads, cars require parking space. Imagine a parking lot for 214 million cars and trucks. If that is a stretch, try visualizing a parking lot for 1,000 cars and then imagine what 214,000 of these would look like.[28]

However we visualize it, the U.S. area devoted to roads and parking lots covers an estimated 16 million hectares (39 million acres), almost as much as the 20 million hectares that U.S. farmers plant in wheat. But this paving of land in industrial countries is slowing as countries approach automobile saturation. In the United States, there is nearly one vehicle for every person. In Western Europe and Japan, there is typically one for every two people.[29]

In developing countries, however, where automobile

fleets are still small and where cropland is in short supply, the paving is just getting under way. More and more of the 11 million cars added to the world fleet of 531 million are being added in the developing world. This means that the war between cars and crops is being waged over wheat fields and rice paddies in countries where hunger is common. The outcome of this conflict in China and India, which together contain 2.4 billion people, will affect food security everywhere.[30]

Car-centered industrial societies that are densely populated, such as Germany, the United Kingdom, and Japan, which have paved an average of 0.02 hectares per vehicle, have lost some of their most productive cropland in the process. Similarly, China and India also face acute pressure on their cropland base from industrialization. Although China covers roughly the same area as the United States, its 1.3 billion people are concentrated in just one third of the country—a thousand-mile strip on the eastern and southern coast where the cropland is also located.[31]

If China were one day to achieve the Japanese ownership rate of one car for every two people, it would have a fleet of 640 million, compared with only 13 million today. While the idea of such an enormous fleet may seem farfetched, we need only remind ourselves that China has already overtaken the United States in steel production, grain production, and red meat production. It is a huge economy and, since 1980, also the world's fastest growing one.[32]

Assuming the same paved area per vehicle in China as in Europe and Japan, a fleet of 640 million cars would require paving nearly 13 million hectares—most of which would likely be cropland. This would equal almost half of China's 28 million hectares of riceland, which produces 122 million tons of rice, the principal food staple.[33]

The situation in India is similar. While India is geographically only a third the size of China, it too has more than 1 billion people, and it now has 8 million motor vehicles. A land-hungry country projected to add 515 million more people by 2050 cannot afford to cover valuable cropland with roads and parking lots.[34]

There simply is not enough land in China, India, and other densely populated countries such as Indonesia, Bangladesh, Pakistan, Iran, Egypt, and Mexico to support auto-centered transportation systems and to feed their people. The competition between cars and crops for land is becoming a competition between the rich and the poor, between those who can afford automobiles and those who are struggling to buy enough food.

The Land-Hungry Soybean
Sometimes the competition for land to produce grain comes from unexpected sources, such as the soybean, which has emerged as a strategic player in our modern food economy. Widely consumed as food, it is now also the leading vegetable oil for table use and the principal protein supplement for livestock, poultry, and fish rations.

Roughly one tenth of the world soybean harvest is consumed as food, mostly as tofu, as a meat substitute in veggie burgers, or as other products, such as soy sauce—a ubiquitous ingredient in East Asian cuisines. One fifth of the harvest is consumed as vegetable oil. In 2002, the world's soybean harvest exceeded that of all other oilseeds combined, including olives, peanuts, sunflowers, rapeseed, cottonseed, and coconuts. Although coconut oil looms large in the vegetable oil economy of Southeast Asia and olive oil has long been a standby in the Mediterranean countries, it is soybean oil that dominates the world vegetable oil economy.[35]

When crushed, the soybean yields roughly 20 percent

oil and 80 percent meal. Over the last 50 years, soybean meal has emerged as the world's dominant protein supplement in livestock, poultry, and fish rations, exceeding the use of all other high-protein meals combined. The incorporation of small amounts of high-quality soy protein into feed rations boosts sharply the efficiency with which pigs, poultry, and fish convert grain into animal protein, making the soybean invaluable.[36]

The soybean, domesticated in Central China some 5,000 years ago, was imported into the United States in 1804. For nearly a century and a half the soybean languished in the United States, grown largely as a garden novelty crop. But then following World War II, as the global demand for vegetable oil and for animal feed protein supplements soared, U.S. farmers began to expand production rapidly, quickly eclipsing the output in China. In 1973, the soybean harvested area in the United States overtook that of wheat. It surpassed corn in 1999. The U.S. 2002 soybean harvest was worth $13 billion, nearly twice that of wheat.[37]

Rather quickly, the geographic focus of soybean production had shifted to the New World. By 1990, the United States was producing half of the world's soybeans, most of them in the Corn Belt, often in an alternate-year rotation with corn. In Brazil and Argentina, which have discovered in recent decades that the soybean is well adapted to their soils and climate, production has also climbed, collectively overtaking that of the United States in 2003.[38]

Worldwide, the soybean harvest expanded from 17 million tons in 1950 to 194 million tons in 2002. (See Figure 3–1.) This 11-fold gain compares with a threefold gain of the world grain harvest during the same period. Nearly all the growth in grain production since 1950 has come from raising grain yields, whereas the 11-fold

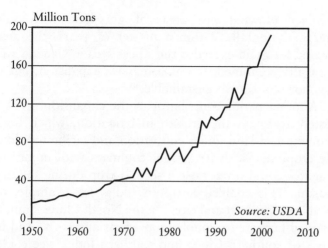

Figure 3–1. *World Soybean Production, 1950–2002*

increase in soybeans depended heavily on a sixfold increase in area. Because the soybean, a legume, devotes much of its metabolic energy to fixing nitrogen in the soil and to producing high-quality protein, yields have risen slowly compared with those of grain. We get more soybeans by planting more soybeans. Given the role of the soybean in boosting the efficiency with which grain is converted into animal protein worldwide, producing more soybeans is essential. But satisfying the growing demand for them will nonetheless take additional land.[39]

Grainland Gains and Losses

The world grain area expanded from 587 million hectares in 1950 to its historical peak of 732 million hectares in 1981. Since then, however, grainland has shrunk, dropping to 647 million hectares in 2002. The first large expansion in grainland after World War II came in the late 1950s with the Soviet Virgin Lands project. Concentrated in what is now the Republic of Kazakhstan, this involved plowing vast areas of grassland with only marginal rainfall. Within a matter of years, the area cleared for grain exceeded the wheat area in Canada and Australia combined. It was a massive expansion, but it was not ecologically sustainable.[40]

Another major contributor to the expansion of harvested area was the growth in irrigation, which both brought arid land under cultivation and facilitated double cropping. With irrigation, countries with moderate climates could often raise a second crop during the dry season. This enabled northern India, for example, to double crop wheat and rice. On the North China Plain, it enabled farmers to double crop wheat and corn. And in parts of southern China and southern India, rice could be double cropped and even occasionally triple cropped. As the century neared its end, the growth in irrigation slowed and in some countries, such as Saudi Arabia, the irrigated land area began to shrink.[41]

Over the last two decades, some countries that had overplowed were forced to pull back. Kazakhstan's grain area, which was roughly 25 million hectares in 1980, had shrunk to 12 million hectares by 2000. In the United States, the Conservation Reserve Program was created in the 1985 Food Security Act to convert highly erodible cropland back into grass or trees. This program retired some 14 million hectares, roughly one tenth of U.S. cropland, from 1985 onward.[42]

As the last century was ending, the Chinese government, concerned about the dust bowl forming in the country's northwest, launched a conservation program similar to that of the United States—one designed to help farmers plant some 10 million hectares of highly erodible grainland in trees. In addition to this planned cropland retirement, China is losing land for other reasons, as noted earlier. Between 1997 and 2002, its grain harvested

area shrank from 90 million to 81 million hectares, partly from irrigation water shortages and the resultant
decline in double cropping and partly from desert
encroachment. By crop, more than 7 million hectares of
the decline was of wheat and 2 million was of rice.[43]

Cropland is also being converted to fish ponds. China,
producer of more than 20 million tons of farmed fish,
which is roughly two thirds of the global total, has devoted 5 million hectares of land—much of it cropland—to
fish ponds. Dominated by a sophisticated freshwater
carp polyculture, this activity is continuing to expand. In
the United States, where aquaculture is dominated by catfish, some 44,000 hectares (109,000 acres) of land in Mississippi are devoted to catfish ponds. Much of this
bottomland was once used to grow rice.[44]

In this new century, some rainforest is being cleared
for oil palm production in Malaysia and Indonesia, but
by far the largest cropland expansion initiative under way
today is in Brazil to the south and west of the Amazon
basin. This savannah-like land, known as the *cerrado*, is
being cleared by Brazilian farmers as they both respond
to the soaring world demand for soybeans and feed a
domestic population of 176 million, which is growing
and becoming more affluent. Thus far, land cleared in the
cerrado has been used largely to produce soybeans. This,
combined with a shift of grainland to soybeans, has
expanded the soybean area from 10 million hectares in
1990 to nearly 18 million in 2002.[45]

This land expansion, combined with rising yields,
has tripled Brazil's soybean harvest since 1990, putting it
in a position to soon eclipse the United States as the
world's leading soybean producer and exporter.
Although the *cerrado* appears well adapted to producing
soybeans, it has not yet contributed much to expanding
the world grain harvest. It might, however, do so if its

farmers adopt a two-year rotation with soybeans and corn, similar to that used in the U.S. Corn Belt.[46]

Argentina is also contributing to the surge in world soybean output by shifting land from grain and by plowing its grasslands. But this grassland cannot be extensively plowed without encountering serious erosion and wildlife problems.

Brazil's expansion into the *cerrado* stands alone in the early twenty-first century as the only large-scale initiative to increase the world's cropland, one that could exceed in scale the Soviet Virgin Lands project of a half-century ago. If earlier expansion efforts in other countries are any guide, however, Brazil will also overexpand and be forced at some point to pull back.[47]

Spreading Land Hunger
Nowhere is the ubiquitous effect of population growth so visible as in its effect on the size of farms. With the world's grainland area changing relatively little over the last half-century and with population more than doubling, grainland per person shrank by more than half from 1950 to 2000. By 2050, it is projected to shrink further—to less than in India today. And because the nearly 3 billion people to be added by then will be born in developing countries, they will experience a disproportionate shrinkage in grainland.[48]

The shrinkage in India, which is projected to add nearly 500 million people by mid-century, is of particular concern. In 1960 India had 48 million farms, but as land was transferred from one generation to the next and then to the next, and divided each time among the heirs, the number of farms multiplied to 105 million by 1990. Farms that averaged 2.7 hectares in 1960 are less than half that size today. Millions of inherited plots are so small that their owners are effectively landless.[49]

The projected shrinkage in Nigeria, Africa's largest country, is even greater, since its population is expected to increase from 121 million today to 258 million in 2050. With a population in 2050 approaching that in the United States today, squeezed into a country only slightly larger than Texas, the handwriting on the wall is clear.[50]

In the western hemisphere, Mexico's grainland area per person has shrunk by half over the last 50 years. With its small plots being divided and then divided again as each successive generation inherits the family farm, land hunger plagues rural areas. The population is projected to grow from 102 million to 140 million by 2050. Some 400 to 600 people per day are fleeing rural areas, making Mexico City one of the world's largest cities and the United States the principal destination of migrants.[51]

Looking ahead, we are encouraged by the slowing of world population growth over the last two decades. But even so, some countries, including Pakistan, Nigeria, Ethiopia, Colombia, the Philippines, Saudi Arabia, and Iraq, are projected to add more people during the next 50 years than they did during the last 50.[52]

In some countries, the land that a family of five has to produce their wheat, rice, or corn in 2050 will be less than 1 acre—less than the living space of an affluent American family with a house in the suburbs. Among the countries in this situation are Bangladesh, China, Ethiopia, India, Mexico, Nigeria, Pakistan, Tanzania, and Uganda. Even worse, in Egypt, Malaysia, and Rwanda, the grainland per person in 2050 will be scarcely half the size of a tennis court.[53]

Except for those in sub-Saharan Africa, virtually all developing countries have benefited from the enormous gains in land productivity over the last half-century. Unfortunately, for many countries where land productivity has already doubled or tripled, such as Mexico,

Egypt, India, and Pakistan, future gains to offset the shrinkage in grainland per person will be difficult to come by.[54]

Eradicating hunger in a world of eroding soils and shrinking cropland per person will not be easy, but it can be done, as described in Plan B, Part II of this book. We know how to conserve soil and raise the land's fertility. We also know how to plan families and stabilize population.

Although the scale of these issues is new, the issues themselves are not. In his classic USDA report, which is still in print, Walter Lowdermilk proposed an eleventh commandment: "Thou shalt inherit the Holy Earth as a faithful steward, conserving its resources and productivity from generation to generation. Thou shalt safeguard thy fields from soil erosion, thy living waters from drying up, thy forests from desolation, and protect thy hills from overgrazing by thy herds, that thy descendants may have abundance forever. If any shall fail in this stewardship of the land, thy fruitful fields shall become sterile stony ground and wasting gullies, and thy descendants shall decrease and live in poverty or perish from off the face of the earth." Lowdermilk was describing in biblical language the basic principles of what today we call sustainable development.[55]

4

Rising Temperatures and Rising Seas

As the earth's temperature rises, it alters the entire climate system, affecting all life on earth. It brings more intense heat waves, more destructive storms, lower crop yields, ice melting, and rising seas, and it shrinks the snowfields and glaciers that feed so many of the world's rivers. Among the industries most affected are agriculture, insurance, and tourism.

Intense heat waves are taking a growing human toll. In 1995, 700 residents of Chicago died in a heat wave. In the summer of 1998, 100 Texans died in a prolonged heat spell. At about the same time, some 2,500 people died in a heat wave in India. In May 2002, in a heat wave in India that reached 50 degrees Celsius (122 degrees Fahrenheit), more than 1,000 people died in the state of Andhra Pradesh alone.[1]

Among the various manifestations of rising temperatures, ice melting, in particular, is drawing attention from scientists. They are particularly concerned because of the effect on sea level. Rising seas that encroach on a continent and shrink the habitable land area while population is growing can only exacerbate an already difficult problem.

More frequent and more destructive storms are now a matter of record. The insurance industry is painfully aware of the relationship between higher temperatures and storm intensity. The last few years have brought a flurry of lowered credit ratings, both for insurance companies and the reinsurance companies that back them up by spreading their risks.

Numerous industries are affected, including many smaller ones. For example, as mountain snow cover shrinks, the ski industry also shrinks, losing revenue and jobs. In the United States, the ski industry has launched its own campaign to reduce carbon emissions by buying wind-generated electricity to operate ski lifts. Industry leaders call their campaign "Keep Winter Cool."[2]

The Temperature Record

Scientists at NASA's Goddard Institute for Space Studies gather data from a global network of some 800 climate-monitoring stations to measure changes in the earth's average temperature. Their temperature records go back 123 years, to 1880.[3]

From 1880 to 1930, the global temperature for almost every year was below the norm (which scientists define as the average from 1950 to 1980). During the 1930s, the first decade when there were several years above the norm, this pattern began to change. It brought record temperatures and drought to the U.S. Great Plains, helping to create the Dust Bowl.[4]

Beginning in 1977, the temperature began to climb and it has been above the norm each year since then. During the 1980s, the average global temperature was 0.26 degrees Celsius above; during the 1990s, it averaged 0.40 degrees above the norm. And during the first three years of the new century, the average temperature has been 0.55 degrees above the norm. If the accelerating rise continues, the jump in this decade will substantially exceed that of each of the preceding ones.[5]

Meteorologists note that the 16 warmest years on record have come since 1980. And since the three warmest years on record have come in the last five years, not only is the earth's temperature rising, but the rise is accelerating. (See Figure 4–1.) Against this backdrop of record increases, the projections of the Intergovernmental Panel on Climate Change (IPCC) that the earth's average temperature will rise 1.4–5.8 degrees Celsius (2.5–10.4 degrees Fahrenheit) during the current century seem all too possible. The IPCC upper-end projected increase of 5.8 degrees Celsius during this century is comparable to the change registered between the last Ice Age and today. Whether the world's temperature trend is more likely to follow the lower or the upper projection, no one knows. But given the recent acceleration in the rise, we may now be on a trajectory that is much closer to the upper end of the range.[6]

At a practical level, the projected rise in temperature of 1.4–5.8 degrees Celsius is a global average. In reality,

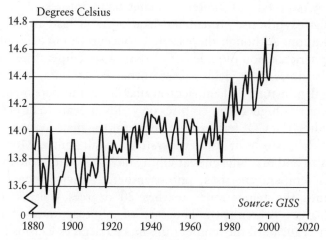

Figure 4–1. *Average Global Temperature, 1880–2002*

the rise will be very uneven. It will be much greater over land than over oceans, in the higher latitudes than over the equator, in the continental interior than in coastal regions. James J. McCarthy, Harvard professor of biological oceanography and co-chair of an IPCC working group, notes that while global average temperature rose roughly 1 degree Fahrenheit during the century that just ended, on Alaska's north slope and in northwestern Canada it rose by 4–7 degrees Fahrenheit (2.2–3.9 degrees Celsius), several times the global average.[7]

The Yield Effect

Among the leading economic trends most sensitive to this warming are crop yields. Crops in many countries are grown at or near their thermal optimum, making them vulnerable to any rise in temperature. Even a minor increase—1 or 2 degrees Celsius—during the growing season can reduce the grain harvest in major food-producing regions, such as the North China Plain, the Gangetic plain of India, or the Corn Belt of the United States.[8]

As noted in Chapter 1, higher temperatures can halt photosynthesis, prevent fertilization, and lead to dehydration. Although the elevated concentrations of atmospheric carbon dioxide (CO_2) that raise temperature can also raise crop yields (absent other constraints, such as soil moisture and nutrient availability), the detrimental effect of higher temperatures on yields appears to be overriding the CO_2 fertilization effect for the major crops.

In a study of local ecosystem sustainability, Mohan Wali and his colleagues at Ohio State University note that as temperature rises, photosynthetic activity increases until the temperature reaches 20 degrees Celsius (68 degrees Fahrenheit). The rate of photosynthesis then plateaus until the temperature hits 35 degrees Celsius (95 degrees Fahrenheit), whereupon it begins to decline, until at 40 degrees Celsius (104 degrees Fahrenheit), it ceases entirely. At this temperature, the plant is in thermal shock, simply trying to survive.[9]

The most vulnerable part of the plant's life cycle is the period when fertilization occurs. Each of the three food staples—rice, wheat, and corn—is vulnerable at this stage of development. Corn is particularly vulnerable. In order for corn to reproduce, pollen must fall from the tassel to the strands of silk that emerge from the end of each ear of corn. Each of these silk strands is attached to a kernel site on the cob. If the kernel is to develop, a grain of pollen must fall on the silk strand and then journey to the kernel site, much as an unfertilized egg moves along the fallopian tube. When temperatures are uncommonly high, the silk strands dry out and quickly turn brown, unable to play their role in the fertilization process.

The effects of temperature on rice fertility have been studied in detail by scientists at the International Rice Research Institute in the Philippines. They report that the fertility of rice falls from 100 percent at 34 degrees Celsius (93 degrees Fahrenheit) to near zero at 40 degrees Celsius, leading to crop failure.[10]

Higher temperatures can also lead to dehydration. While it may take a team of scientists to understand the effects of temperature on the fertilization of the rice plant, anyone can tell when a corn field is suffering from heat stress and dehydration. When a corn plant curls its leaves to reduce exposure to the sun, photosynthesis is reduced. And when the stomata on the underside of the leaves close to reduce moisture loss, CO_2 intake is reduced, thereby restricting photosynthesis. The corn plant, which under ideal conditions is so extraordinarily productive, is highly vulnerable to thermal stress.

K. S. Kavi Kumar of the Madras School of Economics and Jyoti Parikh of the Indira Gandhi Institute of Development Research assessed the effect of higher temperatures on wheat and rice yields in India. Basing their model on data from 10 sites, they concluded that in north India a 1-degree Celsius rise in mean temperature did not meaningfully reduce wheat yields, but a 2-degree rise lowered yields at almost all of the sites. When they looked at temperature change alone, a 2-degree Celsius rise led to a decline in irrigated wheat yields ranging from 37 percent to 58 percent. When they incorporated the negative effects of a higher temperature with the positive effects of CO_2 fertilization, the decline in yields among the various sites ranged from 8 percent to 38 percent.[11]

The decline in rice yields was remarkably similar. A separate study in the South Indian state of Kerala, looking at the effect of temperature on rice yields, concluded that for each 1-degree Celsius rise in temperature, rice yields declined 6 percent. These studies are disturbingly relevant given the projected average temperature rise in India of 2.3–4.8 degrees Celsius following the doubling of atmospheric CO_2 over pre-industrial levels.[12]

As rising temperatures become a reality and as the effect of temperature on crop yields becomes clearer, agricultural scientists are becoming concerned. John Sheehy, a crop ecologist and leading researcher on the effects of climate change on crops, offers a scientific rule of thumb for assessing the effect of higher temperature on the yield of rice plants: "For every 1 degree Celsius increase in temperature between 30 and 40 degrees Celsius during flowering, fertility decreases by 10 percent." At 40 degrees, fertility drops to near zero. L. H. Allen, Jr., one of the scientists who is analyzing the temperature-yield relationship at the U.S. Department of Agriculture, concludes that each rise of 2 degrees Fahrenheit (1.1 degrees Celsius) above ideal levels reduces yield by 10 percent.[13]

A recent study by a team of U.S. scientists at the Carnegie Institution goes further. Based on U.S. corn and soybean yield data from more than 400 counties over the last 17 years, they report that a 1-degree Celsius rise in temperature during the June-August growing season reduces yields of both crops by 17 percent. This may help explain why the record U.S. average corn yield—8.7 tons per hectare in 1994—has not been matched during the eight years since then.[14]

With the global average temperature for 2002 at a near-record high, it is not surprising that the 2002 harvest in several countries suffered from high temperatures. As the temperature climbs, more countries are likely to suffer crop-withering heat waves. The May 2002 heat wave in India that claimed more than 1,000 lives in Andhra Pradesh also stressed crops. So, too, did the heat wave in neighboring Pakistan.[15]

In the United States, intense heat in 2002, particularly in the Great Plains states—often 38 degrees Celsius (100 degrees Fahrenheit) or higher—took its toll on the grain harvest. These near-record temperatures at times extended northward into the Great Plains of Canada during the summer, exacerbating drought there and shrinking the wheat harvest. The higher latitudes and continental interiors where the projected temperature rise is to be greatest neatly defines the North American breadbasket—the Great Plains of the United States and Canada and the U.S. Corn Belt.[16]

The North China Plain, China's principal food-producing region, also suffered from high temperatures in 2002. Even in September, temperatures were soaring into the mid-30s and above. Such high temperatures not only stress crops, they also increase soil moisture evaporation, raising the demand for irrigation water.[17]

Plant breeders will undoubtedly be able to develop

crop strains that are more heat-resistant, but it is doubtful that they can fully offset the effects of rising temperature. And thus far biotechnology has not had any major
success in this strategically important area of plant
breeding.

If we permit atmospheric CO_2 levels to continue rising at recent rates, we will be headed for a world far
warmer than any since agriculture began some 11,000
years ago—a world in which farmers will be struggling to
adjust to an ever-changing climate. They must think
about changing to not only new varieties, as they have
always done to boost production, but also to new crops
in order to adapt to the changing climate. And virtually
all the world's farmers will have to change their farming
practices, keeping in mind this is not just a one-time
adjustment but a continuing change and a guessing game
as to whether shifts are aberrations or a lasting change in
the local climate. In the past, farmers could deal with
aberrations because they knew that sooner or later conditions would return to normal, but now there is no "normal" to return to.

What changes in cropping patterns lie ahead as the
earth becomes warmer? Will the decline in production of
drought-tolerant crops, such as sorghum and millet, over
the last several decades be reversed as they replace wheat
in human diets and in rations for livestock and poultry?
Will rice give way to more water-efficient wheat in our
diets? Will water shortages lead to wheat eventually edg-
ing out rice as the dominant food staple in both India and
China?

Another response will be to move agriculture northward into Canada and Siberia. Unfortunately, the soils in
these regions are not particularly fertile. There is, for
example, a world of difference between the deep fertile
soils south of the Great Lakes and those north of them.

The U.S. Corn Belt is the world's most productive agricultural region, whereas the thin glaciated soils north of the Great Lakes are far less productive. Despite its vast land area, Canada produces less grain than France does. It is a leading exporter only because its population is so small relative to its vast land area.[18]

Temperature rises in some areas could easily be double the global average. In other areas, there might be little or no change. Such is the world of uncertainty now facing the world's farmers.[19]

Reservoirs in the Sky

Snow/ice masses in mountains are nature's freshwater reservoirs. These "reservoirs in the sky" are nature's way of storing water to feed rivers during the summer dry season. Agriculture is heavily dependent on these snow/ice masses, which are a major source of water for irrigated farming. Now they are being threatened by the rise in temperature.

In some agricultural regions, snowmelt is the leading source of irrigation water. These regions include the southwestern United States, where the Colorado River, the primary source of irrigation water, depends on snowfields in the Rockies for much of its flow. California, in addition to depending heavily on the Colorado, also relies on snowmelt from the Sierra Nevada in the eastern part of the state. Both the Sierra Nevada and the coastal range supply irrigation water to California's Central Valley, the world's fruit and vegetable basket.

Preliminary results of an analysis of the effects of rising temperature on three major river systems in the western United States—the Columbia, the Sacramento, and the Colorado—indicate that the winter snow pack in the mountains feeding them will be dramatically reduced and that winter rainfall and flooding will increase accordingly. John Krist, who writes for California's *Ventura County Star*, says that this "will mean less water flowing into reservoirs from snowmelt during dry months but more pouring in during flood-prone winter months when there is no room to store it." Many of the world's river irrigation systems are plagued with the same prospect.[20]

In Central Asia, the agriculture in several former Soviet republics depends heavily on snowmelt from the Hindu Kush mountain range. Among these are Uzbekistan, Turkmenistan, Kyrgyzstan, Kazakhstan, and Tajikistan. Afghanistan also depends on the Hindu Kush. Iran gets much of its water from the snowmelt in the 6,000-meter Elburz Mountains between Tehran and the Caspian Sea.

Largest of all in world food terms is the snow/ice mass in the Himalayas. Every major river in Asia originates in the Himalayas, including the Indus, the Ganges, the Mekong, the Yangtze, and the Yellow. If rainfall in the Himalayas increases and snowfall decreases, the seasonal flow of these rivers will change, leading to more flooding during the rainy season and less snowmelt to feed rivers during the dry season.[21]

This melting's impact on the Yellow River will affect China's wheat harvest, the largest in the world. Alterations in the flow of the Yangtze River will directly affect China's rice harvest—also the world's largest. And India's wheat harvest, which is second only to China's, will be affected by the flows of both the Indus and the Ganges. Anything that alters the seasonal flow of the Mekong will reduce the rice harvest of Viet Nam, a leading source of rice for importing countries.[22]

There are many more mountain ranges where the snow/ice cover is melting, including the Alps and the Andes. The snow/ice masses in the world's leading mountain ranges and the water they store as ice and snow has been taken for granted simply because it has always been there. Now that is changing. If we continue burning fossil fuels and raising the earth's temperature, we risk losing these reservoirs in the sky.

Melting Ice and Rising Seas

In its landmark third edition report released in early 2001, the IPCC projected that sea level would rise during this century 0.09–0.88 meters (4–35 inches) as a result of thermal expansion and ice melting. New studies released during the two years since then indicate that the earth's ice cover is melting much faster than IPCC scientists assumed.[23]

A 2002 study by two scientists from the University of Colorado's Institute of Arctic and Alpine Research shows that the melting of large glaciers on the west coast of Alaska and in northern Canada is accelerating. Earlier data had indicated that the melting was raising sea level by 0.14 millimeters per year, but new data for the 1990s indicate that the more rapid melting is now raising sea level by 0.32 millimeters a year—more than twice as fast.[24]

The Colorado study is reinforced by a U.S. Geological Survey (USGS) study that indicates glaciers are now shrinking in all 11 of Alaska's glaciated mountain ranges. An earlier USGS study reported that the number of glaciers in Glacier National Park in the United States had dwindled from 150 in 1850 to fewer than 50 today. The remaining glaciers are projected to disappear within 30 years.[25]

Another team of USGS scientists, which used satellite data to measure changes in the area covered by glaciers worldwide, describes an accelerated melting of glaciers in several mountainous regions, including the South American Andes, the Swiss Alps, and the French and Spanish Pyrenees.[26]

The melting of glaciers is gaining momentum

throughout the Andes. Lonnie Thompson of Ohio State University reports that the Qori Kalis glacier, which is located on the west side of the Quelccaya ice cap in the Peruvian Andes, shrank three times as fast each year from 1998 to 2000 as it did between 1995 and 1998. And the earlier rate, in turn, was nearly double the annual rate of retreat from 1993 to 1995. Thompson also projects that the large Quelccaya ice cap will disappear entirely between 2010 and 2020. The Antisana glacier in Ecuador, which supplies half of the water for Quito, has retreated nearly 100 meters in the last eight years.[27]

Bernard Francou, research director for the French government's Institute of Research and Development, believes that within the next 15 years, 80 percent of South American glaciers will disappear. For countries like Bolivia, Peru, and Ecuador, which rely on glaciers for water for household and irrigation use, this is not good news.[28]

Lonnie Thompson's studies of Kilimanjaro show that between 1989 and 2000, Africa's tallest mountain lost 33 percent of its ice field. He projects that its snowcap could disappear entirely within the next 15 years.[29]

The vast snow/ice mass in the Himalayas is also retreating. Although data are not widely available, those glaciers that have been studied indicate an accelerating retreat. As one example, representatives of the major mountaineering association, The Union Internationale des Associations d'Alpinisme, report that the glacier that ended at the base camp from which Edmund Hillary and Tenzing Norgay launched their history-making ascent of Everest in 1953 has retreated about 5 kilometers (3 miles). Geologist Jeffrey Kargel, who studies the Himalayas, is not surprised by this. "That fits in with the general picture of what's happening in Nepal, India, Bhutan and, to a smaller extent, Tibet," he says.[30]

Both the North and the South Poles are showing the

effects of rising temperature. While the South Pole is covered by a huge continent, the North Pole is covered by the Arctic Ocean. A flurry of papers presented at the annual conference of the American Geophysical Union (AGU) in December 2002 reported dramatic advances in ice melting. They noted that in summer 2002 the Arctic Ocean ice cover had shrunk to the smallest area seen since 1978, when detailed studies began. Mark Serreze of the National Snow and Ice Data Center in Boulder, Colorado, reported that this was the most abrupt change in the ocean's ice cover that scientists have seen during the 24 years they have been monitoring it.[31]

In addition to shrinking, the Arctic sea ice has thinned by 42 percent over the last 35 years—from an average of 3.1 meters to 1.8 meters. The combination of the shrinking and thinning has reduced the mass of sea ice by half. A team of Norwegian scientists projects that the Arctic Sea could be entirely ice-free during the summer within a matter of decades.[32]

If that happens, it would not affect sea level because the ice is already in the water. But it would alter the Arctic heat balance. When sunlight strikes ice and snow, roughly 80 percent of the light is reflected back into space and 20 percent is absorbed as heat. If, however, sunlight strikes land or open water, only 20 percent is bounced back into space and 80 percent is converted into heat, leading to higher temperatures. This is an example of a positive feedback loop, a situation in which a trend feeds on itself.[33]

The melting of Greenland's ice sheet is a different matter. Another report delivered at the AGU conference—this one by Konrad Steffen, a glaciologist at the University of Colorado—indicated that the ice cover on Greenland is also melting much faster over a 686,000-square-kilometer area (roughly a third of the total area) than at any time on record. Steffen described how he and his colleagues, who were camped on the normally frozen Greenland ice, were flooded under a foot of meltwater and had to be rescued by helicopter.[34]

The prospect of much warmer Arctic summers is of concern because Greenland, which is three times the size of Texas, lies partly within the Arctic Circle. An article in *Science* reports that if the entire ice sheet on this huge island were to melt, it would raise sea level 7 meters (23 feet). Such a melting, even under the most rapid warming scenario, would be measured in centuries, not years. Nonetheless, if the Greenland ice sheet does disappear, hundreds of coastal cities will be below sea level, as will the rice-growing river floodplains and deltas of Asia. Many island countries will cease to exist.[35]

At the other end of the earth, the Antarctic ice sheet, which covers a continent the size of the United States and is 2.6 kilometers (1.6 miles) thick on average, contains over 90 percent of the world's fresh water. The immediate concern here is not the ice that covers the continent but the ice shelves that extend from the continent into the surrounding seas, which are beginning to break up at an alarming pace.[36]

The ice shelves surrounding Antarctica are formed by the flow of glaciers from the continent to lower levels. This flow of ice, fed by the continuous formation of new ice on land and culminating in the breakup of the shelves on the outer fringe and the calving of icebergs, is not new. What is new is the pace of this process. When Larsen A, a huge ice shelf on the east coast of the Antarctic Peninsula, broke up in 1995, it was a signal that all was not well in Antarctica. In 2000, a huge iceberg nearly the size of Connecticut—11,000 square kilometers, or 4,250 square miles—broke off the Ross Ice Shelf.[37]

After Larsen A broke up, it was only a matter of time,

given the rise in temperature in the region, before Larsen B would do the same. In November 2001, an alert went out to the scientific community from a researcher at the Instituto Antártico Argentino, who noted the unusually warm spring temperature and the 20-percent acceleration in the flow of the ice shelf. So when the northern part of the Larsen B ice shelf collapsed into the sea in March 2002, it did not come as a surprise. At about the same time, a huge chunk of ice broke off the Thwaite Glacier. Covering 5,500 square kilometers, this iceberg was the size of Rhode Island.[38]

Even veteran ice watchers are surprised at how quickly the disintegration is occurring. "The speed of it is staggering," said Dr. David Vaughan, a glaciologist at the British Antarctic Survey, which has been monitoring the Larsen Ice Shelf closely. Along the Antarctic Peninsula, in the vicinity of the Larsen ice shelf, the average temperature has risen 2.5 degrees Celsius over the last five decades. Higher temperatures lead to ice melting on the surface of the ice shelves. Scientists theorize that as the melted water on the surface penetrates fractures it weakens the ice, making it vulnerable to further fracturing.[39]

As the ice shelves, already in the water, break off from the continental ice mass, this does not affect sea level per se. What is of concern to scientists is that without the ice shelves to impede the flow of glacial ice, typically at a rate of 400–900 meters a year, the flow of ice from the continent could accelerate, leading to a thinning of the ice sheet on the edges of the Antarctic continent. If this were to happen, it would raise sea level. Dr. Neal Young of the Antarctic Cooperative Research Centre at the University of Tasmania in Australia notes that after Larsen A broke off, the upstream rate of glacial flow at least doubled.[40]

Experts now say it is getting harder to avoid the conclusion that there is a link between the buildup of greenhouse gases and the accelerating breakup of Antarctic ice shelves. As Dr. Theodore A. Scambos of the National Snow and Ice Data Center at the University of Colorado observes, "With the disappearance of ice shelves that have existed for thousands of years, you rather rapidly run out of other explanations."[41]

The accelerated melting of ice, which is consistent with the accelerating rise in temperature that has occurred since 1980, is of great concern in low-lying regions of coastal countries and low-lying island countries. In 2000 the World Bank published a map showing that a 1-meter rise in sea level would inundate half of Bangladesh's riceland. With a rise in sea level of up to 1 meter forecast for this century, tens of millions of Bangladeshis would be forced to migrate. In a country with 144 million people—already one of the most densely populated on earth—this would be a traumatic experience. Rice-growing river floodplains in other Asian countries would also be affected, including India, Thailand, Viet Nam, Indonesia, and China. With a 1-meter rise in sea level, more than a third of Shanghai would be under water. For China as a whole, 70 million people would be vulnerable to a 100-year storm surge.[42]

The most easily measured effect of rising sea level is the inundation of coastal areas. Donald F. Boesch, with the University of Maryland's Center for Environmental Sciences, estimates that for each 1-meter rise in sea level, the shoreline will retreat by an average 1,500 meters, or nearly a mile. With such a rise, the United States would lose 36,000 square kilometers (14,000 square miles) of land—with the middle Atlantic and Mississippi Gulf states losing the most. Large portions of Lower Manhattan and the Mall in the center of Washington, D.C., would be flooded with seawater during a 50-year storm surge. New Orleans would be under water.[43]

Thermal expansion of the oceans and ice melting are raising sea level at a measurable rate. It has become an indicator to watch—a trend that could force a human migration of unimaginable dimensions. It also raises questions about responsibility to other nations and to future generations that humanity has never before faced.

More Destructive Storms

Rising seas are not the only threat. Higher temperatures in the surface water in the tropical oceans mean more energy radiating into the atmosphere to drive storm systems, leading to more frequent, more destructive storms. The combination of rising seas, more powerful storms, and stronger storm surges can be devastating. Such a combination would wreck havoc with low-lying coastal cities, such as Shanghai and New Orleans.

In the fall of 1998, Hurricane Mitch—one of the most powerful storms ever to come out of the Atlantic, with winds approaching 200 miles per hour—hit the east coast of Central America. As atmospheric conditions stalled the normal progression of the storm to the north, some 2 meters of rain were dumped on parts of Honduras and Nicaragua within a few days. The deluge collapsed homes, factories, and schools, leaving them in ruins. It destroyed roads and bridges. Seventy percent of the crops and much of the topsoil in Honduras were washed away—topsoil that had accumulated over long stretches of geological time. Huge mudslides destroyed villages, sometimes burying the entire population.[44]

The storm left 11,000 dead and thousands more missing. The basic infrastructure—the roads and bridges in Honduras and Nicaragua—was largely destroyed. President Flores of Honduras summed it up this way: "Overall, what was destroyed over several days took us 50 years to build." The damage from this storm, exceeding the

annual gross domestic product of the two countries, set
their economic development back by 20 years.[45]

Munich Re, the world's largest reinsurer, a company
that spreads risks among the insurance companies, is
worried about the effects of climate change on the financial viability of the industry. It has published a list of
storms with insured losses of $1 billion or more. The first
such natural disaster came in 1983, when Hurricane Ali-
cia struck the United States, racking up $1.3 billion in
insured losses. Of the 34 natural catastrophes with $1 bil-
lion or more of insured losses recorded through the end
of 2001, two were earthquakes; the other 32 were atmo-
sphere-related—storms, floods, or hurricanes. During
the 1980s, there were three such events. But during the
1990s, there were 25.[46]

The two largest events in terms of total damage were
Hurricane Andrew in 1992, which took down 60,000
homes and racked up $30 billion worth of damage, and
the flooding of China's Yangtze river basin in 1998, which
also cost an estimated $30 billion. This sum is equal to
the value of the harvest of China's two food staples,
wheat and rice, combined. Part of this growth in damage
is due to greater development in coastal areas and river
floodplains. But part is due to more frequent, more
destructive storms.[47]

The regions most vulnerable to more powerful storms
are the Atlantic and Gulf coasts of the United States and
the Caribbean and Central American countries. In Asia,
it is East and Southeast Asia, including countries like the
Philippines, Taiwan, Japan, China, and Viet Nam, that
are likely to bear the brunt of the powerful storms crossing the Pacific. Further west in the Bay of Bengal,
Bangladesh and the east coast of India are particularly
vulnerable.

Western Europe, traditionally experiencing a heavily

damaging winter storm perhaps once in a century, had its first winter storm to exceed a billion dollars in 1987—one that wreaked $3.7 billion in destruction, $3.1 billion of which was covered by insurance. Since then, it has had seven winter storms with insured losses ranging from $1.3 billion to $5.9 billion.[48]

Andrew Dlugolecki, a senior officer at the CGMU Insurance Group, the largest insurance company in the United Kingdom, notes that damage from atmospherically related events has increased by roughly 10 percent a year. "If such an increase were to continue indefinitely," he notes, "by 2065 storm damage would exceed the gross world product. The world obviously would face bankruptcy long before then." In the real world, few trends continue at a fixed rate over a period of several decades, but Dlugolecki's basic point is that climate change can be destructive, disruptive, and enormously costly.[49]

Insurance companies are convinced that with higher temperatures and more energy driving storm systems, future losses will be even greater. They are concerned about whether the industry can remain solvent under this onslaught of growing damages. So, too, is Moody's Investors Services, which in early 2002 downgraded the credit-worthiness of four of the world's leading reinsurance companies.[50]

Subsidizing Climate Change

At a time of mounting public concern about climate change driven by the burning of fossil fuels, the fossil fuel industry is still being subsidized by taxpayers to the tune of $210 billion per year. Fossil fuel subsidies belong to another age, a time when development of the oil and coal industries was seen as a key to economic progress—not as a threat to our future. Once in place, subsidies lead to special interest lobbies that fight tooth and nail against eliminating them, even those that were not appropriate in the first place.[51]

In the United States, oil and gas companies are now perhaps the most powerful lobbyists in Washington. Between 1990 and 2002, they amassed $154 million in campaign contributions in an effort to protect special tax rates worth billions. In testimony before the House Ways and Means Committee in 1999, Donald Lubick, U.S. Treasury Assistant Secretary for Tax Policy, said in reference to the oil and gas industry, "This is an industry that probably has a larger tax incentive relative to its size than any other industry in the country." That such profitable investments are possible is a measure of the corruption of the U.S. political system, and of the capacity of those with money to shape the economy to their advantage.[52]

Subsidies permeate and distort every corner of the global economy. Germany's coal mining subsidy was initially justified in part as a job protection measure, for example. At the peak, the government was subsidizing the industry to the tune of nearly $90,000 per year for each worker. In purely economic terms, it would have made more sense to close the mines and pay miners not to work.[53]

Many subsidies are largely hidden from taxpayers. This is especially true of the fossil fuel industry, which includes such things as a depletion allowance for oil production in the United States. Even more dramatic are the routine U.S. military expenditures to protect access to Middle Eastern oil, which are calculated by analysts at the Rand Corporation to fall between $30 billion and $60 billion a year, while the oil imported from the region is worth only $20 billion.[54]

A 2001 study by Redefining Progress shows U.S. taxpayers subsidizing automobile use at $257 billion a year, or roughly $2,000 per taxpayer. This means that taxpayers who do not own automobiles, including those too poor to afford them, are subsidizing those who do.[55]

Another hidden subsidy is that provided in the form of free parking for employees, including even those who work for government agencies. Free parking encourages the use of automobiles and thus the use of gasoline. It is a form of income, but it is not taxed.[56]

One of the bright spots about this subsidization of fossil fuels is that it provides a reservoir of funding that can be diverted to climate-benign, renewable sources of energy, such as wind, solar, and geothermal energy. Shifting these subsidies from fossil fuels to the development of renewable sources would be a win-win situation, as described in Chapter 11. To subsidize the use of fossil fuels is to subsidize rising temperatures, which lead to crop-withering heat waves, melting ice, rising seas, and more destructive storms. Perhaps it is time for the world's taxpayers to ask if this is how they want their tax monies to be used.

5

Our Socially Divided World

The social and economic gap between the world's richest 1 billion people and its poorest 1 billion has no historical precedent. Not only is this gap wide, it has been widening for half a century. The differences between the world's most affluent and its poorest can be seen in the contrasts in nutrition, education, disease patterns, family size, and life expectancy.

World Health Organization (WHO) data indicate that roughly 1.2 billion people are undernourished, underweight, and often hungry. At the same time, roughly 1.2 billion people are overnourished and overweight, most of them suffering from exercise deprivation. So while a billion people spend their time worrying whether they will eat, another billion worry about eating too much.[1]

Perhaps not surprisingly, education levels reflect the deep divide between the rich and the poor. In some industrial countries, more than half of all young people now graduate from college. By contrast, although five centuries have passed since Gutenberg invented the printing press, 875 million adults are illiterate. Unable to read, they are also excluded from the use of computers and the Internet. Because they cannot read or write, their prospects of escaping poverty are not good.[2]

Disease patterns also reflect the widening gap. The billion poorest suffer mostly from infectious diseases—malaria, tuberculosis, dysentery, and AIDS. Malnutrition leaves infants and small children vulnerable to infectious diseases. Unsafe drinking water takes a heavier toll on those with hunger-weakened immune systems, resulting in millions of fatalities each year. In contrast, among the billion at the top of the global economic scale, it is diseases related to aging, obesity, smoking, and exercise deprivation that take the heaviest toll.[3]

Close to a billion people live in countries where population size is essentially stable, neither increasing nor decreasing very much. With another group of comparable size living in countries where population is projected to double by 2050, the demographic divide between rich and poor is wider than at any time in history.[4]

Life Expectancy: A Seminal Indicator
Life expectancy is in many ways the best single measure of economic and social progress. Although income per person is widely used, this measures only average wealth, whereas life expectancy also tells us how widely the benefits of progress are distributed. If these benefits are concentrated in a few hands, life expectancy will be short; if they are broadly distributed, life expectancy will be much longer.

After World War II, life expectancy climbed rapidly throughout the world with advances in public health, vaccines, antibiotics, and food production. But as the twentieth century drew to an end, life expectancy was no longer rising everywhere. The HIV epidemic sharply reduced it in sub-Saharan Africa. Without AIDS, sub-Saharan Africa's 700 million people could expect to live to the age of 62, but in fact their life expectancy has dropped to 47 years. And millions of infants born with the virus are likely to die by the age of 5.[5]

In Botswana and Swaziland, 39 percent of all adults are HIV-positive and the infection is continuing to spread. In Botswana, life expectancy was expected to reach 70 years by now but instead is projected to drop to 40 years by 2005. In Zimbabwe, where 34 percent of the adult population was HIV-positive at the end of 2001, life expectancy is projected to drop to 33 years by 2005—half what it would have been without AIDS. For South Africa, where the epidemic started later, 20 percent of the adult population is now HIV-positive. Life expectancy, which would have been 68 years by 2010, instead will be 42 years.[6]

The decline in life expectancy witnessed thus far in Africa is the beginning, not the end, of the epidemic. A combination of the spread of the virus itself, the deterioration of basic health care as AIDS victims overwhelm the health care system, and the associated fall in food production are combining to further reduce life expectancy. For the first time in history, we see an epidemic that claims primarily able-bodied adults, thus creating a situation where disease begets famine and famine begets disease. The result is a life expectancy more akin to those of the Dark Ages than what we envisaged for the twenty-first century.

The Effects of the HIV Epidemic
Since the human immunodeficiency virus was identified in 1981, this infection has spread worldwide. By 1990, an estimated 10 million people were infected with the virus. By the end of 2002, the number had climbed to 68 million. Of this total, 26 million have died; 42 million are living with the virus. Twenty-nine million HIV-positive people today live in sub-Saharan Africa, but only 30,000 are being treated with anti-retroviral drugs; 6 million live in South Asia, with nearly 4 million of them in India.[7]

Infection rates are climbing. In the absence of effective treatment, the parts of sub-Saharan Africa with the highest infection rates face a staggering loss of life. Adding the heavy mortality from the epidemic to the normal mortality of older adults means that countries like Botswana and Zimbabwe will lose half of their adult populations within a decade.[8]

There is no recent historical example of an infectious disease taking such a heavy toll. To find a precedent for such a potentially devastating loss of life from such a disease, we have to go back to the decimation of New World Indian communities by the introduction of smallpox in the sixteenth century or to the bubonic plague that claimed roughly a fourth of Europe's population during the fourteenth century. HIV should be seen for what it is—an epidemic of epic proportions that, if not checked soon, could claim more lives during the early part of this century than were claimed by all the wars during the last century.[9]

The HIV epidemic is not an isolated health care phenomenon. It is affecting every facet of life, every sector of the economy. Food production, already lagging behind population growth in most countries in sub-Saharan Africa, is now falling fast as the number of field workers shrinks. As food production falls, hunger intensifies among the dependent groups of children and elderly. Malnutrition weakens the immune systems of some, the virus weakens the immune systems of others, and some have immune systems weakened by both. The downward spiral in family welfare typically begins when the first adult falls victim to the illness—a development that is doubly disruptive because for each person who is sick and unable to work, others must devote at least part of their time caring for that family member.[10]

Expenditures for health care and medicine in families

with falling incomes and shrinking food supplies further exacerbate the dire situation. As savings disappear, productive assets must be sold, including livestock and farm implements. Medical and funeral costs for parents often leave children in debt. Hunger leaves those with the virus more vulnerable to infectious diseases.[11]

While the economic fallout from the massive loss of young adults is still poorly understood, the epidemic is already beginning to cut into economic activity. Rising worker health insurance costs are shrinking or even eliminating company profit margins, forcing some firms into the red. In addition, companies are facing increasing sick leave, decreased productivity, and the burden of recruiting and training replacements when employees die.[12]

In these circumstances, companies become less competitive in world markets. Incoming capital flows begin to shrink, and economic growth slows or even turns into economic decline. Both exports and imports are reduced, savings decline, and more countries face the prospect of defaulting on their international debt.[13]

Education is also affected. The ranks of teachers are being decimated by the virus. In some countries, such as Zambia, teachers are dying faster than they can be replaced. When one or both parents die, more children stay home simply because there is not enough money to buy books and support them in school. They must fend for themselves. Universities are also feeling the effects. At the University of Durbin in South Africa, 25 percent of the student body is HIV-positive.[14]

The effects on health care are equally devastating. In many hospitals in eastern and southern Africa, a majority of the beds are now occupied by AIDS victims, leaving less space for those who need care for traditional illnesses. Doctors and nurses are often stretched to the breaking point. With health care systems now unable to provide even basic care, the toll of traditional disease is also rising. Life expectancy is dropping not only due to the lives lost to AIDS, but also due to those lost because of the deterioration in health care.[15]

The epidemic is leaving millions of orphans in its wake. Sub-Saharan Africa is expected to have 20 million "AIDS orphans" by 2010—children who have lost at least one parent to the disease. There is no precedent for millions of street children in Africa. But the extended family, once capable of absorbing these numbers, is now itself being decimated by the loss of adults, leaving children, often small ones, to fend for themselves. For some girls, the only option is what has come to be known as "survival sex." Michael Grunwald of the *Washington Post* writes from Swaziland, "In the countryside, teenage Swazi girls are selling sex—and spreading HIV—for $5 an encounter, exactly what it costs to hire oxen for a day of plowing."[16]

The HIV epidemic in Africa is now a development problem, a matter of whether a society can continue to function as needed to support its people. It is a food security problem. It is a national security problem. It is an educational system problem. And it is a foreign investment problem. Stephen Lewis, the U.N. Special Envoy for HIV/AIDS in Africa, says that the epidemic can be curbed and the infection trends can be reversed, but it will take help from the international community. The failure to fully fund the Global Fund to Fight AIDS, Tuberculosis and Malaria is "mass murder" by complacency. He says, "The pandemic cannot be allowed to continue, and those who watch it unfold with a kind of pathological equanimity must be held to account."[17]

Writing in the *New York Times*, Alex de Waal, an adviser to the U.N. Economic Commission for Africa and to UNICEF, sums up the effects of the epidemic well: "Just as HIV destroys the body's immune system, the epidemic of HIV and AIDS has disabled the body politic. As a result of HIV, the worst hit African countries have undergone a social breakdown that is now reaching a new level: African societies' capacity to resist famine is fast eroding. Hunger and disease have begun reinforcing each other. As daunting as the prospect is, we will have to fight them together, or we will succeed against neither."[18]

Poverty and Hunger

Hunger is the most visible face of poverty. The U.N. Food and Agriculture Organization estimates that 840 million of the world's people are chronically hungry. They are not getting enough food to achieve full physical and mental development and to maintain adequate levels of physical activity.[19]

The majority of the underfed and underweight are concentrated in the Indian subcontinent and sub-Saharan Africa—regions that contain 1.3 billion and 700 million people, respectively. Twenty-five years ago, the nutritional status of Asia's population giants, India and China, was similar, but since then China has eliminated much of its hunger, whereas India has made considerably less progress. The principal difference has not been so much in the rate of agricultural production as in the rate of population growth. During this last quarter-century China has accelerated the shift to smaller families. While most of the gains in food production during this period in India were absorbed by population growth, those in China went to raising consumption and upgrading diets.[20]

Sub-Saharan Africa, the other remaining stronghold of hunger, has been plagued with even faster population growth than India. In the last several decades, its population has grown faster than any other in the world.[21]

Malnutrition takes its heaviest toll among the young, who are most vulnerable during their period of rapid physical and mental development. In both India and Bangladesh, more than half of all children are malnourished. In Ethiopia, 47 percent of children are undernourished and in Nigeria the figure is 27 percent—and these are Africa's two most populous countries.[22]

Although it is not surprising that those who are underfed and underweight are concentrated in developing countries, it is perhaps surprising that most of them live in rural communities. More often than not, the undernourished are landless or live on plots of land so small that they are effectively landless. Those who live on the well-watered plains are usually better nourished. It is those who live on marginal land—land that is steeply sloping or semiarid—who are hungry.

The penalties of being underweight begin at birth. A U.N. report estimates that 20 million underweight infants are born each year to mothers who also are malnourished. The study indicates that these children suffer lasting effects in the form of "impaired immune systems, neurological damage, and retarded physical growth."[23]

Worldwatch Institute's Gary Gardner and Brian Halweil report that if an infant's weight at birth is two thirds or less of normal, the risk of death in infancy is 10 times greater. They cite David Barker of Britain's University of Southampton, who "observes soberly that 60 percent of all newborns in India would be in intensive care had they been born in California." WHO epidemiological data indicate that 54 percent of deaths from the five leading causes of childhood mortality in developing countries have malnutrition as an underlying condition.[24]

University of Toronto economist Susan Horton estimates productivity losses among the moderately undernourished at 2–6 percent and among the severely undernourished at 2–9 percent. Gardner and Halweil note that if Horton's calculations for five countries in South

Asia hold for all developing countries, then "between $64 billion and $128 billion is drained from developing country economies just from productivity losses."[25]

Eradicating hunger in South Asia and sub-Saharan Africa will be difficult, but it is not impossible. It will, however, require a far greater effort and a shift in priorities. India, for example, opted early on to become a nuclear power. As a result, it now has the dubious distinction of being able to defend with nuclear weapons the largest concentration of hungry people in the world.

Poverty and the Burden of Disease

To be poor often means to be sick. Poverty and ill health are closely linked, and they tend to reinforce each other. Health is closely related to access to safe water, something that 1.1 billion people lack. Waterborne diseases claim more than 3 million lives each year, mostly as a result of dysentery and cholera. These and other waterborne diseases take their heaviest toll among children. Infant mortality in the affluent societies averages 6 per thousand; in the 48 poorest countries, it averages 100 per thousand, or nearly 17 times as high.[26]

Another reason for the close coupling of ill health and poverty is the lack of sanitation. Some 2.4 billion people live in villages or urban squatter settlements with no sanitary facilities at either the household or community level.[27]

Many of the world's poor lack knowledge of the basic principles of good hygiene. The poor and uneducated often do not understand the mechanisms of infectious disease transfer and thus cannot take steps to protect themselves. And people with immune systems weakened by hunger are more vulnerable to common infectious diseases. Poverty also means children are often not vaccinated for these routine diseases, even though the cost may be just pennies per child.[28]

Among the leading infectious diseases, malaria claims more than 1.1 million lives each year, 90 percent of them in Africa. The number who carry this disease and often suffer from it most of their lives is several times greater. Thousands of children die from malaria each day. Economists estimate that reduced worker productivity and other costs associated with malaria are cutting economic growth by a full percentage point in countries with heavily infected populations.[29]

Nowhere is the evidence that poverty begets disease and disease begets poverty more dramatically illustrated than with the HIV epidemic in Africa, as described earlier. In this case, we are now witnessing the spread of a fatal disease on a scale that is altering the future of a continent. In addition to the continuing handicaps of a lack of infrastructure and trained personnel, Africa must now contend with the adverse economic effects of the epidemic. AIDS has dramatically raised the dependency ratio—the number of young and elderly who depend on productive adults. This, in turn, makes it much more difficult for a society to save. Reduced savings means reduced investment and slower economic growth, or even decline.

The link between poverty and disease is a strong one, but one that has been broken for most of humanity by economic development. The challenge now is to eradicate this link for that remaining minority who do not have access to safe water, vaccines, education, and basic health care.

The High Cost of Illiteracy

Despite a half-century of unprecedented economic and social development, there are still 875 million adults who are illiterate—unable to take advantage of this basic stepping stone to the modern world. Not only is there a huge

number of illiterate adults, but their ranks are being fed
by the 115 million children who do not attend school.[30]

The world's illiterates are concentrated in a handful of
the more populous countries, most of them in Asia and
Africa. Prominent among these are India, China, Pakistan, Bangladesh, Nigeria, Egypt, Indonesia, Brazil, and
Mexico.[31]

Progress in eradicating illiteracy is uneven, to say the
least. From 1990 to 2000, China and Indonesia made
large gains in reducing illiteracy. Other countries also
making meaningful progress were Mexico, Nigeria, and
Brazil. However, in four other populous countries—
Bangladesh, Egypt, Pakistan, and India—the number of
illiterates increased.[32]

Worldwide, some 60 percent of illiterate adults are
female. In almost all developing countries, the number of
illiterate females exceeds the number of illiterate males.
In some countries the gap is wide. In Pakistan, for example, 40 percent of males are illiterate compared with 69
percent of females. In India, the gender gap is almost as
wide, with 32 percent of males being illiterate and 55 percent of females. These numbers mean that on the Indian
subcontinent a majority of women are unable to read or
write. For China, it is 8 percent males and 24 percent
females. Brazil is the only one of the more populous
developing countries where female illiteracy matches that
of males, with both at 15 percent.[33]

Where there is illiteracy, there is poverty. They tend to
reinforce each other simply because illiterate women have
much larger families than literate women do and because
each year of schooling raises earning power by 10–20 percent. Illiterate women are trapped by large families and
minimal earning power. In Brazil, illiterate women have
more than six children each on average; literate women
have only two.[34]

Even though Brazil has an average per capita gross domestic product of $2,600, its 15-percent illiteracy reflects the heavily skewed distribution of income within the society. When Cristovam Buarque took over as Minister of Education in early 2003, he was aghast to discover that 15 members of the Ministry staff were illiterate.[35]

Those who are not literate are usually not numerate either. Without rudimentary math skills, it is difficult to think quantitatively. A skill that those who are educated take for granted does not exist for many of the world's adults.

It is difficult to have a functioning democracy with a largely illiterate population. Without literacy and a modicum of education, societies are often governed by superstition, making rational democracy difficult. For those who are illiterate, educational horizons and job opportunities are limited.

Environmentally responsible behavior also depends to a great extent on a capacity to understand basic scientific issues, such as the greenhouse effect or the ecological role of forests. Lacking this, it is harder to grasp the link between fossil fuel burning and climate change or between tree cutting and the incidence of flooding or the loss of biological diversity.

Those who never attend school are also often outside the loop in acquiring basic information on nutrition and hygiene. They may have little exposure to HIV education and no understanding of how the disease is spread. Since vaccinations are often administered through schools, those who do not attend classes may not receive these basic shots. If schools provide free lunches, those who are not there will also miss out nutritionally. For the poorer segments of society, this is not a trivial deprivation.[36]

There are two key components in eliminating illiteracy quickly. One is to make sure that all children are in school. The second is to teach adults to read and write. Success in the near-term future means waging the war on illiteracy on both fronts.

Literacy is one of many defining social characteristics of a society, and a steppingstone to other improvements, such as better nutrition and better health. It is the key to breaking the self-reinforcing cycle where illiteracy begets poverty and poverty begets large families, trapping people in poverty. The deteriorating relationship between the global economy and the earth's ecosystem requires an all-out effort to bring literacy to all adults in order to break the poverty cycle and to stabilize population.

6

Plan A: Business as Usual

If we continue with business as usual—Plan A—the troubles described in the preceding five chapters will worsen. Plan A is failing environmentally and, as a result, it will eventually fail economically. The environmental bubble economy created by overdrawing the earth's natural assets will eventually burst unless we deflate it.

As noted in Chapter 1, the food bubble economy is based on the unsustainable use of groundwater and of cropland. If we were to cease overpumping in order to stabilize water tables, the world grain harvest would drop sharply. No one knows by precisely how much, but Sandra Postel of the Global Water Policy Project estimated a decade ago that the world was overpumping its aquifers by 160 billion tons of water a year. This is equal to 160 million tons of grain, or 8 percent of the world grain harvest. In effect, 8 percent of the world's people—some 500 million people—are fed with grain produced with the unsustainable use of water.[1]

Global assessments such as Postel's are difficult partly because the extent of overpumping varies widely by country. A World Bank report indicates that the pumping of water in Yemen's Sana'a Basin is four times the rate of recharge. In India, some analysts think that pumping may be nearly double the rate of recharge. In Saudi Arabia and the southern Great Plains of the United States, where pumping is from fossil aquifers, virtually all pumping is overpumping since there is little or no recharge. Once a fossil aquifer is depleted, pumping ends.[2]

A similar situation exists with cropland. To produce the current grain harvest of nearly 1.9 billion tons, many farmers are tilling land that is too steeply sloping or too dry to sustain cultivation. In some countries, this share of cropland is negligible; in others, it is large. For the world, it could easily be 10 percent. Kazakhstan, an extreme case, has abandoned half of its grainland since 1980. The United States and China, the world's largest grain producers, are returning highly erodible cropland to grass or planting it to trees before it becomes wasteland. In each country, roughly one tenth of cropland is going into grass and trees. The United States has largely completed its land use conversion. China is just getting under way.[3]

With oceanic fisheries, long the world's leading protein source, no one knows exactly how much the catch exceeds the sustainable yield. In its *State of the World's Fisheries* annual report, the U.N. Food and Agriculture Organization reports that 75 percent of all fisheries are fished at or beyond capacity, some to the point of collapse. A Canadian study based on 10 years of painstaking research, which was published in *Nature* in May 2003, reports that 90 percent of world stocks of the larger predatory species, including cod, halibut, tuna, swordfish, and marlin, disappeared over the last half-century. No one knows the extent of overfishing, but like overpumping aquifers, it is a practice designed to expand food production in the short term that will almost certainly lead to a decline over the long term.[4]

Although rangeland deterioration does not get much media attention, overgrazing is at least as common as overfishing. Data on the extent of overgrazing by country are hard to find. We do know that the demands of the world's 3.1 billion cattle, sheep, and goats are overwhelming the sustainable forage yields of rangelands. In China, where the government is asking its pastoralists to voluntarily reduce their flocks of sheep and goats by 40 percent as it tries to halt advancing deserts, we at least get a hint of the perceived extent of overgrazing.[5]

With carbon emissions, we have a better sense of the excess. Of the 6.5 billion tons of carbon released into the atmosphere each year from fossil fuel burning, roughly half is fixed by nature. The other half accumulates in the atmosphere, feeding the greenhouse effect. In this case, carbon emissions are now double nature's carbon-fixing capacity.[6]

In sum, no one knows exactly the extent of our excessive claims on the earth in this bubble economy. The most sophisticated effort to calculate this, the one by Mathis Wackernagel and his team, estimates that in 1999 our claims on the earth exceeded its regenerative capacity by 20 percent. If this overdraft is rising 1 percent a year, as seems likely, then by 2003 it was 24 percent. As we consume the earth's natural capital, the earth's capacity to sustain us is decreasing. We are a species out of control, setting in motion processes we do not understand with consequences that we cannot foresee.[7]

Accelerating Environmental Decline

Most disruptive environmental trends, whether it be shrinking forests, falling water tables, or rising temperature, are accelerating. For example, atmospheric carbon dioxide (CO_2) levels rose from an estimated 280 parts per million (ppm) at the beginning of the industrial era in 1760 to 316 ppm in 1960. By 2002, the CO_2 concentration had climbed to 373 ppm. After rising at less than 0.2 ppm each year during the preceding two centuries, it has climbed by 1.3 ppm per year since 1960—more than six times as fast.[8]

Each decade, the rise in global average temperature has been greater than the decade before. As the earth's temperature rise accelerates, so does ice melting, as described in Chapter 4. Within a decade the melting of large glaciers on the west coast of Alaska and in northern Canada has gone from raising sea level by 0.14 millimeters a year to raising it by 0.32 millimeters—more than twice as fast.[9]

These studies are reinforced by one from the U.S. Geological Survey that describes an accelerating melting of glaciers in several of the world's mountainous regions. In the Peruvian Andes, for example, data collected on the Qori Kalis glacier show that the rate of retreat since 1995 has been doubling roughly every three years.[10]

As temperatures rise, so does the amount of energy driving storm systems. As noted in Chapter 4, Munich Re reports that the number of weather-related events, including hurricanes, typhoons, and winter storms, with $1 billion or more of insured damage increased from 3 in the 1980s to 25 during the 1990s. Even after adjusting for variables such as a disproportionate share of building in high-risk coastal regions and river floodplains, it is clear that storms are becoming more frequent and more destructive. The meteorological actuaries who project storm frequency and intensity expect this acceleration to continue as long as the temperature keeps rising.[11]

A similar trend exists with water tables. Thirty years ago, reports of falling water tables and wells going dry were rare. Today they are commonplace, as described in Chapter 2. In several places in the southern Great Plains of the United States, water tables have dropped by at least 100 feet (30 meters) over the last few decades. Under the

North China Plain, where the annual drop in the water table was 1.5 meters a year during the early 1990s, the decline is now reported to be 3 meters in many areas.[12]

The acceleration of problems can be seen with rivers too: Several decades ago, if the Colorado failed to reach the sea, it was news. Now it would be news if it did so. In China, the Yellow River ran dry for the first time in 1972, and then occasionally in subsequent years, but by the early 1990s it was running dry every year.[13]

The earth's forest cover, another basic indicator of the planet's health, is also shrinking at an accelerating rate. Although it expanded by 36 million hectares in the industrial world between 1990 and 2000, it shrank by 130 million hectares in the developing world. This net loss of 96 million hectares in 10 years far exceeded that of any previous decade.[14]

Over the last 50 years, Indonesia's once vast tropical rainforest shrank from 162 million hectares to 98 million hectares—an average loss of 1.3 million hectares a year. In the new century, it is shrinking by 2 million hectares a year. Iran is also being deforested at an accelerating rate. *The Economist* reports that from 1955 to 1967, northern Iran lost 9,250 hectares a year. Then from 1967 to 1994, forests disappeared at 18,000 hectares per year. Since then the figure has jumped to 29,000 hectares per year. At this exponential pace, it is only a matter of time before Iran is deforested.[15]

In Southeast Asia, Myanmar (formerly Burma) is fast exporting its remaining tropical hardwoods. My colleague Janet Larsen writes that log exports to China are growing much faster than the trees—many of which are hundreds of years old—can be replaced. In the western hemisphere, deforestation is concentrated in Brazil and Mexico, both of which appear to be losing forests at an accelerating rate.[16]

One manifestation of overgrazing, deforestation, and

overplowing is desertification and dust storms. Data for major dust storms in China compiled by the China Meteorological Administration indicate that desertification is accelerating. After increasing from 5 major dust storms in the 1950s to 14 during the 1980s, the number leapt to 23 in the 1990s. The new decade has begun with more than 20 major dust storms in 2000 and 2001 alone. If this rate is sustained throughout the decade, the total will exceed 100—a fourfold increase in just one decade.[17]

A similar acceleration appears to be under way for species extinction, which is now estimated to be at least 1,000 times the natural rate of extinction. Take primate species—some 240 in total, and our closest living relatives. Ten thousand years ago, as the last Ice Age was ending, baboons reportedly outnumbered humans by at least two to one. Now, as our numbers multiply, the numbers of other primates are diminishing, often to the point where their survival is in question. In 1996, the World Conservation Union–IUCN reported that 13 species of primates were critically endangered. By 2000, this number had increased to 19, a gain of one half. During the same period, the number of species endangered (the next most threatened category) went from 29 to 46, also expanding by half.[18]

Spreading Hunger, Growing Unrest

Hunger is concentrated in two regions of the world: the Indian subcontinent and Africa south of the Sahara. Up to a fourth of India's grain harvest may be based on the overpumping of aquifers. This overpumping, which has been instrumental in helping India develop a food bubble economy, virtually assures a future decline in food production.[19]

For the 700 million people in sub-Saharan Africa, the situation is also difficult. The production of grain, which supplies half of the calories humans consume directly and a substantial share of the remainder consumed indirectly as meat, milk, eggs, and farmed fish, is a useful indicator of diet adequacy. Annual grain production per person, which averaged 147 kilograms between 1961 and 1980, fell to 120 kilograms between 2000 and 2002, a drop of 18 percent. Africa's ribs are beginning to show. This unfolding food emergency does not exist in a vacuum. Desperate Africans are turning to bushmeat in an effort to survive, threatening various forms of wildlife—from herbivores to gorillas. Efforts to protect wildlife by setting up parks are breaking down as hungry Africans try to survive.[20]

Africa is not well endowed agriculturally. Its soils are typically thin, depleted of nutrients, low in organic matter, and highly erodible. Except for the Congo basin, nearly all the continent is arid or semiarid. Africa has not had a Green Revolution for the same reason that Australia has not had one: it does not have enough water to use much fertilizer. Now it is also facing the heavy loss to AIDS of able-bodied adults who work in the fields.

With business as usual, the prospect of eradicating world hunger is slim to nonexistent. Too many trends are currently headed in the wrong direction. Grain production per person for the world, which climbed from 250 kilograms in 1950 to the historical high of 344 kilograms in 1984, has been declining since then. In 2002 it fell to 290 kilograms, the lowest in 26 years.[21]

The recent loss of momentum in expanding the grain harvest has been cushioned by drawing down grain reserves. But as of 2003, reserves are at their lowest level in a generation, and they cannot be drawn down much further.[22]

With the prospect of water shortages driving more countries into the world grain market for imports, we may well wake up one morning and discover that there is no longer enough grain to go around—and not enough water to produce enough grain. Such a situation will lead to rapid, potentially dramatic, rises in world grain prices, making it difficult for many low-income, grain-importing countries to procure enough grain to feed their people. Avoiding such a prospect depends on a worldwide reordering of investment and research priorities.

Streams of Environmental Refugees

We are familiar with political refugees who are escaping persecution and with economic refugees seeking jobs, but environmental refugees are not as well known. Such refugees include those whose land is turning to desert, those who are attempting to escape toxic environments, those whose wells are going dry, and those whose land is being submerged by rising seas. In the United States, the first large wave of environmental refugees was formed by those fleeing the Dust Bowl in the southern Great Plains during the 1930s.[23]

A generation later, the United States experienced the first toxic-waste refugees. Love Canal, a small town in New York, part of which was built on a toxic waste disposal site, made national and international headlines during the late 1970s. Beginning in 1942, the Hooker Chemical Company had dumped 21,000 tons of toxic waste, including chlorobenzene, dioxin, halogenated organics, and pesticides. In 1952, it closed the site, capped it over, and deeded it to the Love Canal Board of Education. An elementary school was built on the site, taking advantage of the free land.[24]

But during the 1960s and 1970s people began noticing odors and residues from seeping wastes. Birth defects and other illnesses were common. In August 1978, 239 families were permanently relocated at government expense. They were reimbursed for their homes at market prices.

In September 1979, 300 more families were temporarily relocated. And in October 1980, 900 additional families received government money to move. In all, several thousand people were permanently relocated.[25]

A few years later, the residents of Times Beach, Missouri, began complaining about a rash of health problems. A firm spraying oil on roads to control dust was, in fact, using waste oil laden with toxic chemical wastes. Among other things, investigators discovered dioxin levels many times higher than the tolerance level. The federal government arranged for the permanent evacuation and relocation of more than 2,000 people.[26]

Early one morning in April 1986, a nuclear reactor at the Chernobyl nuclear power plant in Kiev exploded. It started a powerful fire that lasted for 10 days. Massive amounts of radioactivity were spewed into the atmosphere, showering communities in the region with heavy doses of radiation. As a result, the residents of the nearby town of Pripyat and several other communities in Ukraine, Belarus, and Russia were evacuated, requiring the resettlement of 350,400 people. As recently as 1992, Belarus was devoting 20 percent of its national budget to resettlement and the many other costs associated with the accident.[27]

The Dust Bowl refugees, the two U.S. evacuations from toxic waste sites, and the far larger resettlement from the nuclear explosion at Chernobyl were early examples of environmental migration, but they are small compared with what lies ahead if we continue with business as usual. Among the new refugees are those being forced to move because of aquifer depletion and wells running dry. Thus far the evacuations have been of villages, but eventually whole cities might have to be relocated, such as Sana'a, the capital of Yemen, or Quetta, the capital of Pakistan's Baluchistan province. Originally designed for 50,000 people, Quetta now has 1 million, all of whom depend on 2,000 wells pumping water from a deep aquifer, depleting what is believed to be a fossil aquifer. Like Sana'a, Quetta may have enough water for the rest of this decade, but then its future will be in doubt. In the words of one study assessing the water prospect, Quetta will soon be "a dead city."[28]

Water refugees are likely to be most common in arid and semiarid regions where populations are outgrowing the water supply. Villages in northeastern Iran have been abandoned because the villagers could no longer reach water. A similar situation is found in villages in India, especially in the west and parts of the south. Countless villagers in northern and western China and in parts of Mexico may have to migrate because of a lack of water.

Spreading deserts are also displacing people. In China, where the Gobi Desert is expanding by 10,400 square kilometers (4,000 square miles) a year, the refugee stream is swelling. Chinese scientists report that there are now desert refugees in three provinces—Inner Mongolia (Nei Monggol), Ningxia, and Gansu. An Asian Development Bank preliminary assessment of desertification in Gansu province has identified 4,000 villages that face abandonment.[29]

In Iran, villages abandoned because of spreading deserts and a lack of water already number in the thousands. In the eastern provinces of Baluchistan and Sistan, some 124 villages have been buried by drifting sand. In the vicinity of Damavand, a small town within an hour's drive of Tehran, some 88 villages have been abandoned.[30]

Another source of refugees, a potentially huge one, is rising seas. The Intergovernmental Panel on Climate Change, in its early 2001 study, reported that sea level could rise by nearly 1 meter during this century, but research completed since then indicates that ice is melting much faster than earlier reported, suggesting that the possible rise may be much higher. Even a 1-meter rise in sea level would inundate half of Bangladesh's riceland, forcing the relocation of easily 40 million people. In a country with 144 million people, internal relocation would not be easy. But where else can they go? How many countries would accept even 1 million of these 40 million? Other Asian countries with rice-growing river floodplains would also face an exodus from the rising seas. Among them are China, India, Indonesia, Myanmar, Pakistan, the Philippines, South Korea, Thailand, and Viet Nam.[31]

Coastal cities that would be vulnerable to rising sea level include New Orleans, New York, Washington, London, Cairo, and Shanghai. A 1-meter rise would put one third of Shanghai under water.[32]

Today, the refugee flows from wells that are going dry and deserts that are expanding are beginning. How large these flows and those from rising seas will become over time remains to be seen. But the numbers could be huge. In the quiet desperation of trying to survive, people often cross national borders. In some cases, this desperation drives migrants to their deaths—as tragically seen in the bodies of Mexicans who regularly perish trying to enter the United States by crossing the Arizona desert and in the bodies of Africans washing ashore in Spain and Italy when their fragile watercraft come apart as they try to cross the Mediterranean.[33]

Population Growth and Political Conflict

Population growth can lead to political conflict not only between societies but also within them. Some insights into this were offered in an engaging *World Watch* magazine article by James Gasana, who was Minister of Agriculture and Environment in Rwanda in 1990–92 and then

Minister of Defense in 1992–93. As the chair of a national agricultural commission in 1990, he had warned that without "profound transformations in its agriculture, [Rwanda] will not be capable of feeding adequately its population under the present growth rate. Contrary to the tradition of our demographers, who show that the population growth rate will remain positive over several years in the future, one cannot see how the Rwandan population will reach 10 million inhabitants unless important progress in agriculture, as well as other sectors of the economy, were achieved. Consequently, it is time to fear the Malthusian effects that could derive from the gap between food supply and the demand of the population and social disorders, which could result."[34]

Gasana's warning of possible social disorder was prophetic. He further described how siblings inherited land from their parents and how, with an average of seven children per family, plots that were already small got much smaller. Many tried to find new land, moving onto marginal land, including steeply sloping mountains. By 1989, almost half of Rwanda's cultivated land was on slopes of 10 to 35 degrees, land that is universally considered uncultivable.[35]

In 1950, Rwanda's population was 1.9 million. By 1994, it was nearly 8 million, making it the most densely populated country in Africa. As population grew, so did the demand for firewood. By 1991, the demand was more than double the sustainable yield of local forests. As a result, trees disappeared, forcing people to use straw and other crop residues for cooking fuel. With less organic matter in the soil, land fertility declined.[36]

As the health of the land deteriorated, so did that of the people dependent on it. Eventually there was simply not enough food to go around. A quiet desperation developed among the people. Like a drought-afflicted countryside, it could be ignited with a single match. That match was the crash of a plane on April 6, 1994, shot down as it approached the capital of Kigali, killing President Juvenal Habyarimana. The crash unleashed an organized attack by Hutus, leading to an estimated 800,000 deaths, mostly of Tutsis. In the villages, whole families were slaughtered lest there be survivors to claim the family plot of land. Gasana notes that the deaths were concentrated in communities where caloric intake was the lowest. Population pressure contributed to the tensions and the slaughter, although it was by no means the only factor.[37]

He sees four lessons that can be learned from this tragic chapter in Africa's history. First, rapid population growth is the major driving force behind the vicious circle of environmental scarcities and rural poverty. Second, conserving the environment is essential for long-term poverty reduction. Third, to break the links between environmental scarcities and conflict, win-win solutions—providing all sociological groups with access to natural resources—are essential. And fourth, preventing conflicts of the kind that ravaged Rwanda in 1994 will require a rethinking of what national security really means.[38]

Many other countries in Africa face a similar situation, including Nigeria, the continent's most populous country with 121 million people. President Olusegun Obasanjo is trying desperately in his strife-torn country to maintain peace between the Christian south and the Muslim north and among various tribes. However, as the desert claims 350,000 hectares of rangeland and cropland each year, people are forced southward into already densely populated areas. The same population pressures, land degradation, and hunger that ignited social tensions in Rwanda are building in Nigeria.[39]

Many African countries, largely rural in nature, are on a similar demographic track. Tanzania's population of 37 million in 2003 is projected to increase to 69 million by 2050. Eritrea, where the average family has seven children, is projected to go from 4 million to 11 million by 2050. In the Congo, the population is projected to triple, going from 53 million to 152 million.[40]

Africa is not alone. India faces a possible intensification of the conflict between Hindus and Muslims. In India, as a second generation subdivides already small plots, pressure on the land is intense. So, too, is the pressure on water resources.

With India's population projected to grow from just over 1 billion in 2000 to 1.5 billion in 2050, a collision between rising human numbers and falling water tables is inevitable. In the absence of effective leadership, India could face social conflicts that would dwarf those in Rwanda. As Gasana notes, the relationship between population and natural systems is a national security issue, one that can spawn conflicts along geographic, tribal, ethnic, or religious lines.[41]

Disagreements over the allocation of water among countries that share river systems is a common source of international political conflict, especially where populations are outgrowing the flow of the river. Nowhere is this potential conflict more stark than among the three principal countries of the Nile River valley—Egypt, Sudan, and Ethiopia. Agriculture in Egypt, where it rarely rains, is almost wholly dependent on water from the Nile. Egypt now gets the lion's share of the Nile's water, but its current population of 71 million is projected to reach 127 million by 2050, thus greatly expanding the demand for grain and for water. Sudan, whose 33 million people also depend heavily on the Nile, is expected to have 60 million by 2050. And the number of Ethiopians, in the country that controls 85 percent of the headwaters of the Nile, is projected to expand from 69 million to 171 million.[42]

Since little water is left in the Nile when it reaches the Mediterranean Sea, if either Sudan or Ethiopia takes more water, Egypt will get less, making it increasingly difficult to produce food for an additional 55 million people. Although there is an existing water rights agreement among the three countries, Ethiopia receives only a minuscule share. Given its aspirations for a better life, and with the headwaters of the Nile being one of its few natural resources, Ethiopia will undoubtedly want to take more. With income per person there averaging only $90 a year compared with nearly $1,300 in Egypt, it is hard to argue that Ethiopia should not get more of the Nile water.[43]

To the north, Turkey, Syria, and Iraq share the waters of the Tigris and Euphrates river system. Turkey, controlling the headwaters, is developing a massive project on the Tigris to increase the water available for irrigation and power. Syria and Iraq, which are both projected to more than double their respective populations of 17 million and 25 million, are concerned because they too will need more water.[44]

In the Aral Sea basin in Central Asia, there is an uneasy arrangement among five countries over the sharing of the two rivers, the Amu Darya and the Syr Darya, that drain into the sea. The demand for water in Kazakhstan, Kyrgyzstan, Tajikistan, Turkmenistan, and Uzbekistan already exceeds the flow of the two rivers by 25 percent. Turkmenistan, which is upstream on the Amu Darya, is planning to develop another half-million hectares of irrigated agriculture. Racked by insurgencies, the region lacks the cooperation needed to manage its scarce water resources. On top of this, Afghanistan, which controls the headwaters of the Amu Darya, plans to use some of the water for its own development. Geographer Sarah O'Hara of the University of Nottingham, who studies the region's water problems, says, "We talk about the developing world and the developed world, but this is the deteriorating world."[45]

We can now see early signs of potential conflicts emerging. Population pressure and land hunger in northern China are pushing migrants across the border into sparsely populated Russia. Illegal Chinese migrants are seeking jobs in Siberia, much as Mexican workers do in the southwestern United States. Expanding commerce between the two countries is also increasing the Chinese presence, particularly in the Russian communities near the Chinese border. As population pressure drives people across national borders, it can create ethnic conflicts within the recipient societies and strain relations between the countries of origin and destination.[46]

Plan A: Overwhelmed by Problems

One of the biggest risks in this new century is that governments will be overwhelmed by the challenges that are now emerging. Now that we have several decades of unprecedentedly rapid population growth behind us, we can begin to see some of its effects. It comes as no surprise that many governments are showing signs of demographic fatigue. Worn down by the struggle to deal with the consequences of fast-multiplying human numbers, they are unable to respond to new threats, such as the HIV epidemic, aquifer depletion, and land hunger.

One of the first big tests of governments' ability to cope was the HIV epidemic. Many governments moved quickly to contain the virus once it was identified, holding infection rates to less than 1 percent of the adult population. But many others, mainly in Africa, failed to do so. The result is that the countries with the highest infection rates will likely lose close to half of their adult populations over the next decade. Populations in some countries in Africa are declining not because of falling fertility, but because of rising mortality. As noted earlier, this rise in the death rate marks a tragic reversal in world demography as the unthinkable becomes a reality.

Just as scores of countries failed to respond to rising HIV infection rates, scores of others are failing to respond to falling water tables. These countries will be forced to confront overpumping when aquifers are depleted, but by then they may be facing drops in food production.

In countless other countries, continuing population growth is shrinking the cropland per person below the survival level. However hard people work, they will not be able to make it. They will either face hunger and rising death rates or they will join the swelling flow of migrants to cities where they will have at least a slim chance of getting a job or food relief. If we continue with business as usual and let social stresses build, the experience in Rwanda with large-scale social conflict could become all too common. With business as usual, there almost certainly will be other groups who are driven to violence by quiet desperation, by a loss of hope.

Developing countries that were successful in their early efforts to reduce fertility, such as South Korea, Taiwan, and Thailand, are advancing rapidly. Others that are already pressing against the limits of land and water resources and whose populations are projected to double again may face falling living standards that will in turn further reinforce the prevailing high fertility. This reinforcing mechanism, referred to by demographers as the demographic trap, could keep living standards at subsistence level and eventually lead to rising mortality as the land and water resource base deteriorates and food production declines. Among the countries at risk of being trapped if they cannot quickly check their population growth are Afghanistan, Ethiopia, Ghana, Haiti, Honduras, India, Myanmar, Nigeria, Pakistan, Sudan, Tanzania, and Yemen.

Climate change is proving to be an overwhelming challenge for both industrial and developing-country governments. Only one country, Iceland, has a strategy to eliminate fossil fuel use and thus reduce carbon emissions to zero. In contrast to the issues just discussed, climate change is primarily the responsibility of the industrial countries, although its effects will be felt everywhere.[47]

What happens when people lose confidence in their governments? The risk in times of extreme stress is that states will fail and that demagogues will assume power. There is a tendency to assume that in the modern world, social breakdown cannot occur, but this is a dangerous illusion. We have no idea what the psychological effects might be if it becomes clear that we have triggered the melting of the Greenland ice sheet and that we cannot stop it. Nor can we even guess at the international political fallout if the Gulf Stream abruptly shifted southward, leaving Western Europe with a Siberian climate.

Once particular climate change and aquifer depletion thresholds are crossed, change can come rapidly and unpredictably. Whether it be in ocean currents, rainfall patterns, ice melting, or rising grain prices, it could leave a bewildered and frightened world in its wake. Will our political institutions, which could not prevent these mega-scale changes, be able to deal with them as they occur? The one thing that now seems certain is that it is time for a new approach—Plan B.

II

THE RESPONSE—PLAN B

Raising Water Productivity

Water scarcity, a consequence of the sevenfold growth in the world economy over the last half-century, will be a defining condition of life for many in this new century. The simultaneous emergence of fast-growing water shortages in so many countries requires a wholly new approach to water policy, a shift from expanding supply to managing demand. Managing water scarcity will affect what we eat, how we dispose of waste, and even where we live.[1]

Historically, the common response to water scarcity was to expand supply: to build more dams or drill more wells. Now this potential is either limited or nonexistent in most countries. Where rivers are drained dry and water tables are falling, the only option is reducing the growth in demand by raising water productivity and stabilizing population. With most of the 3 billion people projected to be added by 2050 due to be born in countries where wells are already going dry, achieving an acceptable balance between people and water may depend more on slowing population growth than any other single action.[2]

After World War II, as the world looked ahead to the end of the century, it saw a projected doubling of world population and frontiers of agricultural settlement that had largely disappeared. The response was to launch a

major effort to raise land productivity, one that nearly
tripled it between 1950 and 2000. Now it is time to see
what we can do with water.[3]

Adopting Realistic Prices

Water pricing policies today are remnants of another age,
a time when water was abundant, when there was more
water than we could possibly use. During the first six
decades of the last century, growth in irrigation came
from surface water projects, consisting of dams and large
networks of gravity-fed canals. Irrigation water from
these large, publicly funded projects was often heavily
subsidized, provided as a basic service. Because water
was so cheap, there was no incentive to use it efficiently.

In some situations, such as in parts of East and Southeast Asia, water is abundant and there is no need to
charge for it. But for most of humanity, that age of water
abundance is now history. As the world moves into an era
of scarcity, the challenge for governments is to take the
politically unpopular step of adopting prices for water
that reflect its value. Charging for water encourages
greater efficiency by all users, including the adoption of
more-efficient irrigation practices, the use of more water-
efficient industrial processes, and the purchase of more
water-efficient household appliances.

Pricing water to encourage efficiency can also be a
threat to low-income users, however. In response to this,
South Africa introduced lifeline rates, whereby each
household receives a fixed amount of water for basic
needs at a low price. When water use exceeds this level,
the price escalates. This helps ensure that basic needs are
met while discouraging the wasteful use of water.[4]

Some countries saw the value of raising water prices
early on. The government of Morocco, with 30 million
people living in a semiarid environment, made a huge

investment in harvesting its limited rainfall, building 88 large dams, raising storage capacity from 2.3 billion cubic meters of water in 1967 to 14 billion in 1997. But even with this sixfold expansion, Morocco was still facing water shortages, so in 1980 it doubled the price of water nationwide, encouraging efficiency. The effect of price rises on water use varies widely, but as a general matter a 10-percent rise in the price of irrigation water reduces water use by 1–2 percent. For residential and industrial use, the drop is usually higher—ranging from 3 to 7 percent.[5]

China has moved in a similar direction in recent years. With 500 of its 700 largest cities facing water shortages, with water tables falling almost everywhere, and with rivers running dry, China decided in 2001 to raise the price of water. The goal was to have water prices more accurately reflect value. Raising water prices in a country with a history of free water was politically difficult, much like raising gasoline prices in the United States.[6]

Some countries facing acute water scarcity are metering groundwater use. Jordan, a country with only 285 cubic meters of water per person per year—one of the lowest in the world—has installed meters on both new and existing irrigation wells. When the amount of water pumped exceeds that specified in the well permit, owners pay a stiff penalty. Although compliance is not automatic and is often met with resistance, it is widely recognized within the community that the failure to comply will deplete aquifers and undermine local farm economies.[7]

Australia inherited water institutions designed by Europeans, institutions that were more suitable for water-rich countries than for arid Australia. These were replaced by a system of riparian rights with licensing systems that specified how much water could be withdrawn, introduced meters to measure withdrawals, and charged for the amount of water used.[8]

Unfortunately, India moved in the opposite direction in 1997, when the government of Punjab decreed that the state utility should provide free electricity to farmers for irrigation. This populist move in India's breadbasket state lasted three years. *Washington Post* reporter John Lancaster wrote, "With no incentive to curb power use, farmers expanded the acreage devoted to water-intensive crops, especially rice, and ran their pumps indiscriminantly, seriously depleting groundwater reserves." In late 2000, when the state electricity utility was on the brink of bankruptcy, it was instructed to start billing farmers for electricity, a move that should raise Punjab's water productivity and slow the fall of water tables.[9]

Other governments in South Asia, while not so flagrant as the government of Punjab, have nonetheless subsidized the use of both electricity and diesel fuel to irrigators. This, coupled with cheap credit for financing the purchase of pumps and motors, has encouraged the overpumping and wasteful use of water, creating a false sense of food security.[10]

Because surface water is usually available only through large government projects, it is easier to charge for it than for groundwater. But the basic principles for managing the two water sources responsibly are essentially the same: provide economic incentives to use water efficiently and involve local water users' associations in the allocation of the water. Surface water typically belongs to the state and groundwater to the person who owns the land under which it is located. Even though individual farmers drill wells on their land, the pumps can be metered and farmers can be charged for the water. Local acceptance of this approach depends on convincing farmers to work together to stabilize the aquifer for everyone's long-term benefit.

Some countries have introduced tradable water rights so that individuals who have rights to surface water or who own wells can sell their water. This practice, common in the western United States, enables water to move freely to higher value uses, which essentially means the sale of water rights by farmers or local irrigation associations to cities. In India and Pakistan, small landholders often make the large investment needed for an irrigation well and then sell water to neighboring farmers.[11]

Raising Irrigation Water Productivity
Historically, farm productivity was measured in yield per hectare, since land was the constraining resource. But as the twenty-first century begins, policymakers are beginning to look at water as the limiting factor for food production. The common measure that is emerging to measure water productivity is kilograms of grain produced per ton of water.

Since 1950, world irrigated area has nearly tripled. With this growth and with grain yields on irrigated land roughly double those on rainfed land, irrigated land now accounts for easily 40 percent of the world grain harvest. For China and India it is even higher. Four fifths of China's grain harvest and close to three fifths of India's comes from irrigated land. In the United States, one fifth of the grain harvest comes from irrigated land.[12]

The relative contributions of surface water and groundwater irrigation vary widely among countries. Of China's 51 million hectares of irrigated land, 42 million depend on surface water and 9 million on underground water. For India, the breakdown is 44 million hectares and 42 million hectares, respectively, making groundwater even more important to India.[13]

Although China has only 9 million hectares of land irrigated with groundwater, this land is disproportionately productive simply because groundwater is available precisely when the farmer needs it. By contrast, surface water is usually delivered by canal to farmers in local groups, usually on a rotational basis. This timing may or may not coincide with a farmer's needs.

Although there are many ways of raising irrigation water productivity, a few stand out. For those using surface water irrigation, reducing seepage from the canals used to carry water from large reservoirs to farms cuts water use. It is not unusual, particularly where distances are long, for water seepage losses to reach 20–30 percent. This water can be saved if canals are lined with plastic sheeting or concrete—a more costly but more long-term solution.[14]

A second approach is to use a more efficient technology, such as overhead sprinkler systems. Commonly used with center-pivot irrigation systems, their weakness is that some water is lost to evaporation even before it hits the ground, especially in hot, arid settings. Low-pressure sprinklers, which release water at a lower level, close to the soil surface, lose less water through evaporation and drift. These are now widely used in the Texas panhandle of the United States, where aquifer depletion is encouraging farmers to use water much more efficiently.[15]

The gold standard for efficiency is drip irrigation, a method that supplies water directly to the root zone of plants. In addition to cutting water use by up to half, drip irrigation also raises yields because it offers a constant, carefully controlled supply of water. Israel, where water shortages are acute, is the world leader in developing drip technology. It is also now widely used in other countries, including Jordan and Tunisia.[16]

In Jordan, for example, drip irrigation reduced water use an average of 35 percent. Crops such as tomatoes and cucumbers typically yielded 15 percent more. The combination of reduced water use and higher yields raised water productivity by more than half. Tunisia, where drip-irrigated area expanded from 2,000 hectares in 1987 to 36,000 hectares in 1999, has realized similar gains.[17]

India in 1998 was irrigating 225,000 hectares with drip irrigation. Thirteen experiments at Indian research institutes on several different crops showed gains in water productivity ranging from a low of 46 percent to a high of 280 percent. (See Table 7–1.) On average, water productivity was raised by 152 percent, more than doubling.[18]

Drip irrigation may be permanent—that is, with water delivered through pipes installed underground, as is often done for orchards, for example—or flexible, con-

Table 7–1. *Water Productivity Gains When Shifting from Conventional Surface Irrigation to Drip Irrigation in India*

Crop	Changes in Yield[1]	Changes in Water Use	Water Productivity Gain[2]
		(percent)	
Bananas	52	–45	173
Cabbage	2	–60	150
Cotton	27	–53	169
Cotton	25	–60	212
Grapes	23	–48	134
Potato	46	0	46
Sugarcane	6	–60	163
Sugarcane	20	–30	70
Sugarcane	29	–47	143
Sugarcane	33	–65	280
Sweet potato	39	–60	243
Tomato	5	–27	44
Tomato	50	–39	145

[1]Results from various Indian research institutes. [2]Measured as crop yield per unit of water supplied.
Sources: See endnote 18.

sisting of rubber hose or plastic tubing. The latter typically is moved by hand every hour or so across the field and is thus a labor-intensive system of irrigation.

The traditionally high costs of both materials and labor used for drip irrigation are now dropping as new techniques and more flexible materials, including plastic tubing or pipe, become available. With these recent advances, the cost of drip irrigation systems has dropped from $1,200–2,500 per hectare to $425–625. Where water is costly, this is a financially attractive investment. And for countries where unemployment is high and water is scarce, the technology is ideal when it substitutes abundant labor for scarce water.[19]

In recent years, the tiniest small-scale drip-irrigation systems—the size of a bucket—have been developed to irrigate a small vegetable garden with roughly 100 plants (25 square meters). Somewhat larger drum systems irrigate 125 square meters. In both cases, the containers are elevated slightly, so that gravity distributes the water. Small drip systems using plastic lines that can easily be moved are also becoming popular. These simple systems can pay for themselves in one year. By simultaneously reducing water costs and increasing yields, they can dramatically raise incomes of smallholders.[20]

Sandra Postel believes that the combination of these drip technologies at various scales has the potential to profitably irrigate 10 million hectares of India's cropland, or nearly one tenth of the total. She sees a similar potential for China, which is now also expanding its drip irrigation area to save scarce water.[21]

Another technique for raising water use efficiency in both flood- and furrow-irrigated fields is laser leveling of the land, a precise leveling that can reduce water use by 20 percent and increase crop yields by up to 30 percent, boosting water efficiency by half. This practice is widely used for field crops in the United States and for rice production in a number of countries.[22]

Raising crop yields is an often overlooked way of raising water productivity. In Zhanghe Reservoir in the Yangtze River basin, where water was becoming scarce, farmers had to share with urban and industrial users. As a result, they simultaneously reduced water use by using more-efficient irrigation practices and raised rice yields from 4 tons per hectare a year on average in 1966–78 to 7.8 tons per hectare in 1989–98. The combination of lower water use and higher crop yields almost quadrupled water productivity, raising it from 0.65 kilograms of rice per ton of water to 2.4 kilograms.[23]

A comparison of wheat yields between countries also shows how higher crop yields boost water productivity. In California, where irrigated wheat produces some 6 tons per hectare, farmers produce 1.3 kilograms of wheat per ton of water used. But in Pakistan's Punjab, irrigated wheat yields averaged only 2 tons per hectare or 0.5 kilograms per ton of water—less than 40 percent the water productivity in California.[24]

Yet another way of raising water productivity is to shift to more water-efficient grains, such as from rice to wheat. The municipal government of Beijing, concerned about acute water shortages, has decreed that production of rice, a water-thirsty crop, should be phased out in the region surrounding the city. Instead of planting the current 23,300 hectares of rice, farmers will shift to other, less water-demanding crops by 2007. Egypt, facing an essentially fixed water supply, also restricts rice production.[25]

The economic efficiency of water use can also be raised by shifting to higher-value crops, a move that is often market-driven. As water tables fall and pumping becomes more costly, farmers in northern China are switching from wheat to higher-value crops simply because it is the only way they can survive economically.[26]

Institutional shifts, specifically moving the responsibility for managing irrigation systems from government agencies to local water users' associations, can facilitate the more efficient use of water. Farmers in many countries are organizing locally so they can assume this responsibility. Since local people have an economic stake in good water management, they typically do a better job than a distant government agency. In some countries, membership includes representatives of municipal governments and other users in addition to farmers.[27]

Mexico is a leader in this movement. As of 2002, more than 80 percent of Mexico's publicly irrigated land was managed by farmers' associations. One advantage of this shift for the government is that the cost of maintaining the irrigation system is assumed locally, reducing the drain on the treasury. This also means that associations need to charge more for irrigation water. Even so, for farmers the advantages of managing their water supply more than outweigh this additional expenditure.[28]

In Tunisia, where water users' associations manage both irrigation and residential water, the number of associations increased from 340 in 1987 to 2,575 in 1999. Many other countries now have such bodies managing their water resources. Although the early groups were organized to deal with large publicly developed irrigation systems, some recent ones have been formed to manage local groundwater irrigation as well. They assume responsibility for stabilizing the water table, thus avoiding aquifer depletion and the economic disruption that it brings to the community.[29]

Rainwater Harvesting
For many countries, particularly those with monsoonal climates and long dry seasons, water shortages result not

from a lack of rainfall but from a seasonally uneven supply. When annual rainfall is concentrated in a few months, storage is difficult. To illustrate, India has 2.1 trillion cubic meters of fresh water available each year, and the United States has 2.5 trillion cubic meters. While rain falls in the United States throughout the year, in India—which is geographically only one third as large—most of the rainfall comes between mid-June and mid-September. As a result, most of this deluge runs off and is quickly carried back to the sea by the country's rivers. Although there are thousands of dams in India, they can collectively store only a fraction of the rainfall.[30]

The focus on building large dams to capture and store surface water before it runs off dominated most of the last century. But because sites were becoming scarce and because the construction of large dams often inundates large areas, displacing local populations and irreversibly altering local ecosystems, this era has now largely run its course. More and more countries are turning to local water harvesting to ensure adequate supply.

In India, Rajendhra Singh is a leader of this movement. Some 20 years ago, when he was visiting semiarid Rajasthan province, he realized that water shortages were constraining development, preventing people from escaping poverty. As he surveyed the area and talked with villagers, he saw that local earthen dams to collect and store rainwater would help satisfy the need for water, both for residential use and for irrigation.[31]

Singh began working with the villagers, helping them design local water storage facilities. Once villagers helped select a site, they would organize to build an earthen dam. All the materials, the stone and the earth, were local. So, too, was the labor—sweat equity provided by the villagers. Singh would help with the engineering and design. He told villagers that in addition to meeting their daily needs for water, the seepage from the small reservoir would gradually raise the water table, restoring wells that had been abandoned. He also told them this would take time. It worked exactly as he said it would.[32]

Singh's initial success led him to create a local non-governmental organization with 45 full-time employees and 230 part-timers. Funded by the Ford Foundation and other groups, it has not only helped build 4,500 local water storage structures in Rajasthan, it has also raised villagers' incomes and improved their lives.[33]

When the local topography is favorable for building successful small water storage structures, this can be a boon for local communities. This approach works not only in monsoonal climates, but also in arid regions where low rainfall is retained for local use. With a modest amount of engineering guidance, hundreds of thousands of communities worldwide can build water storage works.

Another technique to retain rainfall is the construction of ridge terraces on hillsides to trap rainfall near where it falls, letting it soak into the soil rather than run off. Using a plow to establish the ridges, local farmers can build these terraces on their own, but they are more successful if they are guided by a surveyor who helps establish the ridgelines and determines how far apart the ridges or terraces should be on the hill. Once the terraces are established, the moisture that accumulates behind them can help support vegetation, including trees that can both stabilize the ridges and produce fruit and nuts or fuelwood. The terraces, which are particularly well adapted to the hilly agricultural regions of semiarid Africa, can markedly raise land productivity because they conserve both water and soil.

The water storage capacity of aquifers can also be exploited. In some ways, they are preferable to dams because water underground does not evaporate. As indicated, percolation from locally constructed water storage facilities often helps recharge aquifers. Similarly, land that is covered with vegetation retains rainfall, reducing runoff and enabling water to percolate downward and recharge aquifers. Without vegetative cover, rainfall runs off immediately, simultaneously causing flooding and reducing aquifer recharge, thus contributing to water shortages. In effect, floods and water shortages are often opposite sides of the same coin. Reforestation, particularly in the upper reaches of a watershed, not only helps recharge aquifers but also conserves soil that if washed away might end up behind dams downstream, reducing the storage capacity of reservoirs.

In summary, water harvesting and local water storage behind dams and in aquifers expands the supply and strengthens the local economy. These same initiatives also help conserve soil, since any action that reduces runoff reduces soil erosion. The net effect is conservation of both water and soil: a classic win-win situation.

Raising Nonfarm Water Productivity

Nonfarm water use is dominated by the use of water simply to wash away waste from factories and households or to dissipate heat from thermal power plants. The use of water to disperse wastes is an outmoded practice that is getting the world into trouble. Toxic industrial wastes discharged into rivers and lakes or into wells also permeate aquifers, making water—both surface and underground—unsafe for drinking. And they are destroying marine ecosystems, including local fisheries. The time has come to manage waste without discharging it into the local environment, allowing water to be recycled indefinitely and dramatically reducing both urban and industrial demand.

The current engineering concept for dealing with

human waste is to use vast quantities of water to wash it away in small amounts, preferably into a sewer system where it will be treated before being discharged into the local river. There are four problems inherent in this "flush and forget" system: it is water-intensive; it disrupts the nutrient cycle; most of humanity cannot afford it; and it is a major source of disease in developing countries.

As water scarcity spreads, the viability of water-based sewage systems will diminish. Water-borne sewage systems take nutrients from the land and dump them into rivers, lakes, or the sea. Not only are the nutrients lost from agriculture, but the nutrient overload has led to the death of many rivers, including nearly all of those in India and China. Water-based sewage also contributes to dead zones in coastal oceans. Sewer systems that dump untreated sewage into rivers and streams, as so many do, are a major source of disease and death.[34]

Sunita Narain of the Centre for Science and Environment in India argues convincingly that a water-based disposal system with sewage treatment facilities is neither environmentally nor economically viable for India. She notes that an Indian family of five, producing 250 liters of excrement in a year and using a water toilet, requires 150,000 liters of water to wash away the wastes.[35]

As currently designed, India's sewer system is actually a pathogen-dispersal system. It takes a small quantity of contaminated material and uses it to make vast quantities of water unfit for human use, often simply discharging it into nearby rivers or streams. Narain says both "our rivers and our children are dying." India's government, like that of many other developing countries, is hopelessly chasing the goal of universal water-based sewage systems and sewage treatment facilities—unable to close the huge gap between services needed and provided, but unwilling to admit that it is not an economically viable option. Narain concludes that the "flush and forget" approach is not working.[36]

This dispersal of pathogens is a huge public health challenge. Worldwide, poor sanitation and personal hygiene claim 2.7 million lives per year, second only to the 5.9 million claimed by hunger and malnutrition.[37]

Fortunately there is an alternative to the use of water to wash away human waste: the composting toilet. This is a simple, waterless toilet linked to a small compost facility. Table waste can also be incorporated in the composter. The dry composting converts human fecal material into a soil-like humus, which is essentially odorless and is scarcely 10 percent of the original volume. These compost facilities need to be emptied every year or so, depending on their design and size. Vendors periodically collect the humus and market it for use as a soil supplement, returning the nutrients and organic matter to the soil and reducing the need for fertilizer.[38]

This technology reduces residential water use, thus cutting the water bill and lowering the energy needed to pump and purify water. As a bonus, it also reduces garbage flow if table waste is incorporated, eliminates the sewage water disposal problem, and restores the nutrient cycle. The U.S. Environmental Protection Agency now lists several brands of dry toilets for use. Pioneered in Sweden, these toilets are used in widely varying conditions, including Swedish apartment buildings, U.S. private residences, and Chinese villages.[39]

At the household level, water can be saved by using appliances that are more water-efficient, including showerheads, flush toilets, dishwashers, and clothes washers. Some countries are adopting water efficiency standards and labeling for appliances, much as has been done for energy efficiency. As water costs rise, as they inevitably will, investments in composting toilets and more water-efficient household appliances will become increasingly attractive to individual homeowners.

For cities, the most effective single step to raise water productivity is to adopt a comprehensive water treatment/recycling system, reusing the same water continuously. With this system, a small percentage of water is lost to evaporation each time it cycles through. Given the technologies that are available today, it is quite possible to comprehensively recycle urban water supplies, largely removing cities as a claimant on water resources.

At the industrial level, one of the largest users of water is the energy sector, which uses water to cool thermal power plants. As fossil fuels are phased out and the world turns to wind, solar, and geothermal energy, the need for cooling water in thermal power plants will diminish. In the United States, for example, thermal cooling of power plants accounts for 39 percent of all water withdrawals. With each coal-fired power plant that is closed as a new wind farm comes online, water use for thermal cooling drops, freeing up water for food production.[40]

Many of the industrial processes now used belong to a time when water was an abundant resource. Within the steel industry, for example, water use efficiency may vary among countries by a factor of three. Much of the water used in industry just washes away waste. If this is stopped, and more and more companies move into zero-emissions industrial parks, water use in industry could drop dramatically.[41]

The new reality is that the existing water-based waste disposal economy is not viable. There are too many factories, feedlots, and households to simply try and wash waste away. It is ecologically mindless and outdated—an approach that belongs to an age when there were many fewer people and far less economic activity.

A Global Full-Court Press

As fast-unfolding water shortages translate into food shortages, they will signal that we can no longer rely on incremental business-as-usual change. Three factors— the simultaneous drop in water tables, the exponential nature of that fall, and the globalization of water scarcity—ensure that such a response will not be sufficient. As water shocks become food shocks and as falling water tables translate into higher food prices, we will realize that the world has changed fundamentally. As Asit K. Biswas, Director of the Third World Centre for Water Management, notes, "The world is heading for a water crisis that is unprecedented in human history. Water development and management will change more in the next 20 years than in the last 2,000 years."[42]

Supply-side technological fixes, such as the massive desalting of seawater, do not hold much hope for food production in the foreseeable future. Although the cost of desalting seawater is falling, it is still expensive and thus not yet a viable prospect for irrigation. At present, it costs between $1 and $2 per cubic meter to desalt seawater. Even at the lower cost, producing wheat with desalted seawater would raise its price from $120 to $1,120 per ton.[43]

Some countries are still focusing on supply expansion when it might be less costly to focus on demand management. To get water to the cities in its industrial northern half, including Beijing and Tianjin, China has devised a plan to move water along three routes from the Yangtze River basin to the Yellow River basin, since the latter has only one tenth the flow of the former. These three routes, designated the East, Central, and West, will cost an estimated $59 billion. Construction on the East route began in December 2002. For China, it might be more economical to invest this $59 billion in urban water recycling and irrigation efficiency in the north rather than trying to transport water from the south.[44]

With water shortages now threatening so many countries at the same time, we need a global full-court press, to borrow an expression from basketball, to raise water productivity. This begins with improved irrigation practices and technologies, as described in this chapter. It also includes boosting crop yields on both irrigated and non-irrigated land. The former will raise the productivity of irrigation water and the latter will get more mileage out of existing rainfall. Shifting to more water-efficient crops also helps raise farm water productivity. The shift from rice to wheat, already under way in some countries, can continue wherever it is practical. With feedgrain, shifting from corn to sorghum may make sense in countries where there is not enough water for irrigation.

At the dietary level, shifting to more grain-efficient forms of animal protein can raise the efficiency of grain use, and thus the efficiency of water use. This means moving from feedlot beef and pork to more poultry and herbivorous species of farmed fish, such as carp, tilapia, and catfish. For the world's affluent, moving down the food chain also saves water.

At the consumer level, switching to more water-efficient household appliances raises water productivity. For cities and industry, recycling of water becomes the key to achieving large gains in water productivity. Finally, and perhaps most important, for water-scarce countries facing large projected increases in population, accelerating the shift to smaller families reduces the chance of being trapped in hydrological poverty.

8

Raising Land Productivity

From the beginning of agriculture until 1950 or so, growth in world food production came almost entirely from expanding the cultivated area. Rises in land productivity were negligible, scarcely perceptible from one generation to the next. Then as the frontiers of agricultural settlement disappeared, the world began systematically to raise land productivity. Between 1950 and 2000, grainland productivity climbed by 160 percent while the area planted in grain expanded only 14 percent.[1]

This extraordinary rise in productivity, combined with the modest expansion of cultivated area, enabled farmers to triple the grain harvest over the last half-century. At the same time, the growing demand for animal protein was being satisfied largely by a quintupling of the world fish catch to 95 million tons and a doubling of world beef and mutton production, largely from rangelands. These gains not only supported a growth in population from 2.5 billion to 6.1 billion, they also raised food consumption per person, shrinking the share who were hungry.[2]

As we look ahead at the next half-century, we face a demand situation that is similar in that the world is facing a projected increase of nearly 3 billion people, only slightly less than during the last half-century, but now virtually all the increase is coming in developing countries. In 1950, most of the world wanted to move up the food chain, eating more livestock products. That is also true today, but instead of 2 billion wanting to move up the food chain, there are now close to 5 billion.[3]

With agricultural supply, however, there are sharp differences. The annual rise in land productivity, averaging 2.1 percent from 1950 to 1990, dropped to 1 percent from 1990 to 2002. In addition, oceanic fisheries and rangelands have been pushed to their limits and beyond, which means we cannot expect much, if any, additional output from either system. Future gains in animal protein production will have to come largely from feeding grain to animals, whether they be livestock, poultry, or fish. And this means more demands on the world's croplands.[4]

At the center of the tripling of world grain production during the last century were high-yielding varieties, the dwarf wheats and rices developed originally in Japan and hybrid corn from the United States. Under favorable conditions, these varieties could double, triple, even quadruple the yields of traditional varieties. But there are no new varieties in the pipeline that can lead to similar quantum jumps in yields. Nearly two decades have passed since the first genetically modified crop varieties were released, yet biotechnologists have yet to produce a single variety of wheat, rice, or corn that can dramatically raise yields. Nor does it seem likely that they will, simply because plant breeders, using conventional breeding techniques, have already taken most of the obvious measures to get the big jumps in yields.[5]

Helping to realize the genetic potential of the new high-yield varieties was the growth in irrigation, which expanded from 94 million hectares in 1950 to 272 million in 2000, raising the share of the world's grain harvest from irrigated land to 40 percent. Now growth in the irrigated area is slowing as many countries lose irrigation water from aquifer depletion and its diversion to cities.[6]

As high-yielding varieties spread and irrigated area expanded, fertilizer use climbed from 14 million tons in 1950 to 137 million tons in 2000—a tenfold gain. While irrigation was removing the moisture constraints on crop yields, fertilizer was removing nutrient constraints. Then diminishing returns set in and the growth in fertilizer use slowed markedly. In the United States, Western Europe, and Japan, use has not increased for more than a decade. It may also now be leveling off in China, the world's largest user of fertilizer. There are still many countries that can profitably increase fertilizer use, including India and Brazil. But for much of the world, applying more fertilizer now has little effect on yields.[7]

Looking back, the greatest progress in eradicating hunger came while grain production per person was climbing from 251 kilograms in 1950 to 344 kilograms in 1984. During these 34 years, the rising tide of food production was reducing hunger throughout the world. After 1984, however, growth in the grain harvest slowed, falling behind that of population. By 2002, it had fallen to 290 kilograms per person, a decline of 18 percent from the peak in 1984.[8]

Rethinking Land Productivity

After climbing from 1.1 tons per hectare in 1950 to 2.8 tons in 2002, the world grain yield has reached a level where it is becoming more difficult to sustain a continuing rapid rise. Much of the impressive gain in yields came as scientists boosted the share of photosynthate going to seed from 20 percent in traditional varieties to over 50 percent in modern high-yielding grains, close to the theoretical limit. Efforts to raise yields further are starting to push against the physiological limits of plants. In many countries, the rise in yields is slowing and in some it is leveling off. For example, yields have not risen much in rice in Japan since 1984, in wheat in Mexico since 1980, or in wheat in the United States since 1985. [9]

This loss of momentum is worldwide. While world grainland productivity rose by just over 2 percent a year from 1950 to 1990, it averaged only 1 percent annually from 1990 to 2001. (See Table 8–1.) And in the last five years from 1997 to 2002, the annual yield gain dropped to 0.5 percent.[10]

The rise in grain yields will likely slow further during this decade. In addition to the shrinking backlog of technology to draw upon, many farmers also must deal with a loss of irrigation water, and farmers worldwide are facing the prospect of record-high temperatures—all of which could make it difficult to sustain a steady rise in land productivity.

Although the rise in yields is slowing, there are still many opportunities for increasing yields, but in most situations the potential for doing so is modest. In Africa, for example, where fertilizer use is restricted by aridity and

Table 8–1. *Gains in World Grain Yield Per Hectare, 1950–2001*

Year	Yield Per Hectare[1] (tons)	Annual Increase (percent)
1950	1.06	
1990	2.47	2.1
2001	2.79	1.0

[1]Yields for 1990 and 2001 are three-year averages.
Source: See endnote 10.

transport costs, the simultaneous planting of grain and leguminous trees is showing promise. The trees start slowly, permitting the grain crop to mature and be harvested. Then they grow to several feet in height. The leaves dropped from the trees provide nitrogen and organic matter—both sorely needed in African soils. The wood is then cut and used for fuel. This simple, locally adapted technology, developed by Pedro Sanchez, head of the International Centre for Research in Agroforestry in Nairobi, often enables farmers to double their grain yields within a matter of years as soil fertility builds.[11]

The magnitude of the challenge ahead is unmistakable. It will force us to think about both limiting the growth in demand and using the existing harvest more productively. On the demand side, achieving an acceptable balance between food and people may now depend on stabilizing world population as close to 7 billion as possible and reducing the unhealthily high level of consumption of livestock products in industrial countries. But we must also think more broadly about land productivity, considering not only the individual crop but how we can increase the number of crops harvested and how to use them better.

Multiple Cropping

In North America and Western Europe, which in the past have restricted cropped area in order to avoid surpluses, there is a potential for double cropping that has not been fully exploited. Indeed, the tripling in the world grain harvest since 1950 is due in part to impressive increases in multiple cropping in Asia. As noted in Chapter 3, some of the more common multiple cropping combinations are wheat and corn in northern China, wheat and rice in northern India, and the double or triple cropping of rice in southern China and southern India.[12]

The double cropping of winter wheat and corn in the North China Plain helped make China the world's leading grain producer. Winter wheat grown there yields close to 4 tons per hectare. Corn averages 5 tons. Together these two crops, grown in rotation, can yield 9 tons of grain per hectare per year. Double cropping of rice yields 8 tons per hectare.[13]

A generation ago in India, land in the north was devoted to producing only wheat, but with the advent of earlier maturing, high-yielding wheats and rices, it became possible to harvest the wheat in time to plant rice. This wheat/rice combination is now widely used throughout Punjab, Haryana, and parts of Uttar Pradesh. The rice yield of 2 tons per hectare and the wheat yield of 3 tons combine for 5 tons of grain per hectare, making it a key to feeding India's 1 billion people.[14]

The area that can be multiple cropped is limited by the availability of irrigation water, early-maturing varieties, and, in developing countries, enough labor to quickly harvest one crop and plant another. The loss of low-cost rural laborers through the processes of industrialization can sharply reduce multiple cropping and therefore the harvested area. In Japan, for example, the grain-harvested area in 1961 reached a peak of nearly 5 million hectares, because farmers were harvesting an average of two crops per year. As of 2002, the harvested area had dropped to 2 million hectares, partly because of cropland conversion to nonfarm uses, but mostly because of a dramatic decline in double cropping as industry pulled labor from agriculture. Even a rice-support price four times the world market price could not keep enough workers in agriculture to support extensive multiple cropping.[15]

South Korea's harvested area has shrunk by half since peaking in 1965. Taiwan's has declined nearly two thirds since 1975. As industrialization progresses in China and India, the more prosperous regions of these countries may see similar declines in multiple cropping. In China, where incomes have quadrupled since 1980, this process already appears to be reducing production.[16]

In the United States, the lifting of planting area restrictions in 1996 opened new opportunities for multiple cropping. The most common U.S. double cropping combination is winter wheat with soybeans as a summer crop. Six percent of the soybean harvest comes from land that also produces winter wheat. One benefit of this rotation is that soybeans fix nitrogen, reducing the amount of fertilizer needed for wheat.[17]

A concerted U.S. effort to both breed earlier maturing varieties and develop cultural practices that would facilitate multiple cropping could substantially boost crop output. If China's farmers can extensively double crop wheat and corn, then U.S. farmers, at a similar latitude and with similar climate patterns, might be able to do the same if agricultural research and farm policy were reoriented in support of such an initiative.

Western Europe, with its mild winters and high-yielding wheat, might also be able to double crop more with a summer grain, such as corn, or with an oilseed crop. Elsewhere in the world, Brazil and Argentina have an extended frost-free growing season climate that supports extensive multiple cropping, often wheat or corn with soybeans.[18]

Raising Protein Efficiency

The second way to raise land productivity in a world where literally billions of people want to diversify their diets by consuming less plant starch and more animal protein is to produce animal protein more efficiently. With some 37 percent of the world grain harvest, or nearly 700 million tons, used to produce animal protein, the potential for more efficient grain use is large.[19]

World meat consumption increased from 47 million tons in 1950 to 240 million tons in 2002, more than doubling consumption per person from 17 kilograms to 40 kilograms. Consumption of milk and eggs has also risen. In every society where incomes have risen, meat consumption has too, perhaps reflecting a taste that evolved over 4 million years of hunting and gathering.[20]

As both the oceanic fish catch and the production of beef on rangelands have leveled off, the world has shifted to grain-based production of animal protein to expand output. And as the demand for animal protein climbs, the mix of protein products consumed is shifting toward those that convert grain into protein most efficiently, the lower-cost products. Health concerns have also prompted some people to shift consumption from beef and pork to poultry and fish.

The efficiency with which various animals convert grain into protein varies widely. With cattle in feedlots, it takes roughly 7 kilograms of grain to produce a 1-kilogram gain in live weight. For pork, the figure is close to 4 kilograms of grain per kilogram of weight gain, for poultry it is just over 2, and for herbivorous species of farmed fish (such as carp, tilapia, and catfish), it is less than 2. As the market shifts production to the more grain-efficient products, it raises the productivity of both land and water.[21]

Global beef production, most of which comes from rangelands, grew less than 1 percent a year from 1990 to 2002. Growth in the number of cattle feedlots was minimal. Pork production grew by 2.5 percent annually, and poultry by nearly 5 percent. (See Table 8–2.) The rapid growth in poultry production, going from 41 million tons in 1990 to 72 million tons in 2002, enabled poultry to

Table 8–2. *Annual Growth in World Animal Protein Production, by Source, 1990–2002*

Source	1990	2002	Annual Growth
	(million tons)		(percent)
Aquacultural Output[1]	13	38	10.2
Poultry	41	72	4.8
Eggs	38	58	3.6
Pork	70	94	2.5
Mutton	10	12	1.5
Oceanic Fish Catch[1]	86	91	0.5
Beef	53	58	0.8

[1]Oceanic fish catch and aquacultural output figures for 2001.
Source: See endnote 22.

eclipse beef in 1995, moving it into second place behind pork. (See Figure 8–1.) World pork production, half of it in China, overtook beef production in 1979 and has continued to widen the lead since then. World beef production, handicapped by inefficient feedlot conversion, is continuing to expand, but just barely. Indeed, within the next decade or so, fast-growing aquacultural output may overtake beef production.[22]

The big winner in the animal protein sweepstakes has been aquaculture, largely because fish are highly efficient at converting feed into protein. Aquacultural output expanded from 13 million tons in 1990 to 38 million tons in 2002, growing by more than 10 percent a year. China is the leading producer, accounting for two thirds of the global output in 2000. Its output, rather evenly divided between coastal and inland areas, is dominated by finfish (mostly carp), which are produced inland in freshwater ponds, lakes, reservoirs, and rice paddies, and by shellfish

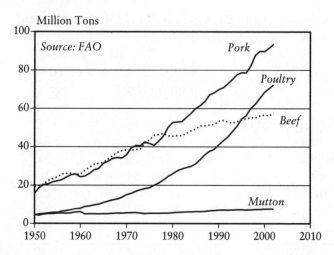

Figure 8–1. *World Meat Production by Type, 1950–2002*

(mostly oysters, clams, and mussels), which are produced in coastal regions.[23]

Over time, China has evolved a remarkably efficient fish polyculture using four types of carp that feed at different levels of the food chain, in effect emulating natural aquatic ecosystems. Silver carp and bighead carp are filter feeders, eating phytoplankton and zooplankton respectively. The grass carp, as its name implies, feeds largely on vegetation, while the common carp is a bottom feeder, living on detritus on the bottom. China's aquaculture is often integrated with agriculture, enabling farmers to use agricultural wastes, such as pig or duck manure, to fertilize ponds, thus stimulating the growth of plankton. Fish polyculture, which typically boosts pond productivity over that of monocultures by at least half, also dominates fish farming in India.[24]

As land and water become ever more scarce, China's fish farmers are feeding more grain concentrates in order to raise pond productivity. Using this technique, China's farmers raised the annual pond yield per hectare from 2.4 tons of fish in 1990 to 4.1 tons in 1996.[25]

In the United States, catfish, which require less than 2 kilograms of feed per kilogram of live weight, is the leading aquacultural product. U.S. annual catfish production of 240,000 tons (or two pounds per person) is concentrated in four states: Mississippi, Louisiana, Alabama, and Arkansas. Mississippi, with easily 60 percent of U.S. output, is the catfish capital of the world.[26]

Public attention has focused on aquacultural operations that are environmentally disruptive, such as the farming of salmon, a carnivorous species, and shrimp. Yet these operations account for only 1.5 million tons of output. World aquaculture is dominated by shellfish and by herbivorous species—mainly carp in China and India, but also catfish in the United States and tilapia in several countries. This is where the potential for growth lies.[27]

A Second Harvest

Another initiative that can have the effect of raising land productivity involves ruminants, such as cattle, sheep, and goats. Although rangelands are being grazed to capacity and beyond, there is a large unrealized potential for feeding agricultural residues—rice straw, wheat straw, and corn stalks—to ruminants, which have a complex digestive system that enables them to convert roughage, which humans cannot digest, into animal protein. This means that a given grain crop can yield a second harvest—the meat or the milk that is produced with straw and corn stalks.

India has been uniquely successful in using cattle and water buffalo to convert crop residues into milk, expanding production from 20 million tons in 1961 to 85 million tons in 2002—a more than fourfold increase. Following a

path of steady growth, milk became India's most valuable farm product in 1994, eclipsing rice. In 1997, India
overtook the United States to become the world's leading
milk producer. (See Figure 8–2.) Remarkably, it did so
almost entirely by using farm byproducts and crop
residues, avoiding the diversion of grain from human
consumption to cattle.[28]

Between 1961 and 2002, India's milk production per
person increased from 0.9 liters per week to 1.6 liters, or
roughly a cup of milk per day. Although this is not a great
deal by western standards, it is a welcome expansion in a
protein-hungry country.[29]

India's milk is produced almost entirely by small
farmers with one to three cows. Milk production is integrated with crop production, involving an estimated 70
million farmers for whom it is a highly valued source of
supplemental income. Ownership of a few cows also
means a supply of manure for fertilizer.[30]

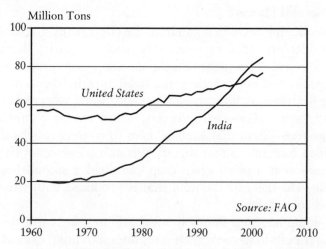

Figure 8–2. *Milk Production in India and the
United States, 1961–2002*

In China, where double cropping of winter wheat and corn is common, wheat straw and corn stalks are removed from the land because there is not enough time for them to decompose before the next crop is planted. As the world's leading producer of both rice and wheat and the second largest producer of corn, China annually harvests an estimated 500 million tons of straw, corn stalks, and other crop residues. At present, with much of this either burned, simply to dispose of it, or used as fuel for cooking, there is a large potential for China to follow India's lead in using crop residues to raise protein productivity.[31]

The ammoniation of crop residues (the incorporation of nitrogen) in the roughage helps microbial flora in the rumen of the cattle and sheep to digest the roughage more completely. The use of this technology in the major crop-producing provinces of east central China—Hebei, Shandong, Henan, and Anhui—has already created a "Beef Belt." Beef output in these four provinces now dwarfs that of the grazing provinces of Inner Mongolia, Qinghai, and Xinjiang.[32]

The achievements of China in aquaculture, of India in expanding its milk production, and of other countries in producing protein more efficiently hold out hope for being able to satisfy the growing world demand for protein without clearing additional land for agriculture, assuming that we can stabilize population soon.

Saving Soil and Cropland

The world's farmers are literally losing ground on two fronts—the loss of soil from erosion and the conversion of cropland to nonfarm uses, as described in Chapter 3. Both are well-established trends that reduce agricultural output, but since both are gradual processes, they are often not given the attention that they deserve.

The 1930s Dust Bowl that threatened to turn the U.S.

Great Plains into a vast desert was a traumatic experience that led to revolutionary changes in American agricultural practices, such as the planting of tree shelterbelts— rows of trees planted beside fields to slow wind and thus reduce wind erosion. Perhaps the most lasting change is strip cropping, the planting of wheat on alternate strips with fallowed land each year. This permits soil moisture to accumulate on the fallowed strips, while the planted strips reduce wind speed and hence the wind erosion on the idled strips. The key to controlling wind erosion is to keep the land covered with vegetation as much as possible and to slow wind speeds at ground level.[33]

One of the time-tested methods of dealing with water erosion is terracing to reduce runoff. On land that is less steeply sloping, as in the midwestern United States, contour farming has also worked well.[34]

Another newer, highly effective tool in the soil conservation toolkit is conservation tillage, which includes both no tillage and minimum tillage. In conventional farming, land is plowed, disked, or harrowed to prepare the seedbed, seed is drilled into the soil with a planter, and row crops are cultivated with a mechanical cultivator two or three times to control weeds. With minimum tillage, farmers simply drill seeds directly into the soil without any preparation at all. Weeds are controlled with herbicides. The only tillage is a one-time disturbance in a narrow band of soil where the seeds are inserted, leaving the remainder of the soil undisturbed, covered by crop residues and thus resistant to both water and wind erosion.[35]

In the United States, where farmers during the 1990s were required to implement a soil conservation plan on erodible cropland to be eligible for commodity price supports, the no-till area went from 7 million hectares in 1990 to nearly 21 million hectares (51 million acres) in 2000, tripling within a decade. An additional 23 million hectares were minimum-tilled, for a total of 44 million hectares of conservation tillage. This total included 37 percent of the corn crop, 57 percent of soybeans, and 30 percent of the wheat. Outside the United States, data for crop year 1998–99 show Brazil using conservation tillage on 11 million hectares and Argentina with 7 million hectares. Canada, at 4 million hectares, rounds out the "big four." And now no-till farming is catching on in Europe, Africa, and Asia. In addition to reducing soil losses, minimum-till and no-till practices also help retain water and reduce energy use.[36]

The U.S. method of controlling soil erosion by both converting highly erodible cropland back to grassland and adopting conservation practices to reduce erosion offers a model for the rest of the world. In 1985, the U.S. Congress, with strong support from the environmental community, created the Conservation Reserve Program (CRP) to reduce soil erosion and control overproduction. The CRP aimed to put up to 45 million acres of highly erodible land into permanent vegetative cover under 10-year contracts. Under this program, farmers were paid to plant fragile cropland to grass or trees. The retirement of 35 million acres under the CRP, together with adoption of conservation practices on 37 percent of all cropland, reduced U.S. soil erosion from 3.1 billion tons in 1982 to 1.9 billion tons in 1997.[37]

Saving cropland is sometimes more difficult than saving the topsoil on the cropland. This is particularly the case when dealing with urban sprawl, where strong commercial forces have influence. With cropland becoming scarce, efforts to protect prime farmland from urban spread are needed everywhere. Here Japan is the model. It has successfully protected rice paddies even within the boundaries of Tokyo, thus enabling it to remain self-sufficient in rice, its staple food.[38]

In the United States, Portland, Oregon, provides another model. The state adopted boundaries to urban growth 20 years ago, requiring each community to project its growth needs for the next two decades and then, based on the results, draw an outer boundary that would accommodate that growth. Richard Moe, head of the National Trust for Historic Preservation, observes, "This has worked in Oregon because it forced development back to the city. Lot sizes are smaller. There is more density, which is made possible by mass transit. There has been a doubling of the workforce in downtown Portland over the last 20 years without one new parking lot, without one new parking space."[39]

Moe's point about Oregon draws attention to still another threat to the world's cropland, namely the automobile. In a land-hungry world, the time has come to reassess the future of the automobile and to design transportation systems that provide mobility for entire populations, not just affluent minorities, and that do this without threatening food security. When Beijing announced in 1994 that it planned to make the auto industry one of the growth sectors for the next few decades, a group of eminent scientists—many of them members of China's National Academy of Sciences—produced a white paper challenging this decision. They identified several reasons why China should not develop a car-centered transport system, but the first was that the country did not have enough land to both feed its people and accommodate the automobile.[40]

The scientists recommended that instead of building an automobile infrastructure of highways, roads, and parking lots, China should concentrate on developing state-of-the-art urban light-rail systems augmented by buses and bicycles. This would not only provide mobility for far more people than a congested auto-centered system, it would also protect cropland.[41]

There are many reasons to question the goal of building auto-centered transportation systems everywhere, including climate change, air pollution, and traffic congestion. But the loss of cropland alone is sufficient. Future food security now depends on restructuring transportation budgets—investing less in highway infrastructure and more in a land-efficient rail, bus, and bicycle infrastructure.

Restoring the Earth

The trends in soil erosion, grainland productivity, and urbanization discussed here and in Chapter 3 suggest a need to stabilize world population at a low level. The advantages of stabilizing at 7.4 billion (the low end of U.N. projections for 2050) rather than 8.9 billion (the medium projection) are clear. But it will require a substantial investment in education, health, and family planning in poor countries. Although at first glance it might appear to be costly, it will be far more costly if we fail to do so.[42]

Paralleling the effort to quickly stabilize population size is the need for the world's affluent to eat lower on the food chain and lighten the pressure on the earth's land and water resources. In a country where starchy subsistence diets prevail, as in India, annual grain consumption per person is roughly 200 kilograms, or a bit over a pound a day. At this level, nearly all the grain must be consumed directly to meet basic caloric needs, leaving little for conversion into animal protein. At the other end of the scale is the United States, where grain consumption per person exceeds 800 kilograms per year. Of this, only a small part is consumed directly in the form of bread, pastry, and breakfast cereals. The bulk is eaten indirectly as meat, milk, and eggs. Unfortunately for most Americans, consumption of fat-rich livestock products is excessive, leading to numerous health problems.[43]

The world's healthiest people are not those living at the top or the bottom of the grain consumption ladder, but rather those somewhere in the middle. In Italy, for example, grain consumption per person is less than 400 kilograms a year. Italians eat some animal protein, including meat and a variety of cheeses, but meat is more of a condiment than an entrée in Italian cuisine. Even though far less is spent on health care per person in Italy than in the United States, Italians live longer. People on the so-called Mediterranean diet live longer than either those with a diet that is heavy in fat-rich livestock products or those who get 70 percent of their calories from a single starchy staple, such as rice. If the more affluent of the earth's inhabitants who are living high on the food chain consume less animal protein, not only will they be healthier but so will the earth.[44]

In reviewing the literature on soil erosion, references to the "loss of protective vegetation" occur again and again. Over the last half-century, we have removed so much of that protective cover by clearcutting, overgrazing, and overplowing that we are losing soil accumulated over long stretches of geological time almost overnight. Arresting this and the resultant decline in the earth's biological productivity depends on a worldwide effort to restore the earth's vegetative cover. Efforts to reverse this degradation are now under way in some countries.

As of 2003, for example, some 14 million hectares of U.S. cropland—roughly one tenth of the total—have been planted to grass and trees under the Conservation Reserve Program. And Algeria, trying to halt the northward advance of the Sahara Desert, is concentrating its orchards and vineyards in the southern part of the country, hoping that these perennial plantings will halt the desertification of its cropland. Only time will tell if this program, launched by Ministry of Agriculture officials in December 2000, will succeed.[45]

China may be facing the biggest challenge on the land degradation front. At the heart of its effort to halt the advance of existing deserts and the formation of new ones is a program to pay farmers in the threatened provinces to plant their cropland in trees. By 2010, 10 million hectares of grainland are to be covered with trees, representing easily one tenth of China's current grainland area.[46]

In Inner Mongolia (Nei Monggol), efforts to halt the advancing desert and to reclaim the land for productive uses initially involved planting desert shrubs to stabilize the sand dunes. And in many situations, sheep and goats are banned entirely and cattle are brought in instead. In Helin County, south of the provincial capital of Hohhot, such a strategy is yielding results. The planting of desert shrubs on abandoned cropland has now stabilized the county's first 7,000-hectare reclamation plot. Based on this success, the reclamation effort is being expanded.[47]

The Helin County strategy is centered on a shift from sheep and goats to dairy cattle, increasing the number of dairy animals from 30,000 in 2002 to 150,000 by 2007. The cattle will be largely stall-fed, eating cornstalks, wheat straw, and the harvest from a drought-tolerant leguminous forage crop resembling alfalfa, which is growing on reclaimed land. Local officials estimate that this program will double incomes within the county during this decade.[48]

To relieve pressure on the country's rangelands, Beijing is asking herders to reduce their flocks of sheep and goats by 40 percent. But in communities where wealth is measured in livestock numbers and where most families are living in poverty, such cuts are not easy or likely unless alternative livelihoods are offered along the lines proposed in Helin County. Indeed, unless governments, with support from the international community, can devise comprehensive programs to bring the size of grazing flocks and herds down to the carrying capacity of the land, grasslands will continue to deteriorate.[49]

One of the big challenges is to eliminate overgrazing on the two fifths of the earth's land surface classified as rangelands. The only viable option in many cases is to reduce the size of flocks and herds. But this is not easy in pastoral communities where livestock are the sole means of livelihood. Not only do the growing numbers of cattle, and particularly sheep and goats, remove the vegetation, but their hoofs pulverize the protective crust of soil that is formed by rainfall and that checks wind erosion. Here the solution is to shift to stall feeding of animals, cutting the forage and bringing it to them. Stall-feeding is labor-intensive and thus is a good fit for developing countries with many small holdings, an excess of labor, and a shortage of productive land. As noted, India has been a leader in adopting this practice, particularly within its thriving dairy industry.[50]

Another way to reduce pressure on the land is to shift from the use of fuelwood to renewable energy sources— everything from solar cookers to wind-generated electricity. Protecting the earth's remaining vegetation also warrants a ban on clearcutting forests in favor of selective cutting, simply because with each clearcut, the land typically suffers heavy soil losses until the forest regenerates. Thus with each cutting, productivity declines further.

Restoring the earth's tree and grass cover protects soil, reduces flooding, and sequesters carbon. It is one way we can restore the earth so that it can support not only us, but our children and grandchildren as well.

9

Cutting Carbon Emissions
in Half

When the Kyoto Protocol was negotiated in 1997, the proposed 5-percent reduction in carbon emissions from 1990 levels in industrial countries by 2012 seemed like an ambitious goal. Now it is seen by more and more people as being out of date. Even before the treaty has entered into force, many of the countries committed to carrying it out have discovered that they can do even better.[1]

National governments, local governments, corporations, and environmental groups are coming up with ambitious plans to cut carbon emissions. Prominent among these is a plan developed by the British government to reduce carbon emissions 60 percent by 2050, the amount that scientists deem necessary to stabilize atmospheric carbon dioxide (CO_2) levels. Building on this, Prime Minister Tony Blair and Sweden's Prime Minister Göran Persson are jointly urging the European Union to adopt the 60-percent goal.[2]

A plan developed for Canada by the David Suzuki Foundation and the Climate Action Network would halve carbon emissions by 2030 and would do it only with investments in energy efficiency that are profitable. And in early April 2003, the World Wildlife Fund released a peer-reviewed analysis by a team of scientists that proposed reducing carbon emissions from U.S. electric power generation 60 percent by 2020. This proposal centers on a shift to more energy-efficient power generation equipment, the use of more-efficient household appliances and industrial motors and other equipment, and in some situations a shift from coal to natural gas. If implemented, it would result in national savings averaging $20 billion a year from now until 2020.[3]

In Canada's most populous province, an environmental group—the Ontario Clear Air Alliance—has devised a plan to phase out the province's five coal-fired power plants, the first one in 2005 and the last one by 2015. The plan is supported by all three major political parties. Jack Gibbons, director of the Alliance, says of coal burning, "It's a nineteenth century fuel that has no place in twenty-first century Ontario."[4]

Germany, which has set the pace for reducing carbon emissions among industrial countries, is now talking about lowering its emissions by 40 percent by 2020. And this is a country that is already far more energy-efficient than the United States. Contrasting goals for cutting carbon emissions in Germany and the United States are due to a lack of leadership in the latter—not a lack of technology.[5]

U.S.-based Interface, the world's largest manufacturer of industrial carpeting, cut carbon emissions in its Canadian affiliate during the 1990s by two thirds from the peak. It did so by examining every facet of its business—from electricity consumption to trucking procedures. The company has saved more than $400,000 a year in energy expenditures. CEO Ray Anderson says, "Interface Canada has reduced greenhouse gas emissions by 64 percent from the peak, and made money in the process, in no small measure because our customers support environmental responsibility." The Canadian plan to cut carbon emissions in half by 2030 was inspired by the profitability of the Interface initiative.[6]

Although stabilizing atmospheric CO_2 levels is a staggering challenge, it is entirely doable. Detailed studies by governments and by various environmental groups are beginning to reveal the potential for reducing carbon emissions while saving money in the process. With advances in wind turbine design and the evolution of the fuel cell, we now have the basic technologies needed to shift quickly from a carbon-based to a hydrogen-based energy economy. Cutting world carbon emissions in half by 2015 is entirely within range. Ambitious though this might seem, it is commensurate with the threat that climate change poses.

Raising Energy Productivity
The enormous potential for raising energy productivity becomes clear in comparisons among countries. Some countries in Europe have essentially the same living standard as the United States yet use scarcely half as much energy per person. But even the countries that use energy most efficiently are not close to realizing the full potential for doing so.[7]

In April 2001, the Bush administration released a new energy plan and called for construction of 1,300 new power plants by 2020. Bill Prindle of the Washington-based Alliance to Save Energy responded by pointing out how the country could eliminate the need for those plants and save money in the process. He ticked off several steps that would reduce the demand for electricity: Improving efficiency standards for household appliances would eliminate the need for 127 power plants. More stringent residential air conditioner efficiency standards would eliminate 43 power plants. Raising commercial air conditioner standards would eliminate the need for 50 plants.

Using tax credits and energy codes to improve the efficiency of new buildings would save another 170 plants. Similar steps to raise the energy efficiency of existing buildings would save 210 plants. These five measures alone from the list suggested by Prindle would not only eliminate the need for 600 power plants, they would save money too.[8]

Of course, each country will have to fashion its own plan for raising energy productivity. Nevertheless, there are a number of common components. Some are quite simple but highly effective, such as banning the use of nonrefillable beverage containers, eliminating the use of incandescent light bulbs, doubling the fuel efficiency of automobiles, and redesigning urban transport systems to raise efficiency and increase mobility.

We know that it is possible to ban the use of nonrefillable beverage containers because Canada's Prince Edward Island has already done so. And Finland has a stiff tax on nonrefillables that has lead to 98-percent container reuse for soft drinks. These actions reduce energy use, water use, and garbage generation. A refillable glass bottle used over and over again requires about 10 percent as much energy per use as an aluminum can, even if the can is recycled. Cleaning, sterilizing, and relabeling a used bottle requires little energy, but recycling aluminum, which has a melting point of 660 degrees Celsius (1220 degrees Fahrenheit), is an energy-intensive process. Banning nonrefillables is a win-win policy initiative because it cuts both energy use and the flow of garbage.[9]

Another simple step is to replace all incandescent light bulbs with compact fluorescent bulbs (CFLs), which use only one third as much electricity and last 10 times as long. In the United States, where 20 percent of all electricity is used for lighting, if each household replaced commonly used incandescents with compact fluorescents, electricity for lighting would be cut in half. The combination of lasting longer and using less electricity greatly outweighs the higher costs of the CFLs, yielding a risk-free return of some 25–40 percent a year. Worldwide, replacing incandescent light bulbs with CFLs would save enough electricity to close hundreds of coal-fired power plants, and it could be accomplished easily within three years if we decided to do it.[10]

A third obvious area for raising energy efficiency is automobiles. In the United States, for example, if all motorists were to shift from their current vehicles with internal combustion engines to cars with hybrid engines, like the Toyota Prius or the Honda Insight, gasoline use could be cut in half. Sales of hybrid cars, introduced into the U.S. market in 1999, reached an estimated 46,000 in 2003. (See Table 9–1.) Higher gasoline prices and a tax deduction of up to $2,000 for purchasing a low-emission vehicle are boosting sales. With U.S. auto manufacturers coming onto the market on a major scale soon, hybrid vehicle sales are projected to reach 1 million in 2007.[11]

A somewhat more complex way to raise energy pro-

Table 9–1. *Sales of Hybrid Cars in the United States, 1999–2003*

Year	Sales
	(number)
1999	17
2000	9,350
2001	20,282
2002	35,835
2003 (est.)	46,000

Source: See endnote 11.

ductivity is to redesign urban transport systems. Most systems, now automobile-centered, are highly inefficient, with the majority of cars carrying only the driver. Replacing this with a more diverse system that would include a well-developed light-rail system complemented with buses as needed and that was bicycle- and pedestrian-friendly could increase mobility, reduce air pollution, and provide exercise. This is a win-win-win situation. Mobility would be greater, the air would be cleaner, and it would be easier to exercise. Fewer automobiles would mean that parking lots could be converted into parks, creating more civilized cities.

In order to begin shifting the mix away from automobiles, some cities now charge cars entering the city. Pioneered by Singapore many years ago, this approach is now being used in Oslo and Melbourne. And in February 2003, London introduced a similar system to combat congestion as well as pollution, charging $8 for any vehicle entering the central city during the working day. This immediately reduced traffic congestion by 24 percent.[12]

Harnessing the Wind

Shifting to renewable sources of energy, such as wind power, opens up vast new opportunities for lowering fossil fuel dependence. Wind offers a powerful alternative to fossil fuels—a way of dramatically cutting carbon emissions. Wind energy is abundant, inexhaustible, cheap, widely distributed, climate-benign, and clean—which is why it has been the world's fastest-growing energy source over the last decade.

The modern wind industry was born in California in the early 1980s as a result of a federal tax credit for renewable energy, combined with a generous state tax credit. For most of the industry's first 15 years, growth was relatively slow, but in recent years, generating capacity has exploded. In 1995, world wind-generating capacity was 4,800 megawatts. By the end of 2002, it had increased sixfold to 31,100 megawatts. (See Figure 9–1.) World wind generating capacity today is sufficient to meet the residential needs of Norway, Sweden, Finland, Denmark, and Belgium combined.[13]

Germany, with over 12,000 megawatts of wind power at the end of 2002, leads the world in generating capacity. Spain and the United States, at 4,800 and 4,700 megawatts, are second and third. Tiny Denmark is fourth with 2,900 megawatts, and India is fifth with 1,700 megawatts. Today Denmark gets 18 percent of its electricity from wind. In Schleswig-Holstein, the northernmost state in Germany, the figure is 28 percent. And in Spain's northern industrial province of Navarra, it is 22 percent. Although a score of countries now generate elec-

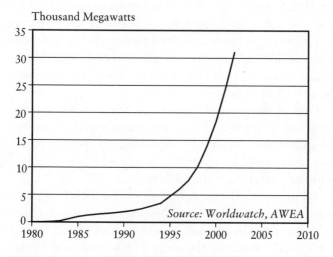

Figure 9–1. *World Wind Energy Generating Capacity, 1980–2002*

tricity from wind, a second wave of major players is coming onto the field, including the United Kingdom, France, Italy, Brazil, and China.[14]

Wind energy is both abundant and widely distributed. In densely populated Europe, there is enough easily accessible offshore wind energy to meet all of the region's electricity needs. China can easily double its current electricity generation from wind alone. In the United States, a national wind resource inventory published in 1991 indicated that there is enough harnessable wind energy in just three of the 50 states—North Dakota, Kansas, and Texas—to satisfy national electricity needs. But this now greatly understates U.S. potential. Recent advances in wind turbine design and size, enabling the turbines to operate at lower wind speeds and to harness the wind's energy more efficiently and at greater heights, have dramatically expanded the harnessable wind resource.[15]

Wind is also clean. Wind energy does not produce sulfur dioxide emissions or nitrous oxides to cause acid rain. Nor are there any emissions of health-threatening mercury that come from coal-fired power plants. No mountains are leveled, no streams are polluted, and there are no deaths from black lung disease. Wind does not disrupt the earth's climate.

One of the great attractions of wind is that it is inexhaustible. Once wind farms are developed, they can operate indefinitely simply by replacing equipment parts as they wear out. In contrast to oil, which is eventually depleted, wind is inexhaustible.

Wind is also cheap. Advances in wind turbine design, drawing heavily on the technologies of the aerospace industry, have dropped the cost of wind power from 38¢ per kilowatt-hour in the early 1980s to less than 4¢ at prime wind sites in 2001. Some recent long-term wind supply contracts were signed at 3¢ per kilowatt-hour. The cost of wind-generated electricity is well below that of nuclear power. On prime wind sites, it can now undercut coal and compete with gas, currently the cheapest source of electricity generation.[16]

Even more exciting, with each doubling of world generating capacity, costs fall by 15 percent. With recent growth rates of 31 percent a year, costs are dropping by 15 percent every 30 months or so. While natural gas prices are highly volatile, the costs of wind are declining. And there is no OPEC for wind.[17]

Cheap electricity from wind brings the option of electrolyzing water to produce hydrogen, which offers a way of both storing wind energy and transporting it via pipelines. It can be stored and used in lieu of natural gas in power plants to provide electricity when the wind ebbs.

Hydrogen is also the fuel of choice for the new fuel cell engines that every major automobile manufacturer is now working on. Honda and Toyota both made it to the market with their first fuel cell–powered automobiles at the end of 2002. DaimlerChrysler plans to be in the market in 2003 and Ford in 2004. In a country like the United States, the advances in wind turbine design and the evolution of fuel cells hold out the hope that farmers and ranchers, who own most of the country's wind rights, could one day be supplying not only the country's electricity, but much of the fuel for its cars as well.[18]

Countries that are rich in wind could end up exporting hydrogen in liquefied form in the same way that natural gas is liquefied and exported today. Among the countries that are both richly endowed in wind and rather sparsely populated are Canada, Argentina (with world-class winds in Patagonia), and Russia. Eastern Siberia could supply vast amounts of hydrogen to densely populated, heavily industrialized China, South Korea, and Japan.

Given the enormous wind-generation potential and

the associated benefits of climate stabilization, it is time to consider an all-out effort to develop wind resources. Instead of doubling every 30 months or so, perhaps we should be doubling wind electric generation each year for the next several years, much as the number of computers linked to the Internet doubled each year from 1985 to 1995. If this were to happen, then costs would drop precipitously, giving wind-generated electricity an even greater advantage over power from fossil fuels.[19]

Energy consultant Harry Braun made an interesting proposal at a Hydrogen Roundtable in April 2003 for quickly shifting to a wind/hydrogen economy. From a manufacturing point of view, he noted, wind turbines are similar to automobiles: each has a brake, a gearbox, an electrical generator, and an electronic control system. Braun noted that if wind turbines are mass-produced like automobiles, the capital costs of wind-generated electricity would drop from $1,000 a megawatt to roughly $300, reducing the cost of electricity to 1¢ or 2¢ per kilowatt-hour.[20]

Rather than wait for fuel cell engines, Braun suggests using hydrogen in internal combustion engines of the sort developed by BMW. He notes that converting a gasoline engine to hydrogen is relatively simple and inexpensive. This would also facilitate the early development of hydrogen stations in wind-rich areas while waiting for the mass production of fuel cell cars. Braun calculates that the electrolysis of water to produce hydrogen and its liquefaction, along with the high efficiency of a hydrogen-fueled internal combustion engine, would bring the cost of hydrogen down to $1.40 per equivalent gallon of gasoline. Assembly-line production of wind turbines at "wartime" speed would quickly end urban air pollution, oil spills, and the need for oil wars.[21]

The incentives for such a growth could come in part

from simply restructuring global energy subsidies—shifting the $210 billion in annual fossil fuel subsidies to the development of wind energy, hydrogen generators, and the provision of kits to convert engines from gasoline to hydrogen. The investment capital could come from private capital markets but also from companies already in the energy business. Shell, for example, has become a major player in the world wind energy economy. BP has also begun to invest in wind power. Other major corporations now in the wind power business include General Electric and ABB. BP's planned investment of $15 billion in developing oil resources in the Gulf of Mexico could also be used to develop 15,000 megawatts of wind-generating capacity, enough to satisfy the residential needs of 15 million people in industrial countries.[22]

These goals may seem farfetched, but here and there around the world ambitious efforts are beginning to take shape. As noted earlier, Germany announced at international climate discussions in India in October 2002 that it wants to cut its greenhouse gas emissions 40 percent by 2020. It is proposing a 30-percent cut throughout Europe by that date. Developing the continent's offshore and onshore wind energy resources will be at the heart of this carbon reduction effort.[23]

In the United States, a 3,000-megawatt wind farm is in the early planning stages. Located in South Dakota near the Iowa border, it is being initiated by Dehlsen Associates, led by James Dehlsen, a wind energy pioneer in California. Designed to feed power into the industrial Midwest around Chicago, this project is not only large by wind power standards, it is one of the largest energy projects of any kind in the world today.[24]

Cape Wind is planning a 420-megawatt wind farm off the coast of Cape Cod, Massachusetts. And a newly formed energy company, called Winergy, has plans for some 9,000 megawatts in a network of wind farms stretching along the Atlantic coast. These are but a few of the more ambitious wind energy projects that are now beginning to emerge in the United States, a country rich in wind energy.[25]

The question is not whether wind is a potentially powerful technology that can be used to stabilize climate. It is. But will we develop it fast enough to head off economically disruptive climate change?

Converting Sunlight into Electricity

When a team of three scientists at Bell Labs discovered in 1952 that sunlight striking a silicon surface could generate electricity, they gave the world access to a vast new source of energy. No country uses as much energy as is contained in the sunlight that strikes its buildings each day, writes Denis Hayes, former Director of the U.S. government's Solar Energy Research Institute.[26]

Solar cells were initially used to provide electricity in remote sites in industrial countries, such as in national forests or parks, offshore lighthouses, and summer homes in remote locations. In recent years, a vast new market has opened up in developing-country villages that are not yet linked to an electrical grid. In many such situations, the cost of building a centralized power plant and a grid to deliver relatively small amounts of electricity is prohibitive, which helps explain why 1.7 billion people in developing countries still do not have electricity. As the cost of solar cells has declined, however, it is now often cheaper to provide electricity from solar cell installations than from a centralized source.[27]

In Andean villages, solar installations are replacing candles as a source of lighting. For villagers who are paying for the installation over 30 months, the monthly payment is roughly the same as the cost of a month's supply of candles. Once the solar cells are paid for, the villagers then have an essentially free source of power—one that can supply electricity for decades. In villages in India, where light now comes from kerosene lamps, kerosene may cost more than solar cells.[28]

At the end of 2002, more than 1 million homes in villages in the developing world were getting their electricity from solar cells. If families average six members, then 6 million people are getting their residential electricity from solar cells. But this is less than 1 percent of the 1.7 billion who do not yet have electricity. The principal obstacle to the spread of solar cell installations is not the cost per se, but the lack of small-scale credit programs to finance them. As this credit shortfall is overcome, village purchases of solar cells could climb far above the rate of recent years.[29]

The residential use of solar cells is also expanding in some industrial countries. In Japan, where companies have commercialized a solar roofing material, some 70,000 homes now have solar installations. Consumers in Germany receive low-interest loans and a favorable guaranteed price when feeding excess electricity into the grid. In industrial countries, most installations are designed to reduce the consumer's dependence on grid-supplied electricity, much of it from coal-fired power plants.[30]

The governments with the strongest incentives for the use of solar cells are also those with the largest solar cell manufacturing industries. In Japan, for example, residential installations totaled roughly 100 megawatts in 2001. The comparable figure for Germany was 75 megawatts. The United States, a far larger country, was third—with 32 megawatts of installations. India was fourth with 18 megawatts. Japan leads the world in solar cell manufacturing, with some 43 percent of the market. The European Union, led by Germany's vigorous program, has

moved into second place with 25 percent of output. The
United States, with 24 percent, is now third.[31]

The cost of solar cells has been dropping for several
decades, but the falling cost curve lags wind by several
years, making solar-generated electricity much more costly than power from wind or coal-fired power plants. Industry experts estimate that with each doubling of cumulative
production, the price drops roughly 20 percent.[32]

Over the last seven years, solar cell sales have expanded an average of 31 percent annually, doubling every 2.6
years. (See Table 9–2.) Since there is little doubt that solar
cells will one day be an inexpensive source of electricity
as the scale of manufacturing expands, the challenge for
governments is to leapfrog into the future by accelerating
growth of the industry. Only very modest government
incentives are needed to do that. If we can quickly reduce
the cost of solar cells, they will join wind as a major player in the world energy economy.[33]

Table 9–2. *Trends in Energy Use by Source, 1995–2002*

Energy Source	Annual Rate of Growth (percent)
Solar Photovoltaics	30.9
Wind Power	30.7
Geothermal Power[1]	3.1
Natural Gas	2.1
Oil	1.5
Hydroelectric[2]	0.7
Nuclear Power	0.7
Coal	0.3

[1]Data available through 2000.   [2]Data available through 2001.
Sources: See endnote 33.

Energy from the Earth

When we think of renewable energy, we typically think of sources derived from the sun, either directly or indirectly, such as solar heating, solar electricity, wind power, and hydropower, or sources of biological origin, such as wood and crop residues. But the earth itself is a source of heat energy (mostly from radioactivity within the earth), which gradually escapes either through conduction or through hot springs and geysers that bring internal heat to the earth's surface. The use of geothermal energy is sustainable as long as its use does not exceed the rate of generation. It is also inexhaustible and will last as long as the earth itself.

Geothermal energy is used both to generate electricity and as a source of heat for direct use, such as with space heating for greenhouses, aquaculture, and industrial processes, and with heat pumps. After Italy pioneered the use of geothermal energy to generate electricity in 1904, the practice spread to some 22 countries. The global capacity of 8,000 megawatts in 2000 represents a 37-percent growth over the 5,800 megawatts available in 1990.[34]

Two countries—the United States with 2,200 megawatts and the Philippines with 1,900 megawatts—account for half of world generating capacity. (In the Philippines, geothermal provides 27 percent of the country's electricity supply.) Most of the remainder is concentrated in five countries: Italy, Mexico, Indonesia, Japan, and New Zealand.[35]

The direct use of geothermal heat for various purposes is even larger, equivalent to 12,000 megawatts of electricity generation. Some 30 countries account for most of the world's direct use of geothermal energy. Its use in heat pumps, which extract and concentrate heat from warm water for various uses, is the largest single use.[36]

Iceland and France dominate the use of geothermal

energy for space heating. In Iceland, 85 percent of the country's 290,000 people use geothermal energy to heat their homes, saving $100 million per year from avoiding oil imports. Geothermal energy accounts for more than one third of Iceland's energy use. During the decade following the two oil price hikes in the 1970s, some 70 geothermal heating facilities were constructed in France, providing both heat and hot water for some 200,000 housing units. In the United States, individual homes are supplied directly with geothermal heat in Reno, Nevada, and in Klamath Falls, Oregon. Other countries that have extensive geothermally based district-heating systems include China, Japan, and Turkey.[37]

Geothermal energy is an ideal source of heat for greenhouses, particularly in northern climes. Russia, Hungary, Iceland, and the United States all use geothermally heated greenhouses to produce fresh vegetables in winter.[38]

Some 16 countries use geothermal energy for aquaculture. Among these are China, Israel, and the United States. In California, for example, 15 fish farms produce tilapia, striped bass, and catfish with warm water from underground. This enables farmers to produce larger fish in a shorter period of time and to produce without interruption during the winter. Collectively these California farms produce 4.5 million kilograms of fish per year.[39]

The number of countries turning to geothermal energy both for electricity and for direct use is increasing rapidly. So, too, is the range of uses. Once the value of geothermal energy is discovered, its use is often quickly diversified. Romania, for example, uses its geothermal energy for district heating, for greenhouses, to produce hot water for dwellings, and to supply industrial hot water for factories. With heat pumps, it is now possible to treat the earth as both a heat source and a sink to provide heating in winter and cooling in summer.[40]

Geothermal energy is widely used for bathing and swimming. Japan, for example, has 2,800 spas, 5,500 public bathhouses, and 15,600 hotels and inns that use hot geothermal water. Iceland has some 100 public swimming pools heated with geothermal energy. Most are open-air pools used the year-round. Hungary heats 1,200 swimming pools with geothermal energy.[41]

The potential of geothermal energy is extraordinary. Japan alone has an estimated geothermal electric-generating capacity of 69,000 megawatts, enough to satisfy one third of its electricity needs. Other countries bordering the Pacific with a vast potential—in the so-called Ring of Fire—include Chile, Peru, Ecuador, Colombia, all of Central America, Mexico, the United States, and Canada in the East Pacific and Russia, China, South Korea, the Philippines, Indonesia, Australia, and New Zealand in the West Pacific. Other geothermally rich countries include those along the Great Rift of Africa and the Eastern Mediterranean. Fortunately, many countries now have enough experience and engineering capacity to tap this vast resource.[42]

Building the Hydrogen Economy

The evolution of the fuel cell—a device that is powered by hydrogen and uses an electro-chemical process to convert hydrogen into electricity, water vapor, and heat—is setting the stage for the evolution of a hydrogen-based economy. The fuel cell is twice as efficient as the internal combustion engine and it is clean, emitting only water vapor.[43]

The great attraction of the fuel cell is that it facilitates the shift to a single fuel, hydrogen, that neither pollutes the air nor disrupts the earth's climate. Stationary fuel cells can be installed in the basements of buildings, for example, to generate electricity and heat that can be used both for heating and cooling. Mobile fuel cells can be used to power cars and portable electronic devices, such as cell phones and laptop computers.

Hydrogen can come from many sources, including the electrolysis of water or the reformulation of natural gas or gasoline, a process that extracts the hydrogen from these hydrocarbons. If the hydrogen comes from water, then electricity from any source can be used to electrolyze the water. If the electricity comes from a wind farm, hydropower station, geothermal power station, or solar cells, the hydrogen will be clean—produced without carbon emissions or air pollutants.

One country, Iceland, already has a plan to convert from fossil fuels to hydrogen. The government, working with a consortium of companies led by Shell and DaimlerChrysler, is taking the first step in 2003 as DaimlerChrysler begins converting Reykjavik's fleet of 80 buses from internal combustion to fuel cell engines. Shell has built a hydrogen station to service the buses, using cheap hydroelectricity to electrolyze water and produce hydrogen. This is clean hydrogen. In the next stage, Iceland's automobiles will be converted to fuel cell engines. And in the final stage, the Icelandic fishing fleet—the centerpiece of its economy—will also convert to fuel cells. Already heating most of its homes and buildings with geothermal energy and getting most of its electricity from hydropower and geothermal power, Iceland plans to be the first modern economy to declare its independence from fossil fuels.[44]

On the other side of the world, in Japan, retired corporate executive Masatsugu Tanaguichi is also planning to create a hydrogen economy. He is working on 875-square-kilometer Yakushima Island off the southern tip of Japan whose principal defining characteristic is 8 meters of rainfall a year. Much of the island is part of a huge nature preserve. Tanaguichi plans to build a series of small dams on the island to convert its abundant hydropower into electricity to power hydrogen generators, electrolyzing water to produce hydrogen. The first goal will be to meet the needs of the 14,000 residents of the island. Once that is done, he plans to ship the excess hydrogen to mainland Japan, transporting it in liquefied form aboard tankers, much as natural gas is transported. He believes the island can export enough hydrogen to run 500,000 automobiles.[45]

Elsewhere, some 30 hydrogen stations have opened. In the Munich airport, for example, a hydrogen station fuels 15 airport buses that have hydrogen-burning internal combustion engines. California now has at least two hydrogen stations—one, built by Honda, uses solar cell electricity to electrolyze water. This station was built to service the five fuel cell cars Honda has sold to the city of Los Angeles. The other hydrogen station in California uses wind-generated electricity to produce the hydrogen. Both are clean-hydrogen stations.[46]

One of the challenges for fuel cell vehicles is how to store the hydrogen. It can be stored in compressed form, liquefied form, or chemically with metal hydrides. It is also possible to store natural gas or gasoline on board and then use reformers to extract the hydrogen. The pros and cons of these various approaches are numerous. In the end, the central question is whether the hydrogen that is used in fuel cell vehicles is clean hydrogen made using renewable energy to electrolyze water or climate-disrupting hydrogen made using fossil fuels.[47]

Fuel cells are initially being used more widely in buildings simply because hydrogen storage is much simpler with stationary fuel cells than with those used in vehicles. Fuel cells will probably proliferate rapidly in larger structures, such as office and apartment buildings, and then, as the technology matures, be installed in private homes. These fuel cells will provide buildings with electricity, heating, and cooling.

Natural gas will likely be the main source of hydrogen in the near term, but, given its abundance, wind is likely to become the principal source in the new energy economy, as mentioned earlier. The hydrogen storage and distribution system, most likely an adaptation of existing natural gas systems, provides a way of both storing wind energy and transporting it efficiently. It is a natural marriage.

One of the big questions today is which of the companies involved in today's multidimensional energy economy will be the principal players in the hydrogen economy? Will it be the oil companies, the natural gas companies, and gas utilities? Will wind companies invest in hydrogen generators and become major hydrogen suppliers? Will companies that control today's natural gas pipelines be the dominant players, delivering hydrogen both to individual buildings and to fueling stations for vehicles?

These are but a few of the questions emerging as the world faces the need to move quickly into the new economy, one in which wind farms replace coal mines and where hydrogen generators replace oil refineries. In making technological choices, there will be winners and there will be losers. A century ago, some automobile companies opted for steam engines and others opted for the newer, less well understood internal combustion engine. Today steam-powered vehicles are found only in museums.

The stakes in this competition are high. The aircraft industry faced a similar situation in the late 1960s as the world appeared to be moving toward supersonic air transport (SST). There were three entries in the race: Russian, Anglo-French, and American. The United States withdrew under pressure from the environmental community, which cited an economic analysis by the Environmental Defense Fund that concluded the technology was too fuel-inefficient to be economically viable. The Russians dropped out of the competition, leaving Europe alone to build the first SST, the Concorde. In the United States, Boeing decided to go with size rather than speed and built the 747. Today, 35 years later, not a single Concorde has been sold commercially. Only the national airlines of the two countries that developed the SST—Air France and British Airways—have bought them. And in April 2003, these companies announced they would ground the Concorde by the end of October 2003. Boeing, meanwhile, has sold more than 1,300 of its 747s.[48]

Today's corporations also will be choosing among various energy sources and technologies as they move into this new energy era. Some companies will underestimate the political pressures to phase out fossil fuels that will likely develop as the costs of climate change become more apparent. Some will choose wisely; others will not. Some will prosper; others will disappear.

Cutting Carbon Emissions

The accelerating rise in the earth's temperature calls for simultaneously raising efficiency and shifting to renewables in order to cut carbon emissions in half, recognizing that the initial large gains are likely to come in efficiency improvements. An important government measure is to mandate efficiency standards for household appliances, automobiles, and the construction of new buildings—taking advantage of recent technological advances.

Moving away from auto-centered urban transport to a system that would prominently feature public transport in a bicycle- and pedestrian-friendly environment would cut fuel use in cities. It would also reduce air pollution and increase the opportunities for exercise—something much needed in a world where 3 million people die each

year from urban air pollution and where half or more of
the adults in exercise-deprived, affluent societies are overweight.[49]

At the corporate level, firms are now looking at the
expense of traffic congestion when deciding where to
locate offices and plants. Similarly, young people deciding
where to settle down are looking for communities that
have bicycle-friendly transportation systems with jogging
and hiking trails.

In looking at new energy sources, wind seems certain
to be the centerpiece in the new energy economy for the
reasons outlined earlier. Its wide distribution offers an
alternative to the current heavy global dependence on
one region for oil. The wind energy industry has now
evolved to the point where it has the requisite technological capacity to expand wind electric generation dramatically over the next decade, making it the world's leading
electricity source.

In considering this prospect, it is instructive to look at
the recent adoption of other popular new technologies,
such as cellular phones. In 1990, there were 11 million cell
phones in use in the world, compared with 519 million
fixed-line phones. Just six years later—in 1996—sales of
cell phones reached 53 million, eclipsing the sales of 51 million fixed-line phones. Within another six years—by 2002—
the cell phones in use had reached 1.2 billion, outnumbering
the 1.1 billion fixed-line phones. In 12 years cell phones
went from being a novelty to dominating the market.[50]

Although the capital requirements for cell phones are
small compared with those for electrical generating
capacity, their sales growth nonetheless illustrates how
market forces can drive the adoption of an appealing new
technology. The cell phone market grew by 50 percent a
year during the 1990s; wind power has been growing at
31 percent a year since 1995.[51]

If we decided for climate stabilization reasons that we wanted to double wind electric generation each year, it would not be long before wind would be the dominant source of electricity. The United States, for example, now has nearly 5,000 megawatts of wind-generating capacity. Doubling that each year would take it to 640,000 megawatts in seven years, making it the leading source of electricity. Again, this is not beyond the capacity of the industry. In 2001, the strongest year to date in the United States, wind electric-generating capacity grew by 67 percent. The total investment to reach this level of generation, using the rule of thumb of $1 million per megawatt (which is now on the high side), would be $640 billion over a seven-year span, or roughly $90 billion a year. For perspective, Americans currently spend $190 billion each year on gasoline.[52]

There are many policy instruments for accelerating the shift from a carbon- to a hydrogen-based energy economy, including the shift of subsidies from fossil fuels to wind, solar, and geothermal energy sources. Some of these subsidies might also be used for investments in efficiency. For example, each car with a gasoline/battery hybrid engine purchased in the United States currently is eligible for a federal tax deduction of up to $2,000. This helps to make these cars more competitive price-wise, since they are still being manufactured on a relatively small scale. Thus far, the only companies that are marketing hybrid cars are Toyota and Honda, both Japanese. U.S. automakers are scrambling to get on the bandwagon so as not to miss out on this fast-growing market.[53]

While subsidies are being shifted from fossil fuels to renewables and the hydrogen economy infrastructure, it would make eminent sense to reduce income taxes and raise those on climate-disrupting energy sources at the same time. This tax shifting, already under way in several countries in Europe, helps consumers of energy—both individuals and corporations—to understand the full costs of burning fossil fuels. (See also Chapter 11.)

Although shifting subsidies and taxes are at the heart of the energy transformation that is needed, other policy tools can either increase efficiency or accelerate the shift to renewables and the hydrogen-based economy. These include formal as well as informal procurement policies. National and local governments, corporations, universities, and individual homeowners can buy green power. In the United States, even if green power is not offered locally, there is a national Green Power Partnership electricity market operated by the U.S. Environmental Protection Agency (EPA) that enables anyone to buy green power. As more users sign up, the incentive to produce green power at premium rates increases.[54]

The Earth Policy Institute, for example, purchased Green Tags for new wind-generated electricity from wind farms in Washington and Oregon. This electricity will not be delivered to our office in Washington, D.C., but that is not necessary, since each Green Tag matches a seller and a buyer, all cleared through EPA's national computer databank. For every buyer there must be a seller. Green power marketing makes it easy for anyone to contribute to the energy transformation. Some churches are now buying green power, for example, and urging their members to do the same.[55]

One approach adopted by several countries and by 36 states in the United States is known as two-way or net metering. Whenever consumer-owned solar cells or wind turbines produce more electricity than is needed, a two-way electric meter enables individual homeowners to sell electricity back to the utility. Net metering has the added advantage of putting back into the system clean energy produced from the sun, which can displace electricity generated from more traditional sources. It also promotes energy efficiency, as users are in effect paid for electricity that they generate but do not use.[56]

As wind electric generation expands, the first step would be to back out coal-fired power plants, either closing them or using them as a backup for wind. Coal-fired plants are the most climate-disruptive energy source simply because coal is almost pure carbon. Coal burning is also the principal source of the mercury deposits that contaminate freshwater lakes and streams. The prevalence of mercury-contaminated fish has led 44 state governments in the United States to issue warnings to consumers to limit or avoid eating fish because of the effect of mercury on the central nervous system. The Centers for Disease Control and Prevention issued a warning in 2001 indicating that an estimated 375,000 babies born each year in the United States are at risk of impaired mental development and learning disabilities because of exposure to mercury.[57]

While it is fashionable for some industries and industry groups to complain that reducing carbon emissions, even by the very modest 5 percent required by the Kyoto Protocol, would be costly and a burden on the economy, the reality is that reducing carbon emissions is one of the most profitable investments that many companies can make. Study after study has concluded that it is possible to reduce carbon emissions while making money in the process.

The experience of individual companies confirms this. Dupont, one of the world's largest chemical manufacturers, has already cut its greenhouse gas emissions from their 1990 level by 65 percent. In an annual report, CEO Chad Holliday, Jr., proudly reports savings of $1.5 billion in energy efficiency gains from 1990 to 2002.[58]

10

Responding to the Social Challenge

Early in this new century, the world is facing many long-standing social challenges, including hunger, illiteracy, and disease. If developing countries add nearly 3 billion people by mid-century, as projected, population growth will continue to undermine efforts to improve the human condition. National food bubbles based on overplowing and overpumping will move toward the bursting point. The gap between the billion richest and the billion poorest will continue to widen, putting even more stress on the international political fabric.[1]

As a species, our failure to control our numbers is taking a frightening toll. Slowing population growth is the key to eradicating poverty and its distressing symptoms, and, conversely, eradicating poverty is the key to slowing population growth. With time running out, the urgency of moving simultaneously on both fronts seems clear.

The challenge is to create quickly the social conditions that will accelerate the shift to smaller families. Among these conditions are universal education, good nutrition, and prevention of infectious diseases. We now have the knowledge and the resources to reach these goals. In an increasingly integrated world, we also have a vested interest in doing so.

Stabilizing Population

Some 36 countries now have populations that are either stable or declining slowly. All are in Europe, except Japan. In countries with the lowest fertility rates, including Japan, Russia, Germany, and Italy, populations will actually decline over the next half-century. But other countries are projected to more than double their populations by then, including Pakistan, Nigeria, and Ethiopia. India, growing at nearly 2 percent a year, is projected to reach 1.5 billion people by 2050, adding 515 million in just 50 years—roughly twice as many people as currently live in the United States. Well before then it will become the world's most populous country.[2]

A larger group of countries has reduced fertility to the replacement level or just below. They are headed for population stability after large groups of young people move through their reproductive years. Included in this group are China, the world's most populous country, and the United States, the third most populous one.

U.N. projections show world population growth under three different assumptions about fertility levels. The medium projection, the one most commonly used, has world population reaching 8.9 billion by 2050. The high projection has population going to 10.6 billion. The low projection, which has population peaking at 7.5 billion in 2039 and then declining, assumes that the world will quickly move below replacement-level fertility to 1.7 children per couple. If the goal is to eradicate hunger and illiteracy, we have little choice but to strive for the lower projection.[3]

Slowing world population growth means that all women who want to plan their families should have access to the family planning services needed to do so. Unfortunately, at present more than 100 million couples cannot obtain the services they need to limit the size of their families. Since most of them are in countries where water scarcity is already a major issue, filling the family planning gap may be the most urgent item on the global agenda. The benefits are enormous and the costs are minimal.[4]

The good news is that countries that want to reduce the size of families quickly and stabilize their population can do so. For example, my colleague Janet Larsen describes how, in just one decade, Iran dropped its population growth rate from one of the world's fastest to one similar to that in the United States. When Ayatollah Khomeini assumed leadership in Iran in 1979, he immediately dismantled the family planning programs that the Shah had put in place in 1967 and advocated large families. At war with Iraq between 1980 and 1988, Khomeini wanted large families to increase soldiers for Islam. His goal was an army of 20 million. In response to his pleas, fertility levels climbed, pushing Iran's population growth up to 4.4 percent per year, a level approaching the biological maximum. As this enormous growth began to burden the economy and overburden the environment, Iran's leaders began to see that overcrowding, environmental degradation, and unemployment were becoming serious problems.[5]

In 1989 the government did an about-face and Iran restored its family planning program. In May 1993, a national family planning law was passed. The resources of several government ministries, including education, culture, and health, were mobilized to encourage smaller families. Iran Broadcasting was given the responsibility for raising awareness of population issues and of the availability of family planning services. Some 15,000 "health houses" were established to provide rural populations with health services and family planning.[6]

Religious leaders were directly involved in what

amounted to a crusade for smaller families. Iran introduced a full panoply of contraceptive measures, including male sterilization—a first among Muslim countries. All forms of birth control, including contraceptives such as the pill and sterilization, were free of charge. In fact, Iran became a pioneer—the only country to require couples to take a class on modern contraception before receiving a marriage license.[7]

In addition to the direct health care interventions, a broad-based effort was made to increase female literacy, boosting it from 25 percent in 1970 to more than 70 percent in 2000. Female school enrollment increased from 60 to 90 percent. Television was used to disseminate information on family planning throughout the country, taking advantage of the 70 percent of rural households that had television. As a result of the impressive effort launched in 1989, the average family size in Iran has dropped from seven children to less than three. During the seven years from 1987 to 1994, Iran cut its population growth rate by half, setting an example for other countries whose populations are still growing rapidly. The overall population growth rate of 1.2 percent in 2001 is only slightly higher than that of the United States.[8]

If a country like Iran, with a strong tradition of Islamic fundamentalism, can move quickly toward population stability, other countries should be able to do the same. Countries everywhere have little choice but to strive for an average of two children per couple. There is no feasible alternative. Any population that increases or decreases continually over the long term is not sustainable. The time has come for world leaders—including the Secretary-General of the United Nations, the President of the World Bank, and the President of the United States—to publicly recognize that the earth cannot easily support more than two children per family.

The costs of providing reproductive health and family planning services are not that high. At the International Conference on Population and Development held in 1994 in Cairo, it was estimated that a fully funded population and reproductive health program for the next 20 years would cost roughly $17 billion annually by 2000 and $22 billion by 2015. Developing countries agreed to cover two thirds of this, while industrial countries were to cover one third. Unfortunately, developing countries have fallen short of their pledge by roughly one third, while donor countries have fallen short by two thirds, leaving a combined gap of roughly $10 billion per year.[9]

The United Nations calculated that these shortfalls were leading to a cumulative 122 million unintended pregnancies by 2000. Of these, an estimated one third ended in abortion. The remaining two thirds led to 65,000 deaths during childbirth and 844,000 women who suffered chronic or permanent injury from their pregnancies. The social costs of not filling the family planning gap are high.[10]

Reinforcing these U.N. calculations are data from the grassroots showing how access to family planning services helps couples achieve their desired family size. Surveys in Honduras show poor women having twice as many children as they want, while women in high socioeconomic groups are highly successful at having the number of children they desire. (See Table 10–1.)[11]

The benefits of restricting family size have been calculated for Bangladesh, where analysts concluded that the $62 spent by the government to prevent an unwanted birth saved $615 on other social services. Investing in reproductive health and family planning leaves more fiscal resources for education and health care. These numbers suggest that, for donor countries, providing the additional $10 billion or so needed to ensure that all cou-

Table 10–1. *Honduras: Ideal and Actual Number of Children Born per Woman, According to Socioeconomic Level*

Socio-economic Level	Children Born Per Woman	Desired Family Size	Difference
		(number of children)	
Low	6.9	3.4	3.5
Middle	4.1	2.9	1.2
High	2.7	2.7	0.0

Source: See endnote 11.

ples who wanted to limit family size have access to the services they need would yield high social returns in improved education and health care.[12]

Universal Basic Education

One way of narrowing the gap between rich and poor is universal education, but currently some 115 million children between the ages of 6 and 12 do not attend school. They are starting life with a severe handicap, one that virtually ensures that they will remain in abject poverty and that the gap between the poor and the rich will continue to widen.[13]

Recognizing this, the United Nations set universal primary education by 2015 as one of its Millennium Development Goals. Some 88 countries will fail to achieve this if they stay on the present course. The need for much greater effort is obvious. The World Bank has taken the lead with its Education for All plan. If fully implemented, all children in poor countries would get a primary school education by 2015. No child would be deprived of education because his or her parents cannot afford books and school fees.[14]

The benefits of education are many. The educational level of females is the principal determinant of the achievement level of their children. Children of educated mothers are better nourished not necessarily because the family income is higher but because the mother's better understanding of nutrition leads to a better choice of foods and healthier methods of preparation. It is the educational level of the mother that sets the tone for the family. Educating her is the key to breaking out of poverty.[15]

The education of girls leads to smaller families. In every society for which data are available, fertility falls as female educational levels rise. Simply stated, the more education women have, the fewer children they bear. And mothers with at least five years of school lose fewer infants during childbirth or due to early illnesses than their uneducated peers do. Among other things, these women can read the instructions on medications and they understand better how to take care of themselves during pregnancy. Economist Gene Sperling, the head of the Forum on Universal Education at the Brookings Institution, reports on a study of 72 countries that concluded that "the expansion of female secondary education may be the single best lever for achieving substantial reductions in fertility."[16]

Basic education increases agricultural productivity. Agricultural extension services that cannot use printed materials to disseminate information on improved agricultural practices are severely handicapped. So too are farmers who cannot read the instructions on a bag of fertilizer. The inability to read the instructions on a pesticide container can be life-threatening.

Under the World Bank's Education for All program, any country with a well-designed plan to achieve universal primary education should receive financial support. The three principal requirements are that a country submit a sensible plan to reach universal basic education, commit a meaningful share of its own resources to the plan, and have transparent budgeting and accounting practices. Monitoring 10 fast-track countries, singled out because they quickly submit solid plans for achieving the Education for All goals, could provide useful information on what works and what does not work in various social situations.[17]

At a time when HIV is spreading throughout the world, schools provide the institutional means to educate young people about the risks of infection. The time to inform and educate about the virus and about the lifestyles that foster its spread is when children are young, not when they are in their teens and often already infected. Young people can also be mobilized to conduct educational campaigns among their peers.

One great need in developing countries, particularly those where the ranks of teachers are being decimated by AIDS, is more teacher training. Providing scholarships for promising students from poor families to attend these training institutes in exchange for a commitment to teach for a fixed period of time, say five years, could be a highly profitable investment. It would help ensure that the human resources are available to reach the universal primary education goal, and it would also open the way for an upwelling of talent from the poorest segments of society.

Sperling believes that every plan should provide for getting to the hardest-to-reach segments of society, especially poor girls in rural areas. He notes that Ethiopia has pioneered this with Girls Advisory Committees. Representatives of these groups go to the parents who are seeking early marriage for their daughters and encourage them to keep their children in school. Some countries, Brazil and Bangladesh among them, actually provide small scholarships for girls, thus helping to ensure that girls from poor families get a basic education.[18]

As the world becomes ever more integrated economically, its 875 million illiterate adults are severely handicapped. This deficit can perhaps best be dealt with by launching adult literacy programs using volunteers. The international community could offer seed money to provide the educational materials and the external advisors. But the actual programs would be staffed largely by local volunteers. Bangladesh and Iran, both with successful adult literacy programs, can serve as models.[19]

The World Bank estimates that external funding of $2.5–5 billion a year would be needed if the 47 poorest countries are to achieve universal primary education by 2015. Doing this in the 88 countries that are unlikely to reach universal primary education by 2015 would cost perhaps three times as much. Even if it were to cost $15 billion per year, it would still be a bargain. At a time when personal computers give many schoolchildren access not only to books but also to the vast information resources of the Internet, having other children who never go to school is no longer acceptable.[20]

Curbing the HIV Epidemic

The key to curbing the AIDS epidemic is education about prevention. We know how the disease is transmitted. It is not a medical mystery. In Africa, where once there was a stigma associated even with mentioning the disease, countries are beginning to design effective prevention education programs. The first goal is to quickly reduce the number of new infections below the number of deaths, thus shrinking the number of those who are capable of infecting others.

Concentrating on the groups in a society who are most likely to spread the disease is particularly effective. In Africa, infected truck drivers who travel far from home for extended periods often engage in commercial sex, spreading it from one country to another. They are thus a target group in reducing infections. Sex workers are also centrally involved in the spread of the disease. In India, for example, the country's 2 million female sex workers have an average of two encounters per day, making them a key group to educate about HIV risks and the life-saving value of using a condom.[21]

Another target group is the military. After soldiers become infected, usually from engaging in commercial sex, they return to their home communities and spread the virus further. In Nigeria, where the adult HIV infection rate is 6 percent, President Olusegun Obasanjo requires free distribution of condoms to all military personnel. A third important group, intravenous drug users who share needles, figures prominently in the spread of the virus in the former Soviet Republics.[22]

The Global Fund to Fight AIDS, Tuberculosis and Malaria, established in 2001, needs $10.5 billion for the next five years. Thus far, it has received pledges of just over $3 billion. The stakes in this game are high. These diseases affect national security, social progress, and the global economy. If failed economies default on their debts, it will affect the entire world.[23]

At the most fundamental level, dealing with the HIV threat requires roughly 8 billion condoms a year in the developing world and Eastern Europe. Including those needed for contraception adds another 2 billion. But of the 10 billion condoms needed, only a billion are being distributed, leaving a shortfall of 9 billion. Costing only 3¢ each, or $270 million, the cost/benefit ratio of supplying these condoms must go off the top of the chart. The condom gap is huge, but the costs of filling it are small. In the excellent study entitled *Condoms Count: Meeting the Need in the Era of HIV/AIDS*, Population Action International notes that "the costs of getting condoms into the hands of users—which involves improving access, logistics and distribution capacity, raising awareness, and promoting use—is many times that of the supplies themselves." If we assumed that these costs are six times the price of the condoms themselves, filling this gap would still cost only $1.9 billion.[24]

Sadly, even though condoms are the only technology available to prevent the spread of HIV, the U.S. government is de-emphasizing their use, insisting that abstinence be given top priority. An effective campaign to stop AIDS cannot function without condoms.[25]

One of the few African countries to successfully lower the HIV infection rate after the epidemic became well established is Uganda. Under the strong personal leadership of President Yoweri Museveni, over the last dozen years the share of adults infected has dropped from a peak of 14 percent down to 5 percent. More recently, Zambia appears to be making progress in reducing infection rates among its young people as a result of a concerted national campaign led by church groups. Senegal occupies a position at the front of the pack because it acted early to check the spread of the virus, holding it to less than 1 percent today.[26]

The financial resources and medical personnel currently available to treat those who are already HIV-positive are minuscule compared with the number of people who need treatment. For example, of the 29 million people who were HIV-positive in sub-Saharan Africa at the end of 2002, only 30,000 were receiving the anti-retroviral drug treatment that is widely available in industrial countries. Africa today is a window on the future of other countries, such as India and China, if they do not respond quickly to contain the virus that is already well established within their borders.[27]

Health for All

While heart disease and cancer (largely the diseases of aging), obesity, and smoking dominate health concerns in industrial countries, in developing countries infectious diseases are the overriding health concern. Beyond AIDS, the principal infectious diseases are diarrhea, respiratory illnesses, tuberculosis, malaria, and childhood diseases such as measles.

Hunger amplifies the effects of infectious diseases. Diarrheal disease, which is seldom fatal in industrial countries, claims some 1.5 million lives each year, mostly of children in the developing world. Among well-nourished children, measles are rarely fatal, yet this disease kills some 800,000 children annually, nearly all of them weakened by hunger and easily overwhelmed. Respiratory illnesses, a minor problem in a healthy population, also take a heavy toll among children with weakened immune systems.[28]

Traditional infectious diseases, such as tuberculosis and malaria, annually claim 1.6 million and 1.1 million lives, respectively. Tuberculosis is particularly challenging for doctors because some strains are resistant to antibiotics. It is a leading health issue in Russia and neighboring countries as well as in developing ones.[29]

Malaria has a sharp geographic focus, with 90 percent of the 1 million deaths last year occurring in Africa. A Roll Back Malaria initiative from the World Heath Organization (WHO) is designed to reduce the malaria threat. Among other things, it involves providing low-cost insecticide-treated bednets. New initiatives within Africa in malaria research and drug and vaccine development could also help curb the disease.[30]

Many countries that are no longer able to afford the vaccines for childhood diseases, such as measles, have fallen behind in their vaccination programs. Lacking the funds to invest today, they pay a far higher price tomorrow. There are not many situations where just a few pennies spent per youngster can make as much difference as vaccination programs can.[31]

Along with the eradication of hunger, the provision of safe water is one of the keys to better health for children. The realistic option now may be to bypass efforts to build costly water-based sewage removal and sewage treatment systems and to opt instead for water-free waste disposal systems that do not disperse disease pathogens, like the dry toilets described in Chapter 7. This switch would simultaneously help alleviate water scarcity, reduce the dissemination of disease agents in water systems, and close the nutrient cycle.

Beyond infectious diseases, air pollution, automobiles, and cigarettes claim millions of lives each year. WHO estimates that air pollution, largely from power plants and automobiles, claims 3 million lives a year. While most industrial countries have made progress in reducing urban air pollution, in developing countries this problem is worsening.[32]

Worldwide, automobile accidents kill 1.2 million people a year, making car ownership almost as dangerous as cigarette smoking. And cars are also a major source of the air pollution that kills drivers and nondrivers alike. If we allocate a third of air pollution deaths to pollutants from automobile exhaust, auto fatalities would exceed 2 million.[33]

Some leading sources of premature death are lifestyle-related. Cigarettes take a particularly heavy toll. WHO estimates that 4.9 million people died in 2000 of tobacco-related illnesses. Today there are some 25 known tobacco-related diseases, including heart disease, stroke, respiratory illness, several forms of cancer, and male impotence. Cigarette smoke kills more people each year than all other air pollutants combined—nearly 5 million versus 3 million.[34]

Impressive progress is being made in reducing cigarette smoking. After a century-long buildup of a tobacco habit, the world is turning away from cigarettes, following the U.S. lead and with a strong boost from WHO leadership in its "tobacco free" initiative. This will no doubt be helped by the Framework Convention on Tobacco Control, the first international accord to deal entirely with a health issue, which was adopted unanimously in Geneva in May 2003.[35]

Ironically, the country that gave the world tobacco is now leading us away from it. In the United States, the number of cigarettes smoked per person has dropped from 2,844 in 1976 to 1,593 in 2002—a decline of 44 percent. Worldwide, where the downturn lags that of the United States by roughly a decade, usage has dropped from the historical high of 1,020 cigarettes smoked per person in 1986 to 878 in 2002, a fall of 14 percent.[36]

Indeed, smoking is on the decline in nearly all the major cigarette-consuming countries, including such strongholds as France, China, and Japan. The number of cigarettes smoked per person has dropped 20 percent in France since peaking in 1985, 8 percent in China since 1990, and 14 percent in Japan since 1992.[37]

One of the principal achievements of the international community in recent decades has been the eradication of smallpox, an effort led by WHO. This successful elimination of a feared disease, which required the worldwide immunization of the poorest of the world's poor, not only now saves hundreds of millions of dollars each year in smallpox vaccination programs but also billions of dollars in health care, and has lightened the burden of disease worldwide. Similarly, the WHO-led international campaign to eradicate polio is on the verge of eliminating another of the world's great scourges, one that did not distinguish between the rich and the poor.[38]

Another impressive gain on the health front has come from a campaign led by UNICEF to treat the symptoms of diarrheal disease with oral rehydration therapy. This remarkably simple technique, the oral administration of a mild saline solution, has been extremely effective—reducing deaths from diarrhea among children from 4.6 million in 1980 to 1.5 million in 1999. Few investments have saved so many lives at such a low cost.[39]

A recent study commissioned by WHO Director-General Gro Harlem Brundtland looked at the economics of health care in developing countries and concluded that providing the most basic health care services—the sort that could be supplied by a village-level clinic—would yield enormous economic benefits for the developing countries and for the world as a whole. The authors estimated that providing basic universal health care in developing countries will require donor grants totaling $27 billion in 2007, scaled up to $38 billion in 2015. Of the first commitment, for 2007, $6 billion is already being provided by donors. In addition to basic services, this figure includes funding for the Global Fund to Fight AIDS, Tuberculosis and Malaria and for universal childhood vaccinations. The report estimated that the total program would cost one tenth of 1 percent of the gross national product of industrial countries. Thus health care is a prime example of an ounce of investment being worth a pound of cure.[40]

School Lunches for the Poor

For more than 50 years, every child in public school in the United States has had access to the school lunch program, ensuring one good meal each day. George McGovern and Robert Dole, both former members of the U.S. Senate agricultural committee, believe this program should be exported to the world's poorest countries.[41]

The U.S. national school lunch program was launched in 1946 largely as the result of data accumulated during the war showing that one third of the country's youths were physically unfit for military service, mainly because of a poor diet. In retrospect, there has been no denying the benefits of the national school lunch program that has continued uninterruptedly for 56 years. McGovern writes that shortly after he became director of the Food for Peace program in the early 1960s, the Dean of the University of Georgia called him to say that the school lunch program had done more to develop the South than any other federal program.[42]

The appeal of school lunch programs for children in other countries is even greater than in the United States because these children are hungrier. Children who are ill or hungry miss many days of school. And even when they are there, they do not learn as well. Jeffrey Sachs, director of Columbia University's Earth Institute, notes, "Sick children often face a lifetime of diminished productivity because of interruptions in schooling together with cognitive and physical impairment." But when school lunch programs are launched in low-income countries, school enrollment jumps. The children's attention span increases. Their academic performance goes up. Fewer days are missed from school, and children spend more years there.[43]

Girls benefit especially. Drawn to school by the lunch, they stay in school longer, marry later, and have fewer children. This is a win-win-win situation. Adopting this program in the 44 lowest-income countries would cost an estimated $6 billion per year beyond what the United Nations is now spending in its efforts to reduce hunger. Only one fourth of this, or $1.5 billion, need come from the United States, since other industrial countries would likely cover the remainder.[44]

George McGovern adds that "a women, infants and children (WIC) program, which offers nutritious food supplements to needy pregnant and nursing mothers," should also be extended into the poor countries. With 25 years of experience to draw on, it is clear that the U.S. WIC program has been enormously successful in improving nutrition, health, and the development of preschool children among the poor. If this were expanded to reach pregnant women, nursing mothers, and small children in the 44 poorest countries, it would help to eradicate hunger among millions of small children at a stage in their lives when it could make a huge difference.[45]

These efforts are costly for sure, but not when compared with the annual losses in productivity from hunger. McGovern and Dole have worked together to create the George McGovern–Robert Dole International Food for Education and Child Nutrition Act. They have urged that $5 billion of the $40 billion appropriated by Congress to combat terrorism be used to assist U.N. agencies and nongovernmental organizations in the war against hunger. They acknowledge that better nutrition by itself will not end terrorism, but they do think that this initiative can help "dry up the swamplands of hunger and despair that serve as potential recruiting grounds for terrorists."[46]

Aside from the strategic benefits to the United States and, indeed, all industrial countries of having a better-fed, well-nourished population of young people in the developing world, hunger should be ended because the world can now afford to do so. In a world where vast wealth is accumulating among the rich, it makes little sense for children to be going to school hungry. To quote President Franklin D. Roosevelt, "The test of our progress is not whether we add more to the abundance of those who have enough; it is whether we provide enough for those who have too little."[47]

Breaking Out

Many countries that have experienced rapid population growth for several decades are showing signs of demographic fatigue. Countries struggling with the simultaneous challenge of educating growing numbers of children, creating jobs for swelling ranks of young job seekers, and dealing with the environmental effects of population growth are stretched to the limit. When a major new threat arises—such as the HIV epidemic—governments often cannot cope.

Problems routinely managed in industrial societies are becoming full-scale humanitarian crises in many developing ones. The rise in death rates in many African countries marks a tragic new development in world demography. In the absence of a concerted effort by national governments and the international community to accelerate the shift to smaller families, events in many countries could spiral out of control, leading to spreading political instability and economic decline.

There is an alternative to this bleak prospect, and that is to help countries that want to slow their population growth quickly to do so. This brings with it what economists call a demographic bonus. When countries move quickly to smaller families, with a sharp reduction in births, growth in the number of young dependents—those that need nurturing and educating—declines relative to the number of working adults. In this situation, productivity rises, savings and investment climb, and economic growth accelerates. Japan, which cut its population growth in half between 1951 and 1958, was one of the first countries to benefit from the demographic bonus. South Korea and Taiwan followed, and more recently China has benefited from the earlier sharp reduction in its birth rate. This effect lasts for only a few decades, but it is enough to launch a country into the modern era.[48]

This chapter has discussed the social preconditions for accelerating the shift to smaller families. These include filling several funding gaps—those needed to reach universal primary education; to fight infectious diseases, such as AIDS, tuberculosis, and malaria; to provide reproductive health care; and to contain the HIV epidemic, among others. Collectively, the seven initiatives discussed are estimated to cost another $62 billion a year, which could be shared by the United States and other industrial countries. (See Table 10–2.) Encouragingly, several countries in Europe are convinced of the need to forge ahead in this direction.[49]

The heaviest investments in this effort center on education and health, which are the cornerstones of both human capital development and population stabilization. Education includes both universal primary education and a global campaign to eradicate adult illiteracy. Health care includes the basic interventions involved in controlling infectious diseases, beginning with childhood vaccinations. Adopting the basic health care program outlined in the report to WHO would itself save an estimated 8 million lives per year by 2010. This proposed initiative is a life-transforming one that can literally alter the course of history. It is a way of raising educational levels, improving health, and accelerating the shift to smaller families, a prerequisite of breaking the poverty cycle.

Helping low-income countries break out of the demographic trap is a highly profitable investment for the world's affluent nations. Industrial-country investments

Table 10–2. *Additional Annual Funding Needed to Reach Basic Social Goals*

Goal	Funding
	(billion dollars)
Universal primary education	15
Adult literacy campaign	4
Reproductive health and family planning	10
Closing the condom gap	2
School lunch programs for 44 poorest countries	6
Assistance to preschool children and pregnant women in 44 poorest countries	4
Universal basic health care	21
Total	62

Source: See endnote 49.

in education, health, and school lunches are in a sense a humanitarian response to the plight of the world's poorest countries. But more fundamentally they are investments in the world in which our children will live.

III
THE ONLY OPTION

11

Plan B: Rising to the Challenge

Plan B is a massive mobilization to deflate the global economic bubble before it reaches the bursting point. Keeping the bubble from bursting will require an unprecedented degree of international cooperation to stabilize population, climate, water tables, and soils—and at wartime speed. Indeed, in both scale and urgency the effort required is comparable to the U.S. mobilization during World War II.

Our only hope now is rapid systemic change—change based on market signals that tell the ecological truth. This means restructuring the tax system: lowering income taxes and raising taxes on environmentally destructive activities, such as fossil fuel burning, to incorporate the ecological costs. Unless we can get the market to send signals that reflect reality, we will continue making faulty decisions as consumers, corporate planners, and government policymakers. Ill-informed economic decisions and the economic distortions they create can lead to economic decline.

Plan B is the only viable option simply because Plan A, continuing with business as usual, offers an unacceptable outcome—continuing environmental degradation and disruption and a bursting of the economic bubble.

The warning signals are coming more frequently, whether they be collapsing fisheries, melting glaciers, or falling water tables. Thus far the wake-up calls have been local, but soon they could become global. Massive imports of grain by China—and the rise in food prices that would likely follow—could awake us from our lethargy.

But time is running out. Bubble economies, which by definition are artificially inflated, do not continue indefinitely. Our demands on the earth exceed its regenerative capacity by a wider margin with each passing day.

Deflating the Bubble
Stabilizing world population at 7.5 billion or so is central to avoiding economic breakdown in countries with large projected population increases that are already overconsuming their natural capital assets. Some 36 countries, all in Europe except Japan, have essentially stabilized their populations. The challenge now is to create the economic and social conditions and to adopt the priorities that will lead to population stability in all remaining countries. The keys here are extending primary education to all children, providing vaccinations and basic health care, and offering reproductive health care and family planning services in all countries.[1]

Shifting from a carbon-based to a hydrogen-based energy economy to stabilize climate is now technologically possible. Advances in wind turbine design and in solar cell manufacturing, the availability of hydrogen generators, and the evolution of fuel cells provide the technologies needed to build a climate-benign hydrogen economy. Moving quickly from a carbon-based to a hydrogen-based energy economy depends on getting the price right, on incorporating the indirect costs of burning fossil fuels into the market price.

On the energy front, Iceland is the first country to

adopt a national plan to convert its carbon-based energy economy to one based on hydrogen. It is starting with the conversion of the Reykjavik bus fleet to fuel cell engines and will proceed with converting automobiles and eventually the fishing fleet. Iceland's first hydrogen service station opened in April 2003.[2]

Denmark and Germany are leading the world into the age of wind, as noted in Chapter 9. Denmark, the pioneer, gets 18 percent of its electricity from wind turbines and plans to increase this to 40 percent by 2030. Germany, following Denmark's early lead, has developed some 12,000 megawatts of wind-generating capacity. Its northernmost state of Schleswig-Holstein now gets 28 percent of its electricity from wind. Spain is also moving fast to exploit its wind resources.[3]

Japan has emerged as the world's leading manufacturer and user of solar cells. With its commercialization of a solar roofing material, it leads the world in electricity generation from solar cells and is well positioned to assist in the electrification of villages in the developing world.[4]

The Netherlands leads the industrial world in exploiting the bicycle as an alternative to the automobile. In Amsterdam's bicycle-friendly environment, up to 40 percent of all trips are taken by bicycle. This reflects the priority given to bikes in the design and operation of the country's urban transport systems. At many traffic lights, for example, bicycles are allowed to go first when the light changes.[5]

The Canadian province of Ontario is emerging as a leader in phasing out coal. It plans to replace its five coal-fired power plants with gas-fired plants, wind farms, and efficiency gains. This initiative calls for the first plant to close in 2005 and the last one in 2015. The resulting reduction in carbon emissions is equivalent to taking 4 million cars off the road. This approach, which may soon be adopted in some other Canadian provinces, is a model for local and national governments everywhere.[6]

Stabilizing water tables is particularly difficult because the forces triggering the fall have their own momentum, which must be reversed. Arresting the fall depends on quickly raising water productivity. It is difficult to overstate the urgency of this effort. Failure to stop the fall in water tables by systematically reducing water use will lead to the depletion of aquifers, an abrupt cutback in water supplies, and the risk of a precipitous drop in food production. In pioneering drip irrigation technology, Israel has become the world leader in the efficient use of agricultural water. This unusually labor-intensive irrigation practice, now being used to produce high-value crops in many countries, is ideally suited where water is scarce and labor is abundant.[7]

With soil erosion, we have no choice but to reduce the loss to the rate of new soil formation or below. The only alternative is a continuing decline in the inherent fertility of eroding soils and cropland abandonment. In stabilizing soils, South Korea and the United States stand out. South Korea, with once denuded mountainsides and hills now covered with trees, has achieved a level of flood control, water storage, and hydrological stability that is a model for other countries. Although the two Koreas are separated only by a narrow demilitarized zone, the contrast between them is stark. In North Korea, where little permanent vegetation remains, droughts and floods alternate and hunger is chronic.[8]

The U.S. record in soil conservation is also impressive. Beginning in the late 1980s, U.S. farmers systematically retired roughly 10 percent of the most erodible cropland, planting the bulk of it to grass. In addition, they lead the world in adopting minimum-till, no-till, and other soil-conserving practices. With this combination of programs and practices, the United States has reduced soil erosion by nearly 40 percent in less than two decades.[9]

Thus all the things we need to do to keep the bubble from bursting are now being done in at least a few countries. If these highly successful initiatives are adopted worldwide, and quickly, we can deflate the bubble before it bursts.

A Wartime Mobilization

Adopting Plan B is unlikely unless the United States assumes a leadership position, much as it belatedly did in World War II. The nation responded to the aggression of Germany and Japan only after it was directly attacked at Pearl Harbor on December 7, 1941. But respond it did. After an all-out mobilization, the U.S. engagement helped turn the tide, leading the Allied Forces to victory within three-and-a-half years.[10]

The U.S. conversion to a wartime economy actually began in a modest way in 1940. On May 16th of that year, in a message to Congress, President Franklin Roosevelt said the United States would eventually have to step up its arms production. That spring Congress passed the Lend Lease Act, which authorized the sale of arms to the United Kingdom and allied countries without expectation of payment. And in December the President created the Office of Production Management to facilitate the shift from a peacetime to a wartime economy.[11]

These actions enabled the United States to begin the economic conversion needed for the war effort: to move industries into the manufacture of armaments, to establish the contracting procedures, and to launch the research and development that was needed. When the Japanese attacked Pearl Harbor, the United States was already starting to gear up for war.[12]

In his State of the Union address on January 6, 1942,

one month after Pearl Harbor, President Roosevelt announced ambitious arms production goals. The United States, he said, was planning to produce 60,000 planes, 45,000 tanks, 20,000 anti-aircraft guns, and 6 million tons of merchant shipping. He added, "Let no man say it cannot be done."[13]

Achieving these goals was possible only by converting existing industries and using materials that previously went into manufacturing civilian goods. Nowhere was this shift more dramatic than in the automobile industry, which was at that time the largest concentration of industrial power in the world, producing 3–4 million cars a year. Auto companies initially wanted to continue manufacturing cars and simply to add on production of armaments. They agreed only reluctantly—after pressure from President Roosevelt—to a wholesale conversion to war-support manufacturing.[14]

Aircraft needs were enormous. They included not only fighters, bombers, and reconnaissance planes, but also the troop and cargo transports needed to fight a war on two fronts, each across an ocean. From the beginning of 1942 through 1944, the United States turned out 229,600 aircraft, a fleet so vast it is hard to visualize.[15]

While the aircraft industry did nearly all the assembly, the auto industry supplied some 455,000 aircraft engines and 256,000 propellers. The aircraft industry was given the job of assembling all planes to ease its fears that the auto industry would become firmly entrenched in the manufacture of aircraft and would dominate the industry after the war.[16]

The year 1942 witnessed the greatest expansion of industrial output in the nation's history—all for military use. Early in the year, the production and sale of cars and trucks for private use was banned, residential and highway construction was halted, and driving for pleasure was banned.[17]

In her book *No Ordinary Time*, Doris Kearns Good-win describes how various firms converted. A sparkplug factory was among the first to switch to the production of machine guns. Soon a manufacturer of stoves was producing lifeboats. A merry-go-round factory was making gun mounts; a toy company was turning out compasses; a corset manufacturer was producing grenade belts; and a pinball machine plant began to make armor-piercing shells.[18]

In retrospect, the speed of the conversion from a peacetime to a wartime economy was stunning. The automobile industry went from producing nearly 4 million cars in 1941 to producing 24,000 tanks and 17,000 armored cars in 1942—but only 223,000 cars, and most of them were produced early in the year, before the conversion began. Essentially the auto industry was closed down from early 1942 through the end of 1944. In 1940, the United States produced some 4,000 aircraft. In 1942, it produced 48,000. By the end of the war, more than 5,000 ships were added to the 1,000 that made up the American Merchant Fleet in 1939.[19]

The harnessing of U.S. industrial power tipped the scales decisively toward the Allied Forces, reversing the tide of war. Germany and Japan could not match the United States in this effort. Winston Churchill often quoted Sir Edward Grey, Britain's foreign secretary: "The United States is like a giant boiler. Once the fire is lighted under it, there is no limit to the power it can generate."[20]

A rationing program was also introduced. In addition to an outright ban on the sale of private cars, strategic goods—including tires, gasoline, fuel oil, and sugar—were rationed beginning in 1942. Cutting back on consumption of these goods freed up resources to support the war effort.[21]

This mobilization of resources within a matter of

months demonstrates that a country and, indeed, the world can restructure its economy quickly if it is convinced of the need to do so. Many people—although not yet the majority—are already convinced of the need for a wholesale restructuring of the economy. The issue is not whether most people will eventually be won over, but whether they will be convinced before the bubble economy collapses.

Creating an Honest Market

The key to restructuring the economy is the creation of an honest market, one that tells the ecological truth. The market is an incredible institution—with some remarkable strengths and some glaring weaknesses. It allocates scarce resources with an efficiency that no central planning body can match. It easily balances supply and demand and it sets prices that readily reflect both scarcity and abundance. The market does, however, have three fundamental weaknesses. It does not incorporate the indirect costs of providing goods or services into prices, it does not value nature's services properly, and it does not respect the sustainable-yield thresholds of natural systems such as fisheries, forests, rangelands, and aquifers.

Throughout most of recorded history, the indirect costs of economic activity, the sustainable yields of natural systems, or the value of nature's services were of little concern because the scale of human activity was so small relative to the size of the earth that they were rarely an issue. But with the sevenfold expansion in the world economy over the last half-century, the failure to address these market shortcomings and the irrational economic distortions they create will eventually lead to economic decline.[22]

As the global economy has expanded and as technology has evolved, the indirect costs of some products have become far larger than the price fixed by the market. The price of a gallon of gasoline, for instance, includes the cost of production but not the expense of treating respiratory illnesses from breathing polluted air or the repair bill from acid rain damage. Nor does it cover the cost of rising global temperature, ice melting, more destructive storms, or the relocation of millions of refugees forced from their homes by sea level rise. As the market is now organized, the motorist burning the gasoline does not bear these costs.

Something is wrong. If we have learned anything over the last few years, it is that accounting systems that do not tell the truth can be costly. Faulty corporate accounting systems that overstate income or leave costs off the books have driven some of the world's largest corporations into bankruptcy, costing millions of people their lifetime savings, retirement incomes, and jobs.

Unfortunately, we also have a faulty economic accounting system at the global level, but with potentially far more serious consequences. Economic prosperity is achieved in part by running up ecological deficits, costs that do not show up on the books, but costs that someone will eventually pay. Some of the record economic prosperity of recent decades has come from consuming the earth's productive assets—its forests, rangelands, fisheries, soils, and aquifers—and from destabilizing its climate.

If we want to determine the full cost of burning gasoline, we need to calculate the indirect costs of doing so. A model for doing this is provided by the U.S. Centers for Disease Control and Prevention (CDC), which in April 2002 released a study on the cost to society of smoking a pack of cigarettes. Calculating the expenses of treating smoking-related illnesses and lost employee productivity

due to illness and absenteeism shows that each pack of
cigarettes smoked in the United States costs society $7.18.
This is in addition to the costs of growing the tobacco,
curing it, and manufacturing the cigarettes. The question
is not whether the additional $7.18 is paid. It is paid by
someone—by the smoker, by the employer, or by the taxpayers who fund Medicare programs.[23]

For gasoline, calculating the true costs to society
means including the medical costs of treating those who
are ill from breathing polluted air; the costs of acid rain
damage to lakes, forests, crops, and buildings; and, by far
the largest, the costs of climate change. Higher temperatures can wither crops and reduce harvests. They can
melt ice and raise sea level, inundating coastal cities, low-
lying agricultural lands, and low-lying island countries.
The interesting question is, What is the cost to society of
burning a gallon of gasoline? Is it more or less, for example, than that of smoking a pack of cigarettes?[24]

No one has attempted to assess fully the worldwide
costs of rising temperature and then to allocate them by
gallon of gasoline or ton of coal. Some studies were
done, however, during the early and mid-1990s on the
external cost of automobile use in the United States,
including direct subsidies, such as parking subsidies, and
many local environmental costs. A summary of eight of
these studies by John Holtzclaw of the Sierra Club indicates that if the price were raised enough to make drivers
pay some of the indirect costs of automobile use, a gallon of gas would cost anywhere from $3.03 to $8.64, with
the variations largely due to how many indirect costs
were covered. For example, some studies included the
military costs of protecting petroleum supply lines and
ensuring access to Middle Eastern oil, while others did
not. No studies, unfortunately, incorporated all the costs
of using gasoline—including the future inundation of

coastal cities, island countries, and rice-growing river floodplains.[25]

Some of the looming costs associated with continued fossil fuel burning are not only virtually incalculable, but the outcome is unacceptable. What is the cost of inundating half of Bangladesh's riceland by a 1-meter rise in sea level? How much is this land worth in a country that is the size of New York state and has a population half that of the United States? And what would be the cost of relocating the 40 million Bangladeshis who would be displaced by the 1-meter rise in sea level? Would they be moved to another part of the country? Or would they migrate to less densely populated countries, such as the United States, Canada, Australia, and Brazil?[26]

Another challenge in creating an honest market is to get it to value nature's services. For example, after several weeks of flooding in the Yangtze River basin in 1998—flooding that eventually inflicted $30 billion worth of damage and destruction in the basin—the Chinese government announced that it was banning all tree cutting in the basin. It justified the ban by saying that trees standing are worth three times as much as trees cut. This calculation recognized that the flood control service provided by forests was far more valuable than the timber in them.[27]

Forests also recycle rainfall inland. Some 20 years ago, two Brazilian scientists, Eneas Salati and Peter Vose, published an article in *Science* in which they pointed out that when rainfall coming from clouds moving in from the Atlantic fell on healthy Amazon rainforest, one fourth of the water ran off and three fourths evaporated into the atmosphere to be carried further inland and provide more rainfall. When land was cleared for grazing, however, the numbers were reversed—with roughly three fourths running off and one fourth evaporating for recycling inland.

Ecologist Philip Fearnside, who has made a career of studying the Amazon, observes that the agriculturally prominent south-central part of Brazil depends on water that is recycled inland via the Amazon rainforest. If the Amazon is converted into a cattle pasture, he notes, there will be less rainfall to support agriculture.[28]

Once we calculate all the costs of a product or service, we can incorporate them into market prices by restructuring taxes. If we can get the market to tell the truth, then we can avoid being blindsided by faulty accounting systems that lead to bankruptcy. As Øystein Dahle, former Vice President of Exxon for Norway and the North Sea, has pointed out: "Socialism collapsed because it did not allow the market to tell the economic truth. Capitalism may collapse because it does not allow the market to tell the ecological truth."[29]

Shifting Taxes

The need for tax shifting—lowering income taxes while raising taxes on environmentally destructive activities— in order to get the market to tell the truth has been widely endorsed by economists. The basic idea is to establish a tax that reflects the indirect costs to society of an economic activity. For example, a tax on coal would incorporate the increased health care costs associated with breathing polluted air, the costs of damage from acid rain, and the costs of climate disruption.[30]

With this concept in hand, it is a short step to tax shifting—that is, reducing taxes on income and offsetting this with taxes on environmentally destructive activities. Nine countries in Western Europe have already begun the process of tax shifting, known as environmental tax reform. The amount of revenue shifted thus far is small, just a few percent. But enough experience has been gained to know that it works.[31]

Among the activities taxed in Europe are carbon emissions, emissions of heavy metals, and the generation of garbage (so-called landfill taxes). The Nordic countries, led by Sweden, pioneered tax shifting at the beginning of the 1990s. By 1999 a second wave of tax shifting was under way, this one including the larger economies of Germany, France, Italy, and the United Kingdom. Tax shifting does not change the level of taxes, only their composition. One of the better known changes was a four-year plan adopted in Germany in 1999 to shift taxes from labor to energy. By 2001, this had lowered fuel use by 5 percent. A tax on carbon emissions adopted in Finland in 1990 lowered emissions there 7 percent by 1998.[32]

Environmental tax reform is spreading, with the reform process now under way in Denmark, Finland, France, Germany, Italy, the Netherlands, Norway, Sweden, and the United Kingdom. There are isolated cases elsewhere. The United States, for example, imposed a stiff tax on chlorofluorocarbons to phase them out in accordance with the Montreal Protocol of 1987. At the local level, the city of Victoria, British Columbia, adopted a trash tax of $1.20 per bag of garbage, reducing its daily trash flow 18 percent within one year.[33]

One of the newer taxes gaining in popularity is the so-called congestion tax. City governments are turning to a tax on vehicles entering the city, or at least the inner part of the city where traffic congestion is most serious. In London, where the average speed of an automobile was 9 miles per hour—about the same as a horse-drawn carriage—a congestion tax was adopted in early 2003. The $8 charge on all motorists driving into the center city between 7 a.m. and 6:30 p.m. immediately reduced the number of vehicles by 24 percent, permitting traffic to flow more freely while cutting pollution and noise.[34]

Singapore was the first city to adopt such a tax some

two decades ago. Although it was quite successful, only quite recently have other cities, such as Oslo and Melbourne, done so. London is by far the largest city to join in. Other cities that are becoming unlivable because of congestion, pollution, and noise may also turn to such taxes.[35]

For some products where the external costs are large and obvious, pressure is mounting to impose taxes. By far the most dramatic example of this was the agreement negotiated between the tobacco industry and state governments in the United States. After numerous state governments had launched litigation to force tobacco companies to reimburse them for the Medicare costs associated with treating smoking-related illnesses, the industry decided to negotiate a package reimbursement, agreeing in November 1998 to reimburse the 50 state governments to the tune of $251 billion—nearly $1,000 for every person in the United States. This landmark agreement was, in effect, a retroactive tax on cigarettes smoked in the past, one designed to incorporate some of the indirect costs. In order to pay this enormous bill, cigarette companies dramatically raised the price of their cigarettes, further discouraging smoking.[36]

The CDC study that calculated the social costs of smoking cigarettes in the United States at $7.18 per pack not only justifies raising taxes on cigarettes, it also provides an empirical framework within which to do so. In 2002, a year in which almost every state government in the United States faced a fiscal deficit because of deteriorating economic conditions, 21 states raised cigarette taxes. Perhaps the most dramatic increase came in New York City, where smokers faced an increase of 39¢ in the state tax and $1.42 in the city tax—a total increase of $1.81 per pack. This brought the price of a pack of cigarettes in New York City to roughly $7.50. Since a 10-percent price increase typically reduces smoking by 4 percent, the health benefits of this tax increase should be substantial.[37]

Environmental tax shifting usually brings a double dividend. In reducing taxes on income—in effect, taxes on labor—labor becomes less costly, creating additional jobs while protecting the environment. This was the principal motivation in the German four-year shift of taxes from income to energy. The shift from fossil fuels to more energy-efficient technologies and to renewable sources of energy reduces carbon emissions and represents a shift to more labor-intensive industries. By lowering the air pollution from smokestacks and tailpipes, it also reduces respiratory illnesses, such as asthma and emphysema, and health care costs—a triple dividend.[38]

When it comes to reflecting the value of nature's services, ecologists can calculate the values of services that a forest in a given location provides. Once these are determined, they can be incorporated into the price of trees as a stumpage tax of the sort that Bulgaria and Lithuania have adopted. Anyone wishing to cut a tree would have to pay a tax equal to the value of the services provided by that tree. The market would then be telling the truth. The effect of this would be to reduce tree cutting, since forest services may be worth several times as much as the timber, and to encourage wood and paper recycling.[39]

Tax shifting also helps countries gain the lead in producing new equipment, such as new energy technologies or those used for pollution control. For example, the Danish government's tax incentives for wind-generated electricity have made Denmark, a country of only 5 million people, the world's leading manufacturer of wind turbines.[40]

Some 2,500 economists, including eight Nobel Prize winners in economics, have endorsed the concept of tax shifts. Former Harvard economics professor N. Gregory

Mankiw, who was nominated to be Chairman of the President's Council of Economic Advisors in early 2003, wrote in *Fortune* magazine: "Cutting income taxes while increasing gasoline taxes would lead to more rapid economic growth, less traffic congestion, safer roads, and reduced risk of global warming—all without jeopardizing long-term fiscal solvency. This may be the closest thing to a free lunch that economics has to offer." Mankiw could also have added that it would reduce the military expenditures associated with ensuring access to Middle Eastern oil.[41]

The Economist has recognized the advantage of environmental tax shifting and endorses it strongly: "On environmental grounds, never mind energy security, America taxes gasoline too lightly. Better than a one-off increase, a politically more feasible idea, and desirable in its own terms, would be a long-term plan to shift taxes from incomes to emissions of carbon." In Europe and the United States, polls indicate that at least 70 percent of voters support environmental tax reform once it is explained to them.[42]

Shifting Subsidies

Each year the world's taxpayers underwrite $700 billion of subsidies for environmentally destructive activities, such as fossil fuel burning, overpumping aquifers, clearcutting forests, and overfishing. A 1997 Earth Council study, *Subsidizing Unsustainable Development*, observes that "there is something unbelievable about the world spending hundreds of billions of dollars annually to subsidize its own destruction."[43]

Iran provides a classic example of extreme subsidies when it prices oil for internal use at one tenth the world price, strongly encouraging the consumption of gasoline. The World Bank reports that if this $3.6 billion annual subsidy were phased out, it would reduce Iran's carbon emissions by a staggering 49 percent. It would also strengthen the economy by freeing up public revenues for investment in the country's economic and social development. Iran is not alone. The Bank reports that removing energy subsidies would reduce carbon emissions in Venezuela by 26 percent, in Russia by 17 percent, in India by 14 percent, and in Indonesia by 11 percent.[44]

Some countries are eliminating or reducing these climate-disrupting subsidies. Belgium, France, and Japan have phased out all subsidies for coal. Germany reduced its coal subsidy from $5.4 billion in 1989 to $2.8 billion in 2002, meanwhile lowering its coal use by 46 percent. It plans to phase them out entirely by 2010. China cut its coal subsidy from $750 million in 1993 to $240 million in 1995. More recently, it has imposed a tax on high sulfur coals. Together these two measures helped to reduce coal use in China by 5 percent between 1997 and 2001 while the economy was expanding by one third.[45]

The environmental tax shifting described earlier reduces taxes on wages and encourages investment in such activities as wind electric generation and recycling, thus simultaneously boosting employment and lessening environmental destruction. Eliminating environmentally destructive subsidies reduces both the burden on taxpayers and the destructive activities themselves.

Subsidies are not inherently bad. Many technologies and industries were born of government subsidies. Jet aircraft were developed with military R&D expenditures, leading to modern commercial airliners. The Internet was a result of publicly funded efforts to establish links between computers in government laboratories and research institutes. And the combination of the federal tax incentive and a robust state tax incentive in California gave birth to the modern wind power industry.[46]

But just as there is a need for tax shifting, there is also a need for subsidy shifting. A world facing the prospect of economically disruptive climate change, for example, can no longer justify subsidies to expand the burning of coal and oil. Shifting these subsidies to the development of climate-benign energy sources such as wind power, solar power, and geothermal power is the key to stabilizing the earth's climate. Shifting subsidies from road construction to rail construction could increase mobility in many situations while reducing carbon emissions.

In a troubled world economy facing fiscal deficits at all levels of government, exploiting these tax and subsidy shifts with their double and triple dividends can help balance the books and save the environment. Tax and subsidy shifting promise both gains in economic efficiency and reductions in environmental destruction, a win-win situation.

A Call to Greatness

History judges political leaders by whether they respond to the great issues of their time. For today's leaders, that issue is how to deflate the world's bubble economy before it bursts. This bubble threatens the future of everyone, rich and poor alike. It challenges us to restructure the global economy, to build an eco-economy.

Among national political leaders, none has articulated the new agenda better than U.K. Prime Minister Tony Blair. He believes that environmental degradation is the issue for our generation, noting that climate change is "unquestionably the most urgent environmental challenge." Arguing that the Kyoto Protocol was not radical enough, he calls for a 60-percent reduction in carbon emissions worldwide by 2050. Summing up, he calls for a "new international consensus to protect our environment and combat the devastating impacts of climate change."[47]

Following the terrorist attacks on the World Trade

Towers and the Pentagon on September 11, 2001, several world leaders suggested a twenty-first century variation of the Marshall Plan to deal with poverty and its symptoms, arguing that in an increasingly integrated world, abject poverty and great wealth cannot coexist. Gordon Brown, U.K. Chancellor of the Exchequer, notes that "Like peace, prosperity was indivisible and to be sustained, it had to be shared." Brown sees a Marshall Plan–like initiative not as aid in the traditional sense, but as an investment in the future.[48]

French President Jacques Chirac, a political conservative, told the Earth Summit in Johannesburg in early September 2002 that "the world needed an international tax to fight world poverty." He suggested a tax on either airplane tickets, carbon emissions, or international financial transactions. To illustrate his commitment, Chirac announced that over the next five years France would double its development aid, reaching the internationally agreed upon goal of devoting 0.7 percent of gross domestic product to aid. Going beyond economic issues, he also suggested the creation of a world environment organization to coordinate efforts to build an environmentally sustainable economy.[49]

Some corporate leaders are also beginning to urge efforts to deal with global poverty. Juergen Schrempp, CEO of DaimlerChrysler, said in a speech at the U.S. Chamber of Commerce that the world needed a new Marshall Plan. The question for the industrial world, he said, was not, Can we afford another Marshall Plan? The question is, Can we afford *not* to have another Marshall Plan?[50]

There is a growing sense among the more thoughtful political and opinion leaders worldwide that business as usual is no longer a viable option, that unless we respond to the social and environmental issues that are undermining our future, we may not be able to avoid economic decline and social disintegration. The prospect of failing states is growing as mega-threats such as the HIV epidemic, water shortages, and land hunger threaten to overwhelm countries on the lower rungs of the global economic ladder. Failed states are a matter of concern not only because of the social costs to their people but also because they serve as ideal bases for international terrorist organizations.

We now have some idea of what needs to be done and how to do it. The United Nations has set social goals for education, health, and the reduction of hunger and poverty. The preceding chapters have sketched out a restructuring of the energy economy to stabilize atmospheric carbon dioxide levels, a plan to stabilize population, a strategy for raising land productivity and restoring the earth's vegetation, and a plan to raise water productivity worldwide. The goals are essential and the technologies are available.[51]

We have the wealth to achieve these goals. What we do not yet have is the leadership. And if the past is any guide to the future, that leadership can only come from the United States. By far the wealthiest society that has ever existed, the United States has the resources to lead this effort. Economist Jeffrey Sachs sums it up well, "The tragic irony of this moment is that the rich countries are so rich and the poor so poor that a few added tenths of one percent of GNP from the rich ones ramped up over the coming decades could do what was never before possible in human history: ensure that the basic needs of health and education are met for all impoverished children in this world. How many more tragedies will we suffer in this country before we wake up to our capacity to help make the world a safer and more prosperous place not only through military might, but through the gift of life itself?"[52]

Unfortunately, the United States continues to focus on building an ever-stronger military as though that were the key to addressing these threats. The $343-billion defense budget dwarfs those of other countries—allies and others alike. U.S. allies, most of them North American Treaty Organization members, spend $205 billion a year on the military; Russia spends $60 billion; China, $42 billion; and Iran, Iraq, and North Korea combined spend $12 billion. (See Table 11–1.) The United States is spending more than its allies and possible adversaries combined. As retired admiral Eugene Carroll, Jr., astutely observed, "For forty-five years of the Cold War we were in an arms race with the Soviet Union. Now it appears we are in an arms race with ourselves."[53]

As discussed in Chapter 10, the additional external

Table 11–1. *Military Spending in Key Countries, 2002, and Additional Funding to Reach Social Goals*

Country	Expenditure
	(billion dollars)
United States	343
U.S. allies	205
Russia	60
China	42
Iran, Iraq, and North Korea	12
Total excluding U.S.	319
Additional annual funding to reach global social goals	62

Source: See endnote 53.

funding needed to achieve universal primary education in
the 88 developing countries that require help is conserva-
tively estimated by the World Bank at $15 billion per year.
Funding for an adult literacy program based largely on
volunteers is estimated at $4 billion. Providing for the
most basic health care is estimated at $21 billion by the
World Health Organization. The additional funding
needed to provide reproductive health and family planning services to all women in developing countries is $10
billion a year.[54]

Closing the condom gap and providing the additional
9 billion condoms needed to control the spread of HIV in
the developing world and Eastern Europe requires $2.2
billion—$270 million for condoms and $1.9 billion for
AIDS prevention education and condom distribution.
The cost per year of extending school lunch programs to
the 44 poorest countries is $6 billion per year. An addi-
tional $4 billion per year would cover the cost of assis-
tance to preschool children and pregnant women in these
countries.[55]

In total, this comes to $62 billion. If the United States
offered to cover one third of this additional funding, the
other industrial countries would almost certainly be will-
ing to provide the remainder, and the worldwide effort to
eradicate hunger, illiteracy, disease, and poverty would be
under way.

This reordering of priorities means restructuring the
U.S. foreign policy budget. Stephan Richter, editor of *The
Globalist*, notes, "There is an emerging global standard
set by industrialized countries, which spend $1 on aid for
every $7 they spend on defense.... At the core, the ratio
between defense spending and foreign aid signals whether
a nation is guided more by charity and community—or
by defensiveness." And then the punch line: "If the United States were to follow this standard, it would have to

commit about $48 billion to foreign aid each year." This would be up from roughly $10 billion in 2002.[56]

The challenge is not just to alleviate poverty, but in doing so to build an economy that is compatible with the earth's natural systems—an eco-economy, an economy that can sustain progress. This means a fundamental restructuring of the energy economy and a substantial modification of the food economy. It also means raising the productivity of energy and shifting from fossil fuels to renewables. It means raising water productivity over the next half-century, much as we did land productivity over the last one.

This economic restructuring depends on tax restructuring, on getting the market to be ecologically honest. Hints of what might lie ahead came from Tokyo in early 2003 when Environment Minister Shunichi Suzuki announced that discussions were to begin on a carbon tax, scheduled for adoption in 2005. The benchmark of political leadership in all countries will be whether or not leaders succeed in restructuring the tax system.[57]

It is easy to spend hundreds of billions in response to terrorist threats, but the reality is that the resources needed to disrupt a modern economy are small, and a Department of Homeland Security, however heavily funded, provides only minimal protection from suicidal terrorists. The challenge is not just to provide a high-tech military response to terrorism, but to build a global society that is environmentally sustainable, socially equitable, and democratically based—one where there is hope for everyone. Such an effort would more effectively undermine the spread of terrorism than a doubling of military expenditures.

We can build an economy that does not destroy its natural support systems, a global community where the basic needs of all the earth's people are satisfied, and a world that will allow us to think of ourselves as civilized.

This is entirely doable. To paraphrase Franklin Roosevelt at another of those hinge points in history, let no one say it cannot be done.

The choice is ours—yours and mine. We can stay with business as usual and preside over a global bubble economy that keeps expanding until it bursts, leading to economic decline. Or we can adopt Plan B and be the generation that stabilizes population, eradicates poverty, and stabilizes climate. Historians will record the choice, but it is ours to make.

Notes

CHAPTER 1. A PLANET UNDER STRESS

1. Mathis Wackernagel et al., "Tracking the Ecological Overshoot of the Human Economy," *Proceedings of the National Academy of Sciences*, 9 July 2002, pp. 9266–71.

2. Steven Pearlstein, "How the Bubble Economy Burst," *Washington Post*, 13 November 2002; Thomas F. Cargill, Michael M. Hutchinson, and Takatoshi Ito, *The Political Economy of Japanese Monetary Policy* (Cambridge, MA: The MIT Press, 1997).

3. United Nations, *World Population Prospects: The 2002 Revision* (New York: February 2003); Joint United Nations Program on HIV/AIDS (UNAIDS), *Report on The Global HIV/AIDS Epidemic 2002* (Geneva, July 2002), p. 44.

4. G. Marland, T. A. Boden, and R. J. Andres, "Global, Regional, and National Fossil Fuel CO_2 Emissions," in *Trends: A Compendium of Data on Global Change* (Oak Ridge, TN: Carbon Dioxide Information Analysis Center, Oak Ridge National Laboratory, 2002).

5. U.N. Environment Programme, *Afghanistan: Post-Conflict Environmental Assessment* (Geneva: 2003), p. 60; Forest Watch Indonesia (FWI) and Global Forest Watch (GFW), *The State of the Forest: Indonesia* (Bogor, Indonesia, and Washington, DC: 2002), p. xii; Canadian cod fishery from Clyde H. Farnsworth, "Cod are Almost Gone and a Culture Could Follow," *New York Times*, 28 May 1994; melting glaciers in Andean region from Lonnie G. Thompson, "Disappearing

Glaciers Evidence of a Rapidly Changing Earth," American Association for the Advancement of Science annual meeting proceedings, San Francisco, CA, February 2001; United Nations, "China's Experience With Calamitous Sand-Dust Storms," in Yang Youlin, Victor Squires, and Lu Qi, eds., *Global Alarm Dust and Sandstorms from the World's Drylands* (Bangkok: Secretariat of the U.N. Convention to Combat Desertification, September 2002), pp. 215–53; U.S. aquifer depletion from U.S. Department of Agriculture (USDA), *Agricultural Resources and Environmental Indicators 2000* (Washington, DC: February 2000), chapter 2.1, p. 6.

6. United Nations, op. cit. note 3.

7. Erik Assadourian, "Economic Growth Inches Up," in Worldwatch Institute, *Vital Signs 2003* (New York: W.W. Norton & Company, 2003), p. 44–45.

8. USDA, *Production, Supply, and Distribution*, electronic database, updated 13 May 2003.

9. Water demand from Peter H. Gleick, *The World's Water 2000–2001* (Washington, DC: Island Press, 2000), p. 52.

10. C. D. Keeling, T. P. Whorf, and the Carbon Dioxide Research Group, "Atmospheric Carbon Dioxide Record from Mauna Loa," Scripps Institution of Oceanography, University of California, 13 June 2002, at <cdiac.esd.ornl.gov/ftp/ndp001/maunaloa.co2>.

11. USDA, *World Agricultural Supply and Demand Estimates* (Washington, DC: 12 May 2003), p. 6.

12. Population added each year from United Nations, op. cit. note 3.

13. World Food Summit from U.N. Food and Agriculture Organization (FAO), *The World Food Summit Goal and the Millennium Goals*, Rome, 28 May–1 June 2001, at <www.fao.org/docrep/meeting/003/Y0688e.htm>; FAO, *The State of Food Insecurity in the World 2002* (Rome: 2002), p. 4.

14. FAO, *State of Food Insecurity*, op. cit. note 13.

15. Grain production per person based on USDA, op. cit. note 8.

16. Goddard Institute for Space Studies, NASA Goddard Space Flight Center Earth Sciences Directorate, "Global Temperature Anomalies in .01 C," at <www.giss.nasa.gov/data/

update/gistemp/GLB.Ts.txt>, viewed 15 April 2003.

17. Effect of higher temperatures from John E. Sheehy, International Rice Research Institute, Philippines, e-mail to Janet Larsen, Earth Policy Institute, 2 October 2002.

18. Ibid.

19. U. Cubasch et al., "Projections of Future Climate Change," in Intergovernmental Panel on Climate Change, *Climate Change 2001: The Scientific Basis. Contribution of Working Group I to the Third Assessment Report of the Intergovernmental Panel on Climate Change* (New York: Cambridge University Press, 2001).

20. Grain from USDA, op. cit. note 8; World Bank, *China: Agenda for Water Sector Strategy for North China* (Washington, DC: April 2001), pp. vii, xi; water tables falling from Sandra Postel, *Last Oasis* (New York: W.W. Norton & Company, 1997), pp. 36–37.

21. United Nations, op. cit. note 3; Postel, op. cit. note 20.

22. USDA, op. cit. note 5; U.S. Bureau of the Census, *Projections of the Total Population of States: 1995–2025*, at <www.census.gov>, updated 2 August 2002.

23. David Seckler, David Molden, and Randolph Barker, "Water Scarcity in the Twenty-First Century," *Water Brief 1* (Colombo, Sri Lanka: International Water Management Institute, 1999); population from United Nations, op. cit. note 3.

24. Population from United Nations, op. cit. note 3; livestock population from FAO, *FAOSTAT Statistics Database*, at <apps.fao.org>, with livestock data updated 9 January 2003.

25. Chinese economic expansion from International Monetary Fund (IMF), *World Economic Outlook Database*, at <www.imf.org/external/pubs/ft/weo>, updated April 2003.

26. Livestock population from FAO, op. cit. note 24.

27. Howard W. French, "China's Growing Deserts Are Suffocating Korea," *New York Times*, 14 April 2002.

28. Wang Tao, "The Process and Its Control of Sandy Desertification in Northern China," seminar on desertification in China, Cold and Arid Regions Environmental & Engineering Institute, Chinese Academy of Sciences, Lanzhou, China, May 2002.

29. Ibid.

30. California population from U.S. Bureau of the Census, *1930 Fact Sheet*, at <www.census.gov>, revised 28 March 2002; U.S. Embassy, *Grapes of Wrath in Inner Mongolia* (Beijing: May 2001).

31. Grain trade from USDA, op. cit. note 8.

32. Ibid.; IMF, *International Financial Statistics Yearbook 2001* (Washington, DC: August 2001), p. 184.

33. Annual shortfall from USDA, op. cit. note 8; U.S. soybean embargo on Japan from David Rapp, "Farmer and Uncle Sam: An Old, Odd Couple," *Congressional Quarterly Weekly Report*, 4 April 1987, pp. 598–603; Chinese trade surplus with the United States from U.S. Census Bureau, "U.S. Trade Balance with China," at <www.census.gov/foreign-trade/balance/c5700.html>, updated 13 May 2003; Chinese economic growth from IMF, *World Economic Outlook* (Washington, DC: September 2002), p. 36.

34. People living on $1 a day from World Bank, *World Development Report 2000/2001* (New York: Oxford University Press, 2001), p. 3.

35. Lester R. Brown, *Who Will Feed China?* (New York: W.W. Norton & Company, 1995); Michael McElroy et al., *China Agriculture: Cultivated Land Area, Grain Projections, and Implications* (Washington, DC: National Intelligence Council, November 1997).

36. Lester R. Brown and Erik P. Eckholm, *By Bread Alone* (New York: Overseas Development Council, 1974), pp. 69–72.

37. "Wheat Board Pulls Out of Market," *Canadian Press*, 6 September 2002; "Drought Threat to Australian Summer Crops," *Financial Times*, 27 November 2002.

38. U.S. farm program from USDA, *Agricultural Resources and Environmental Indicators 1996–97* (Washington, DC: July 1997), pp. 255–327; carryover stocks from USDA, op. cit. note 8.

39. Population estimates from United Nations, op. cit. note 3.

40. China from U.S. Embassy, "Desert Mergers and Acquisitions," *Beijing Environment, Science, and Technology Update* (Beijing: 19 July 2002); Nigeria from "Combating Desertification and Deforestation," *Africa News Service*, 23 April 2002;

IRNA (Iranian News Agency), "Official Warns of Impending Desertification Catastrophe in Southeast Iran," *BBC International Reports*, 29 September 2002.

41. Christopher Ward, "Yemen's Water Crisis," based on a lecture to the British Yemeni Society in September 2000, July 2001; "Pakistan: Focus on Water Crisis," *U.N. Integrated Regional Information Networks*, 17 May 2002.

42. Figure of 1.3 billion from UNAIDS, op. cit. note 3.

CHAPTER 2. EMERGING WATER SHORTAGES

1. World Bank, *China: Agenda for Water Sector Strategy for North China* (Washington, DC: April 2001); Christopher Ward, *The Political Economy of Irrigation Water Pricing in Yemen* (Sana'a, Yemen: World Bank, November 1998); U.S. Department of Agriculture (USDA), *Agricultural Resources and Environmental Indicators 2000* (Washington, DC: February 2000).

2. Water use from Peter H. Gleick, *The World's Water 2000–2001* (Washington, DC: Island Press, 2000), p. 52.

3. Colorado, Nile, Indus, and Ganges rivers from Sandra Postel, *Pillar of Sand* (New York: W.W. Norton & Company, 1999), pp. 71–73, 261–62; Yellow River from World Bank, op. cit. note 1, p. viii; Aral Sea from U.N. Environment Programme (UNEP), *Afghanistan: Post-Conflict Environmental Assessment* (Geneva: 2003), p. 60.

4. For a chronology of water conflicts, see Peter H. Gleick, *The World's Water 2002–2003* (Washington, DC: Island Press, 2002), pp. 194–208.

5. Water-to-grain conversion from U.N. Food and Agriculture Organization (FAO), *Yield Response to Water* (Rome: 1979).

6. Jacob W. Kijne, *Unlocking the Water Potential of Agriculture* (Rome: FAO, 2003), p. 26.

7. Water use from Gleick, op. cit. note 2.

8. Grain production from USDA, *Production, Supply, and Distribution*, electronic database, updated 13 May 2003; Table 2–1 from United Nations, *World Population Prospects: The 2002 Revision* (New York: February 2003).

9. Michael Ma, "Northern Cities Sinking as Water Table Falls," *South China Morning Post*, 11 August 2001; share of China's grain harvest from the North China Plain based on Hong Yang and Alexander Zehnder, "China's Regional Water Scarcity and Implications for Grain Supply and Trade," *Environment and Planning A*, vol. 33 (2001), and on USDA, op. cit. note 8.

10. Ma, op. cit. note 9.

11. World Bank, op. cit. note 1, pp. vii, xi.

12. John Wade, Adam Branson, and Xiang Qing, *China Grain and Feed Annual Report 2002* (Beijing: USDA, 21 February 2002).

13. China's grain production from USDA, op. cit. note 8.

14. Wade, Branson, and Qing, op. cit. note 12; grain production from USDA, op. cit. note 8; 2003 rice production is Earth Policy Institute estimate.

15. Figure 2–1 from USDA, op. cit. note 8.

16. World Bank, op. cit. note 1, p. viii.

17. Tushaar Shah et al., *The Global Groundwater Situation: Overview of Opportunities and Challenges* (Colombo, Sri Lanka: International Water Management Institute, 2000); Seckler cited in David Seckler, David Molden, and Randolph Barker, "Water Scarcity in the Twenty-First Century," *Water Brief 1* (Colombo, Sri Lanka: International Water Management Institute, 1999), p. 2.

18. Shah et al., op. cit. note 16.

19. USDA, op. cit. note 1, Chapter 2.1, p. 6.

20. Irrigated area from U.N. Food and Agriculture Organization, *FAOSTAT Statistics Database*, at <apps.fao.org>, updated 9 January 2003; grain harvest from USDA, op. cit. note 8.

21. Population from United Nations, op. cit. note 8; fall in water table from "Pakistan: Focus on Water Crisis," *U.N. Integrated Regional Information Networks,* 17 May 2002.

22. "Pakistan: Focus on Water Crisis," op. cit. note 21; Garstang quoted in "Water Crisis Threatens Pakistan: Experts," *Agence France-Presse*, 26 January 2001.

23. Population from United Nations, op. cit. note 8; overpumping from Chenaran Agricultural Center, Ministry of Agriculture,

according to Hamid Taravati, publisher, Iran, e-mail to author, 25 June 2002.

24. Craig S. Smith, "Saudis Worry as They Waste Their Scarce Water," *New York Times*, 26 January 2003.

25. Ibid.

26. Population from United Nations, op. cit. note 8; Yemen's water situation from Christopher Ward, "Yemen's Water Crisis," based on a lecture to the British Yemeni Society in September 2000, July 2001; Ward, op. cit. note 1; Marcus Moench, "Groundwater: Potential and Constraints," in Ruth S. Meinzen-Dick and Mark W. Rosegrant, eds., *Overcoming Water Scarcity and Quality Constraints* (Washington, DC: International Food Policy Research Institute, October 2001).

27. Population from United Nations, op. cit. note 8; Ward, op. cit. note 26.

28. Deborah Camiel, "Israel, Palestinian Water Resources Down the Drain," *Reuters*, 12 July 2000.

29. Population from United Nations, op. cit. note 8; water table fall from Shah et al., op. cit. note 17; percentage of water extracted from underground from Karin Kemper, "Groundwater Management in Mexico: Legal and Institutional Issues," in Salman M.A. Salman, ed., *Groundwater: Legal and Policy Perspectives, Proceedings of a World Bank Seminar* (Washington, DC: World Bank, 1999), p. 117.

30. Postel, op. cit. note 3, pp. 261–62; Jim Carrier, "The Colorado: A River Drained Dry," *National Geographic*, June 1991, pp. 4–32.

31. Sandra Postel, *Last Oasis* (New York: W.W. Norton & Company, 1997), pp. 38–39.

32. UNEP, op. cit. note 3, pp. 50–59.

33. Ibid., p. 60.

34. Ibid.

35. Lester R. Brown and Brian Halweil, "China's Water Shortages Could Shake World Food Security," *World Watch*, July/August 1998, p. 11.

36. Postel, op. cit. note 3, pp. 71, 146.

37. Ibid., pp. 56–58.

38. Meinzen-Dick and Rosegrant, op. cit. note 26.

39. UNEP, "'Garden of Eden' in Southern Iraq Likely to Disappear Completely in Five Years Unless Urgent Action Taken," news release (Nairobi: 22 March 2003); Hassan Partow, *The Mesopotamian Marshlands: Demise of an Ecosyste*m, Early Warning and Assessment Technical Report (Nairobi: Division of Early Warning and Assessment, UNEP, 2001).

40. Water for steel production from Postel, op. cit. note 31, p. 137.

41. Noel Gollehon and William Quinby, "Irrigation in the American West: Area, Water and Economic Activity," *Water Resources Development*, vol. 16, no. 2 (2000), pp. 187–95.

42. John Krist, "Water Issues Will Dominate California's Agenda This Year," *Environmental News Service*, 21 February 2003.

43. Shah et al., op. cit. note 17.

44. Gershon Feder and Andrew Keck, *Increasing Competition for Land and Water Resources: A Global Perspective* (Washington, DC: World Bank, March 1995), pp. 28–29.

45. Population projections from United Nations, op. cit. note 8; China water demand from World Bank, op. cit. note 1; Brown and Halweil, op. cit. note 35.

46. Postel, op. cit. note 3, pp. 65–66.

47. Brown and Halweil, op. cit. note 35.

48. Population estimates from United Nations, op. cit. note 8.

49. Ibid.; grain imports from USDA, op. cit. note 8.

50. Population from United Nations, op. cit. note 8; grain imports from USDA, op. cit. note 8.

51. Grain surpluses from USDA, op. cit. note 8.

52. Population from United Nations, op. cit. note 8.

53. Andrew Keller, R. Sakthivadivel, and David Seckler, *Water Scarcity and the Role of Storage in Development*, Research Report 39 (Colombo, Sri Lanka: International Water Management Institute, 2000), p. 5.

54. "Pakistan: Focus on Water Crisis," op. cit. note 21.

55. USDA, op. cit. note 1, Chapter 2.1, p. 5.

56. Seckler, Molden, and Barker, op. cit. note 17.

57. Population from United Nations, op. cit. note 8.

CHAPTER 3. ERODING SOILS AND SHRINKING CROPLAND

1. Walter C. Lowdermilk, *Conquest of the Land Through 7,000 Years*, USDA Bulletin No. 99 (Washington, DC: U.S. Department of Agriculture (USDA), Natural Resources Conservation Service, 1939).

2. Ibid., p. 10.

3. U.N. Food and Agriculture Organization (FAO), *FAO/WFP Crop and Food Assessment Mission to Lesotho Special Report*, at <www.fao.org>, viewed 29 May 2002; Michael Grunwald, "Bizarre Weather Ravages Africans' Crops," *Washington Post*, 7 January 2003.

4. Number of hungry from FAO, *The State of Food Insecurity in the World 2002* (Rome: 2002).

5. One third is author's estimate.

6. Lester R. Brown, *Building a Sustainable Society* (New York: W.W. Norton & Company, 1981), p. 3.

7. Yang Youlin, Victor Squires, and Lu Qi, eds., *Global Alarm: Dust and Sandstorms from the World's Drylands* (Bangkok: Secretariat of the U.N. Convention to Combat Desertification, September 2002), pp. 15–28.

8. Asif Farrukh, *Pakistan Grain and Feed Annual Report 2002* (Islamabad, Pakistan: USDA Foreign Agricultural Service (FAS), March 2003).

9. Leon Lyles, "Possible Effects of Wind Erosion on Soil Productivity," *Journal of Soil and Water Conservation*, November/December 1975; USDA, Soil Conservation Service, "Preliminary 1982 National Resources Inventory," unpublished printout (Washington, DC: April 1984).

10. Lester R. Brown and Edward C. Wolf, *Soil Erosion: Quiet Crisis in the World Economy*, Worldwatch Paper 60 (Washington, DC: 1984), p. 20.

11. Author's calculation based on K. G. Tejwani, Land Use Con-

sultants International, New Delhi, private communication, 3 July 1983; Centre for Science and Environment, *The State of India's Environment 1982* (New Delhi: 1982).

12. Ministry of Population and Environment, *Implementation of the UN Convention to Combat Desertification*, National Report (Kathmandu, Nepal: April 2000).

13. Hong Yang and Xiubin Li, "Cultivated Land and Food Supply in China," *Land Use Policy*, vol. 17, no. 2 (2000), p. 5.

14. Richard E. Bilsborrow, "Migration, Population Change, and the Rural Environment," *Environmental Change and Security Project Report*, summer 2002, pp. 69–94.

15. Yang Youlin, "Dust Sandstorms: Inevitable Consequences of Desertification—A Case Study of Desertification Disasters in the Hexi Corridor, NW China," in Youlin, Squires, and Qi, op. cit. note 7, p. 228.

16. United Nations, *World Population Prospects: The 2002 Revision* (New York: February 2003).

17. "Algeria to Convert Large Cereal Land to Tree-Planting," *Reuters*, 8 December 2000.

18. Government of Nigeria, *Combating Desertification and Mitigating the Effects of Drought in Nigeria*, National Report on the Implementation of the United Nations Convention to Combat Desertification (Nigeria: November 1999), p. 6.

19. United Nations, op. cit. note 16; Republic of Kenya Ministry of Environment and Natural Resources, *National Action Programme: A Framework for Combating Desertification in Kenya in the Context of the United Nations Convention to Combat Desertification* (Nairobi: February 2002), pp. 12–14.

20. Iranian News Agency, "Official Warns of Impending Desertification Catastrophe in Southeast Iran," *BBC International Reports*, 29 September 2002.

21. U.N. Environment Programme, *Afghanistan: Post-Conflict Environmental Assessment* (Geneva: 2003), p. 52.

22. Lester R. Brown, "Dust Bowl Threatening China's Future," in Lester R. Brown, Janet Larsen, and Bernie Fischlowitz-Roberts, *The Earth Policy Reader* (New York: W.W. Norton & Company, 2002), pp. 200–04.

23. Economic reforms from Erik Eckholm, "Chinese Farmers See a New Desert Erode Their Way of Life," *New York Times*, 30 July 2000; livestock population from FAO, *FAOSTAT Statistics Database*, at <apps.fao.org>, livestock data updated 9 January 2003.

24. U.S. Embassy, *Grapes of Wrath in Inner Mongolia* (Beijing: May 2001).

25. U.S. Embassy, "Desert Mergers and Acquisitions," *Beijing Environment, Science, and Technology Update* (Beijing: 19 July 2002), p. 2.

26. Addition of cars from *Ward's World Motor Vehicle Data* (Southfield, MI: Ward's Communications, 2000); population from United Nations, op. cit. note 16.

27. Calculations for paved area by Janet Larsen, Earth Policy Institute, based on U.S. Department of Transportation, Federal Highway Administration (FHWA), *Highway Statistics 1999* (Washington, DC: 2001), on Mark Delucchi, "Motor Vehicle Infrastructure and Services Provided by the Public Sector," cited in Todd Litman, *Transportation Land Valuation* (Victoria, BC, Canada: Victoria Transport Policy Institute, November 2000), p. 4, on *Ward's World Motor Vehicle Data*, op. cit. note 26, on Jeffrey Kenworthy, Associate Professor in Sustainable Settlements, Institute for Sustainability and Technology Policy, Murdoch University, Australia, e-mail message, 7 February 2001, and on discussion with David Walterscheid, FHWA Real Estate Office, February 2001.

28. Ibid.

29. Ibid.; grain area from USDA, *Production, Supply, and Distribution*, electronic database, updated 13 May 2003.

30. Automobile production from *Ward's World Motor Vehicle Data*, op. cit. note 26; fleet size from Michael Renner, "Vehicle Production Inches Up," in Worldwatch Institute, *Vital Signs 2003* (New York: W.W. Norton & Company, 2003), pp. 56–57; population from United Nations, op. cit. note 16.

31. Larsen, op. cit. note 27; population from United Nations, op. cit. note 16.

32. Larsen, op. cit. note 27; economy from International Monetary Fund, *World Economic Outlook* (Washington, DC: October 1999).

33. Larsen, op. cit. note 27; rice area harvested and production in China from USDA, op. cit. note 29.

34. Population from United Nations, op. cit. note 16; *Ward's World Motor Vehicle Data*, op. cit. note 26.

35. USDA, op. cit. note 29.

36. Ibid.

37. Grain areas from ibid.; soybean prices from USDA, FAS, *Oilseeds: World Markets and Trade* (Washington, DC: May 2003).

38. Soybean production from USDA, op. cit. note 29.

39. Figure 3–1 from ibid.

40. World grain area from ibid.; Soviet Virgin Lands project from FAO, *The State of Food and Agriculture 1995* (Rome: 1995), p. 175.

41. Craig S. Smith, "Saudis Worry as They Waste Their Scarce Water," *New York Times*, 26 January 2003.

42. Grain area from USDA, op. cit. note 29; USDA, Farm Service Agency Online, "History of the CRP," in *The Conservation Reserve Program*, at <www.fsa.usda.gov/dafp/cepd/12logocv.htm>, viewed 29 April 2003.

43. Chinese conservation program from Xu Jintao, Eugenia Katsigris, and Thomas A. White, *Implementing the Natural Forest Protection Program: Lessons and Policy Recommendations* (Beijing: China Council for International Cooperation on Environment and Development, October 2002), p. 5; grain harvested area from USDA, op. cit. note 29.

44. FAO, *Yearbook of Fishery Statistics: Aquaculture Production 1998* (Rome: 2000); USDA, Economic Research Service-NASS, *Catfish Production* (Washington, DC: February 2003), p. 4; S. F. Li, "Aquaculture Research and Its Relation to Development in China," in World Fish Center, *Agricultural Development and the Opportunities for Aquatic Resources Research in China* (Penang, Malaysia: 2001), p. 26.

45. The *cerrado* from Randall D. Schnepf et al., *Agriculture in Brazil and Argentina* (Washington, DC: USDA, Economic Research Service, November 2001), p. 12; population from United Nations, op. cit. note 16.

46. USDA, op. cit. note 29; Schnepf et al., op. cit. note 45.

47. Soviet Virgin Lands project from FAO, op. cit. note 40.

48. Population from United Nations, op. cit. note 16; grain area harvested from USDA, op. cit. note 29.

49. Population from United Nations, op. cit. note 16; R. K. Pachauri and P. V. Sridharan, eds., *Looking Back to Think Ahead*, GREEN India 2047 Project (New Delhi: Tata Energy Research Institute, 1998), p. 89.

50. United Nations, op. cit. note 16.

51. Grainland per person from USDA, op. cit. note 29; population projection from United Nations, op. cit. note 16; rural exodus from Mary Jordan and Kevin Sullivan, "Trade Brings Riches, But Not to Mexico's Poor," *Washington Post*, 22 March 2003.

52. United Nations, op. cit. note 16.

53. USDA, op. cit. note 29; United Nations, op. cit. note 16.

54. USDA, op. cit. note 29.

55. Lowdermilk, op. cit. note 1, p. 24.

CHAPTER 4. RISING TEMPERATURES AND RISING SEAS

1. Cindy Schreuder and Sharman Stein, "Heat's Toll Worse Than Believed, Study Says at Least 200 More Died," *Chicago Tribune*, 21 September 1995; "Texas-Sized Heat Wave Easing Slightly," *CNN*, 3 August 1998; "India Heat Wave Toll Tops 1,000," *CNN*, 22 May 2002; "India's Heatwave Toll 1,200, No Respite in Sight," *Agence France-Presse*, 23 May 2002.

2. Paul Tolme, "Skiing: Trying to Keep Cool," *Newsweek*, 2 December 2002, p. 8.

3. Data from J. Hansen, NASA's Goddard Institute for Space Studies (GISS), "Global Temperature Anomalies in .01 C," at <www.giss.nasa.gov/data/update/gistemp>, viewed 28 April 2003; weather stations used from Reto A. Ruedy, GISS, e-mail to Janet Larsen, Earth Policy Institute, 14 May 2003.

4. Hansen, op. cit. note 3.

5. Ibid.

6. Figure 4–1 from ibid.; Intergovernmental Panel on Climate

Change (IPCC), *Climate Change 2001: The Scientific Basis. Contribution of Working Group I to the Third Assessment Report of the Intergovernmental Panel on Climate Change* (New York: Cambridge University Press, 2001); comparison to time since Ice Age from Warren Washington, cited in Stephen Phillips, "Ignoring Climate Will Land Us in Hot Water," *Times Higher Education Supplement,* 7 February 2003.

7. Ibid.; McCarthy from Jonathan Shaw, "The Great Global Experiment," *Harvard Magazine,* November–December 2002, p. 35.

8. For data on the world's grain production, see U.S. Department of Agriculture (USDA), *Production, Supply, and Distribution,* electronic database, Washington, DC, updated 13 May 2003.

9. Mohan K. Wali et al., "Assessing Terrestrial Ecosystem Sustainability," *Nature & Resources,* October–December 1999, pp. 21–33.

10. John E. Sheehy, International Rice Research Institute, Philippines, e-mail to Janet Larsen, Earth Policy Institute, 1 October 2002; Pedro Sanchez, "The Climate Change–Soil Fertility–Food Security Nexus," speech, *Sustainable Food Security for All By 2020,* Bonn, Germany, 4–6 September 2002.

11. K. S. Kavi Kumar and Jyoti Parikh, "Socio-Economic Impacts of Climate Change on Indian Agriculture," *International Review for Environmental Strategies,* vol. 2, no. 2 (2001), pp. 277–93.

12. S. A. Saseendran et al., "Effects of Climate Change on Rice Production in the Tropical Humid Climate of Kerala, India," *Climate Change,* vol. 44 (2000), pp. 495–514, cited in Kumar and Parikh, op. cit. note 11, p. 278.

13. Sheehy, op. cit. note 10; Allen's research noted in David Elstein et al., "Leading the Way in CO_2 Research," *Agricultural Research,* October 2002, pp. 12–13; see also L. H. Allen, Jr., et al., "Carbon Dioxide and Temperature Effects on Rice," in S. Peng et al., eds., *Climate Change and Rice* (Berlin: Springer-Verlag, 1995), pp. 258–77.

14. David B. Lobell and Gregory P. Asner, "Climate and Management Contributions to Recent Trends in U.S. Agricultural Yields," *Science,* 14 February 2003, p. 1032; Erik Stokstad,

"Study Shows Richer Harvests Owe Much to Climate," *Science*, 14 February 2003, p. 997; record yield from USDA, op. cit. note 8.

15. Global average temperature from Hansen, op. cit. note 3.

16. Grain harvest from USDA, op. cit. note 8; near-record temperatures from USDA, National Agricultural Statistics Service, "Weekly Weather and Crop Bulletin," at <jan.mannlib. cornell.edu/reports/nassr/field/weather>, and from NOAA/ USDA Joint Agricultural Weather Facility, "International Weather and Crop Summary," updated weekly at <www. usda.gov/agency/oce/waob/jawf/wwcb/inter.txt>; daily temperature reports for the United States and the world from "Weather," *Washington Post*, daily editions.

17. "Weather," op. cit. note 16.

18. Information on world soils from USDA, Natural Resources Conservation Service, at <www.nrcs.usda.gov/technical/ worldsoils>; grain production from USDA, op. cit. note 8.

19. Committee on Abrupt Climate Change, National Research Council, *Abrupt Climate Change: Inevitable Surprises* (Washington, DC: National Academy Press, 2002).

20. John Krist, "Water Issues Will Dominate California's Agenda This Year," *Environmental News Network*, 21 February 2003.

21. For more information, see NASA Goddard Space Flight Center, "Decline of World's Glaciers Expected to Have Global Impacts Over This Century," press release (Greenbelt, MD: 29 May 2002).

22. Crop harvests from USDA, op. cit. note 8.

23. IPCC, op. cit. note 6.

24. University of Colorado at Boulder, "Global Sea Levels Likely to Rise Higher in 21st Century than Previous Predictions," press release (Boulder, CO: 16 February 2002).

25. "Alaska Examines Impacts of Global Warming," *National Geographic News*, 21 December 2001; Myrna H. P. Hall and Daniel B. Fagre, "Modeled Climate-Induced Glacier Change in Glacier National Park, 1850–2100," *BioScience*, February 2003, pp. 131–40.

26. American Institute of Physics, "New Research Shows Moun-

tain Glaciers Shrinking Worldwide," press release (Boston: 30 May 2001).

27. Lonnie G. Thompson, "Disappearing Glaciers Evidence of a Rapidly Changing Earth," American Association for the Advancement of Science annual meeting proceedings, San Francisco, CA February 2001; Eric Hansen, "Hot Peaks," *On Earth*, fall 2002, p. 8.

28. Hansen, op. cit. note 27.

29. Thompson, op. cit. note 27.

30. Kargel quoted in Hansen, op. cit. note 27.

31. David Perlman, "Global Warming Evidence Mounts: Flurry of Reports Show a Withering Ice Cap," *San Francisco Chronicle*, 23 December 2002; M. C. Serreze et al., "A Record Minimum Arctic Sea Ice Extent and Area in 2002," *Geophysical Research Letters*, vol. 30, no. 3, p. 1110.

32. D. A. Rothrock et al., "Thinning of the Arctic Sea-Ice Cover," *Geophysical Research Letters*, 1 December 1999, pp. 3469–72; Lars H. Smedsrud and Tore Furevik, "Towards an Ice-Free Arctic?" *Cicerone*, no. 2, 2000.

33. Richard A. Kerr, "Will the Arctic Ocean Lose All Its Ice?" *Science*, 3 December 1999, p. 1828.

34. Perlman, op. cit. note 31.

35. W. Krabill et al., "Greenland Ice Sheet: High Elevation Balance and Peripheral Thinning," *Science*, 21 July 2000, p. 428.

36. National Science Foundation, Office of Polar Programs, "Ice Sheets," at <www.nsf.gov/od/opp/support/icesheet.htm>, updated March 2001.

37. National Snow and Ice Data Center, "Antarctic Ice Shelf Collapses," at <nsidc.org/iceshelves/larsenb2002>, 19 March 2002; "Breakaway Bergs Disrupt Antarctic Ecosystem,"*Environment News Service*, 9 May 2002; "Giant Antarctic Ice Shelves Shatter and Break Away," *Environment News Service*, 19 March 2002.

38. National Snow and Ice Data Center, op. cit. note 37; "Breakaway Bergs Disrupt Antarctic Ecosystem," op. cit. note 37; "Giant Antarctic Ice Shelves Shatter and Break Away," op. cit. note 37.

39. National Snow and Ice Data Center, op. cit. note 37; "Break-away Bergs Disrupt Antarctic Ecosystem," op. cit. note 37; "Giant Antarctic Ice Shelves Shatter and Break Away," op. cit. note 37; Vaughan quoted in Andrew Revkin, "Large Ice Shelf in Antarctica Disintegrates at Great Speed," *New York Times*, 20 March 2002.

40. Michael Byrnes, "New Antarctic Iceberg Split No Threat," *Reuters*, 20 May 2002; Young quoted in "Giant Antarctic Ice Shelves Shatter and Break Away," op. cit. note 37.

41. Scambos quoted in Revkin, op. cit. note 39.

42. World Bank, *World Development Report 1999/2000* (New York: Oxford University Press, 2000), p. 100; population from United Nations, *World Population Prospects: The 2002 Revision* (New York: February 2003); Shanghai and China as a whole from Stuart R. Gaffin, *High Water Blues: Impacts of Sea Level Rise on Selected Coasts and Islands* (Washington, DC: Environmental Defense Fund, 1997), p. 27.

43. Boesch cited in Bette Hileman, "Consequences of Climate Change," *Chemical & Engineering News*, 27 March 2000, pp. 18–19; James E. Neumann et al., *Sea-level Rise & Global Climate Change: A Review of Impacts to U.S. Coasts* (Arlington, VA: Pew Center on Global Climate Change, 2000); Gaffin, op. cit. note 42.

44. Janet N. Abramovitz, "Averting Unnatural Disasters," in Lester R. Brown et al., *State of the World 2001* (New York: W.W. Norton & Company, 2001), pp. 123–42.

45. Storm death toll from National Climatic Data Center, National Oceanic & Atmospheric Administration, U.S. Department of Commerce, "Mitch: The Deadliest Atlantic Hurricane Since 1780," <www.ncdc.noaa.gov/oa/reports/mitch/mitch.html>, updated 25 January 1999; Flores quoted in Arturo Chavez et al., "After the Hurricane: Forest Sector Reconstruction in Honduras," *Forest Products Journal*, November/December 2001, pp. 18–24; gross domestic product from International Monetary Fund (IMF), *World Economic Outlook Database*, at <www.imf.org/external/pubs/ft/weo>, updated April 2003.

46. Munich Re, *Topics Annual Review: Natural Catastrophes 2001* (Munich, Germany: 2002), pp. 16–17.

47. Ibid.; value of China's wheat and rice harvests from USDA, op. cit. note 8, using prices from IMF, *International Financial Statistics* (Washington, DC: various years).

48. Munich Re, op. cit. note 46.

49. Andrew Dlugolecki, "Climate Change and the Financial Services Industry," speech delivered at the opening of the UNEP Financial Services Roundtable, Frankfurt, Germany, 16 November 2000; "Climate Change Could Bankrupt Us by 2065," *Environment News Service*, 24 November 2000.

50. "Disaster and Its Shadow," *The Economist*, 14 September 2002, p. 71.

51. Bjorn Larsen, *World Fossil Fuel Subsidies and Global Carbon Emissions in a Model with Interfuel Substitution*, Policy Research Working Paper 1256 (Washington, DC: World Bank, February 1994), p. 7; population from United Nations, op. cit. note 42.

52. Contributions from the Center for Responsive Politics, "Oil and Gas: Long Term Contribution Trends," at <www.open secrets.org/industries/indus.asp?Ind=E01>, updated 5 March 2003; Committee on Ways and Means, *Incentives for Domestic Oil and Gas Production and Status of the Industry*, Hearing Before the Subcommittee on Oversight of the Committee on Ways and Means, House of Representatives (Washington, DC: U.S. Government Printing Office, February 1999), p. 16.

53. Kym Anderson and Warwick J. McKibbin, "Reducing Coal Subsidies and Trade Barriers: Their Contribution to Greenhouse Gas Abatement," *Environment and Development Economics*, October 2000, pp. 457–81.

54. Military expenditures from Graham E. Fuller and Ian O. Lesser, "Persian Gulf Myths," *Foreign Affairs*, May–June 1997, pp. 42–53; value of Persian Gulf oil imports from U.S. Department of Energy, Energy Information Administration, *Annual Energy Review* (Washington, DC: 2001), p. 165.

55. Mark M. Glickman, *Beyond Gas Taxes: Linking Driving Fees to Externalities* (Oakland, CA: Redefining Progress, March 2001), p.1; number of taxpayers from Internal Revenue Service, "Number of Returns Filed, by Type of Return and State, Fiscal Year 2000," in *2000 IRS Data Book* (Washington, DC: September 2001).

56. For an overview of pricing parking, see "Parking Pricing: Direct Charges for Using Parking Facilities," *Transportation Demand Management*, online encyclopedia, Victoria Transport Policy Institute, Victoria, BC, at <www.vtpi.org/tdm/tdm26.htm>, updated 30 January 2003.

CHAPTER 5. OUR SOCIALLY DIVIDED WORLD

1. World Health Organization (WHO) cited in Gary Gardner and Brian Halweil, *Underfed and Overfed: The Global Epidemic of Malnutrition*, Worldwatch Paper 150 (Washington, DC: Worldwatch Institute, 2000), p. 7.

2. Hilaire A. Mputu, *Literacy and Non-Formal Education in the E-9 Countries* (Paris: UNESCO, 2001), p. 5.

3. WHO and UNICEF, *Global Water Supply and Sanitation Assessment 2000 Report* (New York: 2000), pp. v, 2; Gardner and Halweil, op. cit. note 1.

4. Population growth rates from Population Reference Bureau (PRB), *2002 World Population Data Sheet*, wall chart (Washington, DC: August 2002).

5. United Nations, *World Population Prospects: The 2002 Revision* (New York: February 2003); Joint United Nations Programme on HIV/AIDS (UNAIDS), *Report on the Global HIV/AIDS Epidemic 2002* (Geneva: July 2002), pp. 44–46.

6. HIV prevalence from UNAIDS, op. cit. note 5, pp. 189–202; Swaziland update by the Ministry of Health cited in "Swaziland: The World's Worst HIV Infection Rate," *U.N. Integrated Regional Information Networks*, 31 December 2002; life expectancies from United Nations, op. cit. note 5, pp. 10–14.

7. Latest regional and world statistics in UNAIDS, *AIDS Epidemic Update* (Geneva: December 2002), p. 6; total deaths and historical estimates calculated using UNAIDS statistics in Worldwatch Institute, *Signposts 2002*, CD-Rom (Washington, DC: 2002); anti-retroviral treatment from UNAIDS, op. cit. note 5, pp. 22–23.

8. UNAIDS, op. cit. note 5.

9. More deaths from AIDS than wars from Lawrence K. Altman, "U.N. Forecasts Big Increase in AIDS Death Toll," *New York Times*, 3 July 2002.

10. AIDS and food security in UNAIDS, op. cit. note 5, pp. 49–50; U.N. Food and Agriculture Organization (FAO), *The Impact of HIV/AIDS on Food Security*, 27th Session of the Committee on World Food Security, Rome, 28 May–1 June 2001.

11. UNAIDS, op. cit. note 5, pp. 49–50; FAO, op. cit. note 10.

12. "Strategic Caring: Firms Strategize About AIDS," *The Economist*, 5 October 2002; UNAIDS, op. cit. note 5.

13. UNAIDS, op. cit. note 5.

14. UNAIDS, *Report on the Global HIV/AIDS Epidemic* (Geneva: June 2000), p. 29; Prega Govender, "Shock AIDS Test Result at Varsity," (Johannesburg) *Sunday Times*, 25 April 1999; "South Africa: University Finds 25 Percent of Students Infected," *Kaiser Daily HIV/AIDS Report*, 27 April 1999.

15. UNAIDS, op. cit. note 14.

16. Mark Dennis, Julia Ross, and Shelley Smith, eds., *Children on the Brink 2002: A Joint Report on Orphan Estimates and Program Strategies* (Washington, DC: UNAIDS, UNICEF, and U.S. Agency for International Development, July 2002), p. 6; Michael Grunwald, "Sowing Harvests of Hunger in Africa," *Washington Post*, 17 November 2002.

17. Stephen Lewis, press briefing (New York: 8 January 2003); Edith M. Lederer, "Lack of Funding for HIV/AIDS is Mass Murder by Complacency, Says U.N. Envoy," *Associated Press*, 9 January 2003.

18. Alex de Waal, "What AIDS Means in a Famine," *New York Times*, 19 November 2002.

19. FAO, *The State of Food Insecurity in the World 2002* (Rome: 2002).

20. Ibid.; population from United Nations, op. cit. note 5.

21. United Nations, op. cit. note 5.

22. FAO, op. cit. note 19.

23. U.N. report cited in Gary Gardner and Brian Halweil, "Nourishing the Underfed and Overfed," in Lester R. Brown et al., *State of the World 2000* (New York: W.W. Norton & Company, 2000), pp. 70–73.

24. Ibid.

25. Ibid.

26. WHO and UNICEF, op. cit. note 3; Peter H. Gleick, *Dirty Water: Estimated Deaths from Water-Related Diseases 2000–2020* (Oakland, CA: Pacific Institute, August 2002); PRB, op. cit. note 4.

27. WHO and UNICEF, op. cit. note 3.

28. Hunger as a risk factor for disease in WHO, *World Health Report 2002* (Geneva: 2002), and in Majid Ezzati et al., "Selected Major Risk Factors and Global and Regional Burden of Disease," *The Lancet*, 30 October 2002, pp. 1–14.

29. WHO/UNICEF, *The Africa Malaria Report 2003* (New York: 2003); Anne Platt McGinn, "Malaria's Lethal Grip Tightens," in Worldwatch Institute, *Vital Signs 2001* (New York: W.W. Norton & Company, 2001), pp. 134–35.

30. Mputu, op. cit. note 2, pp. 5–13.

31. Ibid.

32. Ibid.

33. Ibid.

34. Gene B. Sperling, "Toward Universal Education," *Foreign Affairs*, September/October 2001, pp. 7–13.

35. Ibid.; Minister of Education from "Start at the Beginning: The First Step to Ensuring Brazil's Future Prosperity is to Improve its Schools," *The Economist*, 22 February 2003, pp. 13–14.

36. Schools as a vehicle to administer vaccines, medicines, vitamins, and meals in Sperling, op. cit. note 34.

Chapter 6. Plan A: Business as Usual

1. Sandra Postel, *Pillar of Sand* (New York: W.W. Norton & Company, 1999), p. 80; population from United Nations, *World Population Prospects: The 2002 Revision* (New York: February 2003).

2. Christopher Ward, *The Political Economy of Irrigation Water Pricing in Yemen* (Sana'a, Yemen: World Bank, November 1998); David Seckler, David Molden, and Randolph Barker, "Water Scarcity in the Twenty-First Century," *Water Brief 1*

(Colombo, Sri Lanka: International Water Management Institute, 1999).

3. Grain from U.S. Department of Agriculture (USDA), *Production, Supply, and Distribution*, electronic database, updated 13 May 2003; cropland conversion from USDA, Farm Service Agency Online, "History of the CRP," *The Conservation Reserve Program*, at <www.fsa.usda.gov/dafp/cepd/12logo cv.htm>; Xu Jintao, Eugenia Katsigris, and Thomas A. White, *Implementing the Natural Forest Protection Program: Lessons and Policy Recommendations* (Beijing: China Council for International Cooperation on Environment and Development, October 2002).

4. U.N. Food and Agriculture Organization (FAO), *The State of World Fisheries and Aquaculture 2002* (Rome: 2002), p. 23; Ransom A. Myers and Boris Worm, "Rapid Worldwide Depletion of Predatory Fish Communities," *Nature*, 15 May 2003.

5. FAO, *FAOSTAT Statistics Database*, at <apps.fao.org>, livestock data updated 9 January 2003; China flock reduction from U.S. Embassy, *Grapes of Wrath in Inner Mongolia* (Beijing: May 2001).

6. G. Marland, T. A. Boden, and R. J. Andres, "Global, Regional, and National Fossil Fuel CO_2 Emissions," in *Trends: A Compendium of Data on Global Change* (Oak Ridge, TN: Carbon Dioxide Information Analysis Center, Oak Ridge National Laboratory, U.S. Department of Energy, 2002); Jonathan Shaw, "The Great Global Experiment," *Harvard Magazine*, November-December 2002, pp. 34–43, 87–90.

7. Mathis Wackernagel et al., "Tracking the Ecological Overshoot of Human Economy," *Proceedings of the National Academy of Sciences*, 9 July 2002, p. 9266–71.

8. Intergovernmental Panel on Climate Change (IPCC), *Climate Change 2001: The Scientific Basis. Contribution of Working Group I to the Third Assessment Report of the Intergovernmental Panel on Climate Change* (New York: Cambridge University Press, 2001); Molly Sheehan, "Carbon Emissions and Temperature Climb," *Vital Signs 2003* (New York: W.W. Norton & Company, 2003), p. 41.

9. University of Colorado at Boulder, "Global Sea Levels Likely

to Rise Higher in 21st Century than Previous Predictions," press release (Boulder, CO: 16 February 2002).

10. U.S. Geological Survey cited in American Institute of Physics, "New Research Shows Mountain Glaciers Shrinking Worldwide," press release (Boston: 30 May 2001); Peruvian Andes from Lonnie G. Thompson, "Disappearing Glaciers Evidence of a Rapidly Changing Earth," American Association for the Advancement of Science annual meeting proceedings, San Francisco, CA, February 2001.

11. Munich Re, *Topics Annual Review: National Catastrophes 2001* (Munich, Germany: 2002), pp. 16–17.

12. Great Plains from USDA, *Agricultural Resources and Environmental Indicators 2000* (Washington, DC: February 2000), Chapter 2.1, p. 6; North China Plain from Michael Ma, "Northern Cities Sinking as Water Table Falls," *South China Morning Post*, 11 August 2001.

13. Yellow River from Lester R. Brown and Brian Halweil, "China's Water Shortages Could Shake World Food Security," *World Watch*, July/August 1998, p. 11.

14. FAO, *State of the World's Forests 2001* (Rome: 2001), pp. 58–59.

15. Forest Watch Indonesia and Global Forest Watch, *The State of the Forest: Indonesia* (Bogor, Indonesia, and Washington, DC: 2002), pp. xi, 3; Iran from "The Curse of Westoxification," *The Economist*, 18 January 2003, p. 9.

16. Janet Larsen, "Illegal Logging Threatens Ecological and Economic Stability," in Lester R. Brown, Janet Larsen, and Bernie Fischlowitz-Roberts, *The Earth Policy Reader* (New York: W.W. Norton & Company, 2002), p. 228.

17. U.S. Embassy, op. cit. note 5.

18. Species Survival Commission (SSC), Craig Hilton-Taylor, compiler, *2000 IUCN Red List of Threatened Species* (Gland, Switzerland, and Cambridge, U.K.: World Conservation Union–IUCN, 2000).

19. Overpumping in India from Seckler, Molden, and Barker, op. cit. note 2.

20. USDA, *Production, Supply, and Distribution*, op. cit. note 3; Richard W. Carroll, "Bushmeat Consumption," statement for

the Subcommittee on Fisheries Conservation, Wildlife and Oceans Committee on House Resources, 11 July 2002.

21. USDA, *Production, Supply, and Distribution,* op. cit. note 3.

22. Ibid.

23. Timothy Egan, "Dry High Plains Are Blowing Away, Again," *New York Times*, 3 May 2002.

24. U.S. Environmental Protection Agency (EPA), "Love Canal," Superfund Redevelopment Initiative, at <www.epa.gov/r02 earth/superfund/npl/0201290c.pdf>, viewed 29 April 2003.

25. Ibid.

26. EPA, "Times Beach One-Page Summary," Superfund Redevelopment Initiative, at <www.epa.gov/oerrpage/superfund/ programs/recycle/success/1-pagers/timesbch.htm>, viewed 29 April 2003.

27. Aleg Cherp et al., *The Human Consequences of the Chernobyl Nuclear Accident* (New York: U.N. Development Programme and UNICEF, 25 January 2002).

28. "Pakistan: Focus on Water Crisis," *U.N. Integrated Regional Information Networks (IRIN)*, 17 May 2002.

29. Wang Tao, "The Process and Its Control of Sandy Desertification in Northern China," seminar on desertification in China, Cold and Arid Regions Environmental & Engineering Institute, Chinese Academy of Sciences, Lanzhou, China, May 2002; Asian Development Bank, *Technical Assistance to the People's Republic of China For Optimizing Initiatives to Combat Desertification in Gansu Province* (Manila: Philippines: June 2001).

30. Iranian News Agency, "Official Warns of Impending Desertification Catastrophe in Southeast Iran," *BBC International Reports*, 29 September 2002.

31. IPCC, op. cit. note 8; Bangladesh inundation from World Bank, *World Development Report 1999/2000* (New York: Oxford University Press, September 1999); number of potential migrants is author's calculation based on the distribution of population in Bangladesh.

32. Don Hinrichsen, "The Oceans Are Coming Ashore," *World Watch*, November/December 2000, p. 32.

33. Mexican migration from "Human Approach to Border," *Denver Post*, 24 April 2003; African migration from Ana M. Alaya, "Nine-mile Passage in Flimsy Boats is Full of Risks, Hopes," *San Diego Union Tribune*, 3 October 2002.

34. James Gasana, "Remember Rwanda?" *World Watch*, September/October 2002, pp. 24–32.

35. Ibid.

36. Population from United Nations, op. cit. note 1; demand for firewood from Gasana, op. cit. note 34.

37. Gasana, op. cit. note 34.

38. Ibid.

39. Population from United Nations, op. cit. note 1; conflict from "Nigeria: Focus on Central Region Tiv, Jukun Clashes," *U.N. IRIN*, 24 October 2001, and from "Nigeria; Focus on Indigene-Settler Conflicts," *U.N. IRIN*, 10 January 2002; loss of cropland from Government of Nigeria, *Combating Desertification and Mitigating the Effects of Drought in Nigeria*, National Report on the Implementation of the United Nations Convention to Combat Desertification (Nigeria: November 1999), p. 6.

40. United Nations, op. cit. note 1.

41. Ibid.; Gasana, op. cit. note 34.

42. United Nations, op. cit. note 1.

43. Population from ibid.; income per person from International Monetary Fund, *World Economic Outlook Database*, Washington, DC, updated April 2003.

44. United Nations, op. cit. note 1.

45. Ibid.; O'Hara quoted in Michael Wines, "Grand Soviet Scheme for Sharing Water in Central Asia is Foundering," *New York Times*, 9 December 2002.

46. Chinese migration to Russia from Benjamin Fulford, "When Worlds Collide," *Forbes Global*, 17 February 2003.

47. Seth Dunn, "The Hydrogen Experiment," *World Watch*, November/December 2000, pp. 14–25.

CHAPTER 7. RAISING WATER PRODUCTIVITY

1. Erik Assadourian, "Economic Growth Inches Up," in World-watch Institute, *Vital Signs 2003* (New York: W.W. Norton & Company, 2003), pp. 44–45.

2. Population from United Nations, *World Population Prospects: The 2002 Revision* (New York: February 2003).

3. Land productivity from U.S. Department of Agriculture (USDA), *Production, Supply, and Distribution*, electronic database, updated 13 May 2003.

4. Barbara Schereiner and Dhesigen Naidoo, Department of Water Affairs and Forestry of South Africa, *Water as an Instrument for Social Development in South Africa* (Pretoria, South Africa), 10 December 1999, at <www.dwaf.gov.za/communications/departmentalspeeches/2002/waterasan instrumentfor social dev.doc>.

5. Population from United Nations, op. cit. note 2; Mohamed Ait Kadi, "Irrigation Water Pricing Policy in Morocco's Large Scale Irrigation Projects," paper prepared for the Ajadir Conference on Irrigation Policies: Micro and Macro Economic Considerations, Ajadir, Morocco, 15–17 June 2002, pp. 6, 9; Mark W. Rosegrant, Ximing Cai, and Sarah A. Cline, *World Water and Food to 2025* (Washington, DC: International Food Policy Research Institute, 2002), p. 141.

6. Water shortage in Chinese cities from R. Maria Saleth and Arial Dinar, *Water Challenge and Institutional Response: A Cross-Country Perspective* (Washington, DC: World Bank, 1999), p. 26; Liang Chao, "Officials: Water Price to Increase," *China Daily*, 21 February 2001.

7. Tom Gardner-Outlaw and Robert Engelman, *Sustaining Water, Easing Scarcity: A Second Update* (Washington, DC: Population Action International, 1997).

8. Saleth and Dinar, op. cit. note 6, p. 23.

9. John Lancaster, "Incomplete Reforms Hobble Economic Growth in India," *Washington Post*, 6 November 2002.

10. Ibid.

11. Noel Gollehon and William Quinby, "Irrigation in the American West: Area, Water and Economic Activity," *Water Resources Development*, vol. 16, no.2 (2000), pp. 187–95;

India and Pakistan in K. William Easter and Robert R. Hearne, *Decentralizing Water Resource Management: Economic Incentives, Accountability, and Assurance*, Policy Research Working Paper 129 (Washington, DC: World Bank, November 1993), p. 13.

12. Irrigated area from U.N. Food and Agriculture Organization (FAO), *FAOSTAT Statistics Database*, at <apps.fao.org>, updated 9 January 2003; grain harvest from USDA, op. cit. note 3.

13. Saleth and Dinar, op. cit. note 6, pp. 25, 27.

14. Water losses detailed in Peter H. Gleick, *The World's Water 2002–2003* (Washington, DC: Island Press, 2002), pp. 305–07.

15. Sandra Postel, *Last Oasis* (New York: W.W. Norton & Company, 1997), p. 102.

16. FAO, *Crops and Drops* (Rome: 2002), p. 17; Alain Vidal, Aline Comeau, and Hervé Plusquellec, *Case Studies on Water Conservation in the Mediterranean Region* (Rome: FAO, 2001), p. vii; Israel from World Commission on Dams, *Dams and Development* (London: Earthscan, 2000), p. 141.

17. Jordan from World Commission on Dams, op. cit. note 16, p. 141; Tunisia from World Bank and Swiss Agency for Development and Cooperation (SDC), Summary Report, *Middle East and North Africa Regional Water Initiative Workshop on Sustainable Groundwater Management*, Sana'a, Yemen, 25–28 June 2000, p. 11.

18. Table 7–1 adapted from Sandra Postel et al., "Drip Irrigation for Small Farmers: A New Initiative to Alleviate Hunger and Poverty," *Water International*, March 2001, pp. 3–13.

19. FAO, op. cit. note 16, p. 18.

20. Postel et al., op. cit. note 18.

21. Ibid.

22. Vidal, Comeau, and Plusquellec, op. cit. note 16, p. 15.

23. D. Molden et al., *Increasing Productivity of Water: A Requirement for Food and Environmental Security*, Working Paper 1 (Colombo, Sri Lanka: Dialogue on Water, Food and Environment, 2001), p. 4.

24. Ibid., p. 6.

25. Water efficiency of wheat and rice from Postel, op. cit. note 15, p. 71; Beijing from "Rice Cropped for Water," *China Daily*, 9 January 2002; Egypt from USDA, "Egyptian Rice Acreage Continues to Exceed Government-Designated Limitations," *Foreign Countries' Policies and Programs*, at <www.fas.usda.gov/grain/circular/1999/99-02/dtricks.htm>, posted February 1999.

26. John Wade, Adam Branson, and Xiang Qing, *China Grain and Feed Annual Report 2002* (Beijing: USDA, March 2002).

27. For more information on water users' associations, see Saleth and Dinar, op. cit. note 6.

28. Saleth and Dinar, op. cit. note 6, p. 6.

29. World Bank and SDC, op. cit. note 17, p. 19.

30. Gardner-Outlaw and Engelman, op. cit. note 7, pp. 14–18.

31. Fen Montaigne, "Water Pressure," *National Geographic*, September 2002, pp. 2–34.

32. Ibid.

33. Ibid.

34. Sunita Narain, "The Flush Toilet is Ecologically Mindless," *Down to Earth*, 28 February 2002, pp. 28–32.

35. Ibid.

36. Ibid.

37. Ibid.

38. U.S. Environmental Protection Agency, "Water Efficiency Technology Factsheet—Composting Toilets," information sheet (Washington, DC: September 1999).

39. Ibid.

40. Noel Gollehon, William Quinby, and Marcel Aillery, "Water Use and Pricing in Agriculture," in USDA, *Agricultural Resources and Environmental Indicators 2003* (Washington, DC: February 2003), Chapter 2.1, p. 2.

41. Postel, op. cit. note 15, pp. 136–45.

42. Asit Biswas, "Water Crisis: Current Perceptions and Future Realities," in *Groundwater: Legal and Policy Perspectives, Proceedings of a World Bank Seminar* (Washington, DC: Salman, 1999), p. 1–11.

43. Calculation based on Peter Wolff and Thomas M. Stein, "Efficient and Economic Use of Water in Agriculture—Possibilities and Limits," *National Resources and Development*, vol. 49/50 (1999), pp. 151–59.

44. Erik Eckholm, "Chinese Will Move Water to Quench Thirst of Cities," *New York Times*, 27 August 2002; "Per Head Water Resources on Decline Along Yangtze," *Xinhua News Agency*, 31 December 2002.

CHAPTER 8. RAISING LAND PRODUCTIVITY

1. U.S. Department of Agriculture (USDA), *Production, Supply, and Distribution*, electronic database, updated 13 May 2003.

2. Animal protein from U.N. Food and Agriculture Organization (FAO), *FAOSTAT Statistics Database*, at <apps.fao.org>, livestock data updated 9 January 2003; population from United Nations, *World Population Prospects: The 2002 Revision* (New York: February 2003); world fish catch from FAO, *Yearbook of Fishery Statistics: Capture Production and Aquaculture Production* (Rome: various years).

3. United Nations, op. cit. note 2.

4. Land productivity from USDA, op. cit. note 1.

5. Thomas R. Sinclair, "Limits to Crop Yield," paper presented at the 1999 National Academy Colloquium, *Plants and Populations: Is There Time?* Irvine, CA, 5–6 December 1998.

6. FAO, *FAOSTAT,* op. cit. note 2, irrigation data updated 7 August 2002.

7. Ibid., fertilizer use data updated 1 April 2003.

8. USDA, op. cit. note 1; United Nations, op cit. note 2.

9. Yields from USDA, op. cit. note 1; percent photosynthate to seed from J. T. Evans, *Crop Evolution Adaptation and Yield* (Cambridge: Cambridge University Press, 1993), pp. 242–44.

10. Table 8–1 from USDA, op. cit. note 1.

11. Pedro Sanchez, "The Climate Change–Soil Fertility–Food Security Nexus," summary note (Bonn: International Food Policy Research Institute, 4 September 2001).

12. USDA, op. cit. note 1.

13. John Wade, Adam Branson, and Xiang Qing, *China Grain and Feed Annual Report 2002* (Beijing: USDA, March 2002).

14. Double-cropping yields from USDA, *India Grain and Feed Annual Report 2003* (New Delhi: February 2003); population from United Nations, op. cit. note 2.

15. Grain harvested area from USDA, op. cit. note 1; USDA, *Japan Grain and Feed Annual Report 2003* (Tokyo: March 2003).

16. USDA, op. cit. note 1.

17. Richard Magleby, "Soil Management and Conservation," in USDA, *Agricultural Resources and Environmental Indicators 2003* (Washington, DC: February 2003), Chapter 4.2, p. 14.

18. USDA, op. cit. note 1; Randall D. Schnepf et al., *Agriculture in Brazil and Argentina* (Washington, DC: USDA Economic Research Service (ERS), November 2001), pp. 8–10.

19. USDA, op. cit. note 1.

20. FAO, *FAOSTAT,* op. cit. note 2, updated 9 January 2003.

21. Feed-to-poultry conversion ratio derived from data in Robert V. Bishop et al., *The World Poultry Market—Government Intervention and Multilateral Policy Reform* (Washington, DC: USDA, 1990); conversion ratio of grain to beef based on Allen Baker, Feed Situation and Outlook staff, ERS, USDA, discussion with author, 27 April 1992, on Linda Bailey, Livestock and Poultry Situation staff, ERS, USDA, discussion with author, 27 April 1992, and on data taken from various issues of *Feedstuffs*; pork data from Leland Southard, Livestock and Poultry Situation and Outlook staff, ERS, USDA, discussion with author, 27 April 1992.

22. Table 8–2 compiled from FAO, *1948–1985 World Crop and Livestock Statistics* (Rome: 1987), from FAO, *FAOSTAT,* op. cit. note 2, updated 9 January 2003, from FAO, *Yearbook of Fishery Statistics*, op. cit. note 2, and from FAO, *The State of World Fisheries and Aquaculture 2002* (Rome: 2002); Figure 8–1 and concentration of pork production in China from FAO, *FAOSTAT,* op. cit. note 2, livestock data updated 9 January 2003.

23. FAO, *Yearbook of Fishery Statistics*, op. cit. note 2.

24. China's carp polyculture from Rosamond L. Naylor et al., "Effect of Aquaculture on World Fish Supplies," *Nature*, 29 June 2000, p. 1022; polyculture in India from W. C. Nandee-

sha et al., "Breeding of Carp with Oviprim," in Indian Branch, Asian Fisheries Society, India, Special Publication No. 4 (Mangalore, India: 1990), p. 1.

25. Krishen Rana, "Changing Scenarios in Aquaculture Development in China," *FAO Aquaculture Newsletter*, August 1999, p. 18.

26. Catfish requirements from Naylor et al., op. cit. note 24; U.S. catfish production data from USDA, ERS-NASS, *Catfish Production* (Washington, DC: February 2003), p. 5.

27. FAO, *State of World Fisheries and Aquaculture 2002*, op. cit. note 22.

28. Roughage conversion from A. Banerjee, "Dairying Systems in India," *World Animal Review*, vol. 79/2 (Rome: FAO, 1994), and from S. C. Dhall and Meena Dhall, "Dairy Industry— India's Strength in Its Livestock," *Business Line*, Internet Edition of *Financial Daily* from *The Hindu* group of publications, at <www.indiaserver.com/businessline/1997/11/07/stories/03070311.htm>, 7 November 1997; Figure 8–2 from FAO, *FAOSTAT,* op. cit. note 2, livestock data updated 9 January 2003.

29. Calculation based on FAO, *FAOSTAT,* op. cit. note 2, livestock data updated 9 January 2003.

30. Banerjee, op. cit. note 28.

31. China's crop residue production and use from Gao Tengyun, "Treatment and Utilization of Crop Straw and Strover in China," *Livestock Research for Rural Development*, February 2000.

32. Ibid.; China's Beef Belt from USDA, ERS, "China's Beef Economy: Production, Marketing Consumption, and Foreign Trade," *International Agriculture and Trade Reports: China* (Washington, DC: July 1998), p. 28.

33. United Nations, "The Great North American Dust Bowl: A Cautionary Tale," *Global Alarm Dust and Sandstorms from the World's Drylands* (Bangkok: Secretariat of the U.N. Convention to Combat Desertification, September 2002), pp. 77–121.

34. R. Neil Sampson, *Farmland or Wasteland* (Emmaus, PA: Rodale Press, 1981), p. 242.

35. USDA, Natural Resources Conservation Service, CORE4 *Conservation Practices Training Guide: The Common Sense Approach to Natural Resource Conservation* (Washington, DC: August 1999); Rolf Derpsch, "Frontiers in Conservation Tillage and Advances in Conservation Practice," in D. E. Stott, R. H. Mohtar, and G. C. Steinhardt, eds., *Sustaining the Global Farm*, selected papers from the 10th International Soil Conservation Organization Meeting, at Purdue University and USDA-ARS National Soil Erosion Research Laboratory, 24–29 May 1999 (Washington, DC: 2001), pp. 248–54.

36. Conservation Technology Information Center, Purdue University, *2000 United States Summary*, from 2000 National Crop Residue Management Survey, at <www.ctic.purdue.edu/Core4/ CT/ctsurvey/2000/2000USSummary.html>, updated 20 January 2002; no-till and minimum-till farming from FAO, *Intensifying Crop Production with Conservation Agriculture*, at <www.fao. org/ag/ags/agse/Main.htm>, viewed 20 May 2003.

37. USDA, ERS, *Agri-Environmental Policy at the Crossroads: Guideposts on a Changing Landscape*, Agricultural Economic Report No. 794 (Washington, DC: January 2001); USDA, Farm Service Agency Online, "History of the CRP," in *The Conservation Reserve Program* at <www.fsa.usda.gov/ dafp/cepd/12logocv.htm>, viewed 29 April 2003.

38. USDA, Foreign Agricultural Service, *Grains: World Markets and Trade* (Washington, DC: various years).

39. Richard Moe, President of the National Trust for Historic Preservation, speech on sprawl, 1999 Red Hills Spring Event Dinner, Tall Timbers Research Station, Tallahassee, FL, 24 March 1999.

40. Ding Guangwei and Li Shishun, "Analysis of Impetuses to Change of Agricultural Land Uses in China," *Bulletin of the Chinese Academy of Sciences*, vol. 13, no. 1 (1999).

41. Ibid.

42. United Nations, op. cit. note 2.

43. Ibid.; USDA, op. cit. note 1; Gary Gardner and Brian Halweil, *Underfed and Overfed: The Global Epidemic of Malnutrition*, Worldwatch Paper 150 (Washington, DC: Worldwatch Institute, 2000).

44. Grain consumption per person from USDA, op. cit. note 1; United Nations, op. cit. note 2; life expectancy from Population Reference Bureau, 2002 *World Population Data Sheet*, wall chart (Washington, DC: August 2002).

45. USDA, Farm Service Agency Online, op. cit. note 37; "Algeria to Convert Large Cereal Land to Tree-Planting," *Reuters*, 8 December 2000.

46. Chinese program from Sun Xiufang and Ralph Bean, *China Solid Wood Products Annual Report 2002* (Beijing: USDA, June 2002).

47. Data are from discussion with officials of Helin County, Inner Mongolia (Nei Monggol), 17 May 2002.

48. Ibid.

49. U.S. Embassy, *Grapes of Wrath in Inner Mongolia* (Beijing: May 2001).

50. India's dairy industry from Banerjee, op. cit. note 28.

CHAPTER 9. CUTTING CARBON EMISSIONS IN HALF

1. United Nations, *Kyoto Protocol to the United Nations Framework Convention on Climate Change* (New York: 1997).

2. United Kingdom from Secretary of State for Trade and Industry, *Our Energy Future—Creating a Low Carbon Economy* (Norwich: The Stationery Office, February 2003); goal for the European Union from Tony Blair and Göran Persson, letter to the European Council, London and Stockholm, 25 February 2003, at <statsradsberedningen.regeringen.se/Pdf/gpblair_feb03.pdf>.

3. Ralph Torrie, Richard Parfett, and Paul Steenhof, *Kyoto and Beyond: The Low-Emission Path to Innovation and Efficiency* (Ottawa: The David Suzuki Foundation and Climate Action Network Canada, October 2002); Alison Bailie et al., *The Path to Carbon-Dioxide-Free Power: Switching to Clean Energy in the Utility Sector*, A Study for the World Wildlife Fund (Washington, DC: Tellus Institute and The Center for Energy and Climate Solutions, April 2003).

4. Gibbons quoted in Martin Mittelstaedt, "Putting Out the Fires," (Toronto) *Globe and Mail*, 15 March 2003.

5. Germany's goals cited in Corin Millais, "European Wind Energy Achieves 40% Growth Rate," press release (Brussels: European Wind Energy Association (EWEA), 13 November 2002).

6. Ray Anderson, writing in Torrie, Parfett, and Steenhof, op. cit. note 3, p. 2.

7. Per capita energy consumption in U.S. Department of Energy (DOE), Energy Information Administration (EIA), *EIA Country Analysis Briefs*, at <www.eia.doe.gov/emeu/cabs>, updated May 2003.

8. Bill Prindle, "How Energy Efficiency Can Turn 1300 New Power Plants Into 170," fact sheet (Washington, DC: Alliance to Save Energy, 2 May 2001).

9. Brenda Platt and Doug Rowe, *Reduce, Reuse, Refill!* (Washington, DC: Institute for Local Self-Reliance, April 2002); energy in David Saphire, *Case Reopened: Reassessing Refillable Bottles* (New York: INFORM, Inc., 1994).

10. Howard Geller, "Compact Fluorescent Lighting," *American Council for an Energy-Efficient Economy Technology Brief*, at <www.aceee.org>, viewed 1 May 2003.

11. Gasoline savings based on Malcolm A. Weiss et al., *Comparative Assessment of Fuel Cell Cars* (Cambridge, MA: Massachusetts Institute of Technology, February 2003); hybrid vehicle tax credit from National Renewable Energy Laboratory (NREL), "Tax Deduction: Hybrid Electric Vehicles," fact sheet, from <www.ott.doe.gov/hev/hev.html>, January 2003; sales projections for 2007 based on Drew Winter and Kevin Kelly, "Hybrid Heartburn," *Ward's Auto World*, March 2003, pp. 44–51, and on Matt Nauman, "Hybrid Car Sales, Demand Picking Up," *St. Paul Pioneer Press*, 11 January 2003. Table 9–1 based on estimates by automakers and *Automotive News*, cited in "Hybrid Car Sales, Demand Picking Up," *Contra Costa Times*, 4 January 2003, with projections for 2003 in "Hybrid Demand High," *Financial Times Information Limited*, 29 March 2003.

12. John Whitlegg, editorial, *World Transport Policy and Practice*, vol. 8, no. 4 (2002), p. 5; Randy Kennedy, "The Day the Traffic Disappeared," *New York Times Magazine*, 20 April 2003, pp. 42–45.

13. Wind power history in Peter Asmus, *Reaping the Wind* (Washington, DC: Island Press, 2000); figure from Janet L. Sawin, "Wind Power's Rapid Growth Continues," in Worldwatch Institute, *Vital Signs 2003* (New York: W.W. Norton & Company, 2003), pp. 38–39, updated with American Wind Energy Association (AWEA) and EWEA estimates in AWEA, *Global Wind Energy Market Report* (Washington, DC: updated March 2003); residential needs based on 1 megawatt needed for 350 households or about 1,000 people, using populations from United Nations, *World Population Prospects: The 2002 Revision* (New York: February 2003).

14. AWEA, op. cit. note 13; Soren Krohn, "Wind Energy Policy in Denmark: Status 2002," Danish Wind Energy Association, at <www.windpower.org/articles/energypo.htm>, February 2002; Schleswig-Holstein in AWEA, *Global Wind Energy Market Report* (Washington, DC: March 2002), p. 3; Navarra from Felix Avia Aranda and Ignacio Cruz Cruz, "Breezing Ahead: The Spanish Wind Energy Market," *Renewable Energy World*, May–June 2000.

15. Offshore wind energy in Europe from EWEA and Greenpeace, *Wind Force 12: A Blueprint to Achieve 12% of the World's Electricity From Wind Power by 2020* (Brussels and Amsterdam: 2002), pp. 25–26. According to Debra Lew and Jeffrey Logan, "Energizing China's Wind Power Sector," Pacific Northwest Laboratory, March 2001, at <www.pnl.gov/china/ChinaWnd.htm>, China has at least 275 gigawatts of exploitable wind potential, roughly equal to the current installed electrical capacity in China as reported by DOE, EIA, "China," *EIA Country Analysis Briefs*, at <www.eia.doe.gov/emeu/cabs>, updated June 2002. According to the 1991 assessment of wind energy resources in the United States, Texas, North Dakota, and Kansas would be able to produce 3,470 billion kilowatt-hours (kWh), approaching the 3,779 billion kWh used by the United States in 2001, as reported by DOE, EIA, "United States," *EIA Country Analysis Briefs*, updated November 2002. See D. L. Elliott, L. L. Wendell, and G. L. Gower, *An Assessment of the Available Windy Land Area and Wind Energy Potential in the Contiguous United States* (Richland, WA: Pacific Northwest Laboratory, 1991); maps available from AWEA at <www.awea.org/projects/index.html>, last updated 23 January 2003.

16. Larry Flowers, NREL, "Wind Power Update," at <www.eren. doe.gov/windpoweringamerica/pdfs/wpa/wpa_update.pdf>, viewed 19 June 2002; Glenn Hasek, "Powering the Future," *Industry Week*, 1 May 2000.

17. David Milborrow, "Size Matters—Getting Bigger and Cheaper," *Windpower Monthly*, January 2003, pp. 35–38.

18. Lawrence D. Burns, J. Byron McCormick, and Christopher E. Borroni-Bird, "Vehicle of Change," *Scientific American*, October 2002, pp. 64–73; Honda and Toyota in "Water Electrolysis—No Hydrocarbons Needed," interview with John Slangerup, President and CEO, Stuart Energy Systems of Mississauga, Ontario, Canada, *World Fuels Today*, 28 January 2003; DaimlerChrysler in Ballard Power Systems, Inc., "Ballard Fuel Cell Engines to Power Sixty Mercedes-Benz Vehicles in Global Fleet Demonstrations," news release (Burnaby, BC, Canada: 7 October 2002); Ford Motor Company, "Ford Combines Hybrid and Fuel Cell Technology in All-New Focus Sedan," press release (Detroit, MI: 11 June 2002).

19. Internet from Molly O. Sheehan, "Communications Networks Expand," in Worldwatch Institute, op. cit. note 13, pp. 60–61.

20. Harry Braun, *The Phoenix Project: Shifting From Oil to Hydrogen with Wartime Speed*, prepared for the Renewable Hydrogen Roundtable, World Resources Institute, Washington, DC, 10–11 April 2003, pp. 3–4.

21. Ibid.

22. Fossil fuel subsidies from Bjorn Larsen, *World Fossil Fuel Subsidies and Global Carbon Emissions in a Model with Interfuel Substitution*, Policy Research Working Paper 1256 (Washington, DC: World Bank, 1994), p. 7; companies involved in wind from Birgitte Dyrekilde, "Big Players to Spark Wind Power Consolidation," *Reuters*, 18 March 2002; David Stipp, "The Coming Hydrogen Economy," *Fortune*, 12 November 2001; "BP to Spend $15 Billion in the Gulf of Mexico," *PR Newswire*, 1 August 2002; wind costs from Milborrow, op. cit. note 17.

23. Germany in Millais, op. cit. note 5.

24. Jim Dehlsen, Clipper Wind, discussion with author, 30 May 2001.

25. Cape Wind, "Cape Wind Selects GE Wind Energy," press release (Yarmouth Port, MA: 21 January 2003); Winergy, *Wind Farm Status Reports*, at <www.winergyllc.com>, viewed 9 May 2003.

26. Denis Hayes, "Sunpower," in Energy Foundation, *2001 Annual Report* (San Francisco: February 2002), pp. 10–18.

27. Population without electricity in World Summit on Sustainable Development, Department of Public Information, Press Conference on Global Sustainable Energy Network (Johannesburg: 1 September 2002).

28. "Power to the Poor," *The Economist*, 10 February 2001, pp. 21–23.

29. Bernie Fischlowitz-Roberts, "Sales of Solar Cells Take Off," *Eco-Economy Update* (Washington, DC: Earth Policy Institute, 11 June 2002).

30. European Photovoltaic Industry Association and Greenpeace, *Solar Generation* (Brussels: September 2001).

31. Fischlowitz-Roberts, op. cit. note 29.

32. Robert H. Williams, "Facilitating Widespread Deployment of Wind and Photovoltaic Technologies," in Energy Foundation, op. cit. note 26, pp. 19–30.

33. Paul Maycock, "Annual Survey of PV," *Photovoltaic News*, March 2003, p. 1. Table 9–2 from the following: wind power from Worldwatch Institute, *Signposts 2002*, CD-rom (Washington, DC: 2002), updated with AWEA, op. cit. note 13; solar photovoltaics from Maycock, op. cit. this note; geothermal power from Worldwatch Institute, op. cit. this note; oil from DOE, EIA, "World Oil Demand," *International Petroleum Monthly*, April 2003; natural gas and coal from Janet L. Sawin, "Fossil Fuel Use Up," in Worldwatch Institute, op. cit. note 13, pp. 34–35; nuclear power from Nicholas Lenssen, "Nuclear Power Rises," in ibid, pp. 36–37; hydroelectric power from BP, *Statistical Review of World Energy 2002* (London: Group Media & Publishing, June 2002), p. 36.

34. International Geothermal Association, "Electricity Generation," at <iga.igg.cnr.it/electricitygeneration.php>, updated 27 April 2002.

35. Ibid.; Philippines share from World Bank, "Geothermal Ener-

gy," prepared under the PB Power and World Bank partnership program, at <www.worldbank.org/html/fpd/energy/geothermal>, viewed 23 January 2003.

36. World Bank, op. cit. note 35.

37. John W. Lund and Derek H. Freeston, "World-wide Direct Uses of Geothermal Energy 2000," *Geothermics*, vol. 30 (2001), pp. 34, 51, 53; population from United Nations, op cit. note 13.

38. Lund and Freeston, op. cit. note 37.

39. Ibid.; California in World Bank, op. cit. note 35.

40. World Bank, op. cit. note 35.

41. Lund and Freeston, op. cit. note 37, pp. 46, 53.

42. Japan from Hal Kane, "Geothermal Power Gains, " in Lester R. Brown et al., *Vital Signs 1993* (New York: W.W. Norton & Company, 1993), p. 54; DOE, EIA, "Japan," *EIA Country Analysis Briefs*, at <www.eia.doe.gov/emeu/cabs>, updated April 2002; other potential in World Bank, op. cit. note 35.

43. Stipp, op. cit. note 22.

44. Terry Macalister, "Iceland Turns Greener," (London) *Guardian*, 25 April 2003.

45. Benjamin Fulford, "Mister Natural," *Forbes Global*, 23 December 2002, pp. 64–65.

46. Fuel Cells 2000, "Worldwide Hydrogen Fueling Stations," at <www.fuelcells.org/H2FuelingStations.pdf>, updated February 2003; "Five Years in the Making, $18 Million Hydrogen Production/Fueling Station Opens in Munich," *Hydrogen & Fuel Cell Letter*, June 1999; Art Garner, "Honda Installs Solar Hydrogen Fueling Station Near LA, First for Any Carmaker," *Hydrogen & Fuel Cell Letter*, August 2001.

47. Amory B. Lovins, "A Strategy for the Hydrogen Transition," 16th Annual U.S. Hydrogen Meeting, National Hydrogen Association, Vienna, VA, 7–9 April 1999; DOE, *A National Vision of America's Transition to a Hydrogen Economy—To 2030 and Beyond* (Washington, DC: February 2002), p. 6.

48. Maureen Hinkle, former staff member, Environmental Defense Fund, discussion with author, 5 May 2003; Alan Cowell, "Nostalgia Abounds as the Concorde's End Is Set,"

New York Times, 11 April 2003; "Towards the Wild Blue Yonder," *The Economist,* 27 April 2002, pp. 67–70.

49. Air pollution fatalities from World Health Organization (WHO), "Air Pollution," fact sheet, revised September 2000, at <www.who.int/inf-fs/en/fact187.html>; overweight from WHO, *Obesity: Preventing and Managing the Global Epidemic,* Report of a WHO Consultation, Technical Report Series No. 894 (Geneva: 2000); Peter G. Kopelman, "Obesity as a Medical Problem," *Nature,* 6 April 2000, p. 636; Barry M. Popkin and Colleen M. Doak, "The Obesity Epidemic is a Worldwide Phenomenon," *Nutrition Reviews,* April 1998, pp. 106–14.

50. Sheehan, op. cit. note 19.

51. Ibid.; growth in wind power from Worldwatch Institute, op. cit. note 33.

52. AWEA, "Wind Power Outlook 2003," at <www.awea.org/pubs/documents/Outlook2003.pdf>, viewed 8 May 2003; wind cost from Milborrow, op. cit. note 17; gasoline expenditures in DOE, EIA, *State Energy Data 2000, Price and Expenditure Data,* at <www.eia.doe.gov/emeu/states/_multi_states.html>, updated 8 May 2003.

53. Policy instruments discussed in Robert Rose, *Fuel Cells and Hydrogen: The Path Forward* (Washington, DC: Breakthrough Technologies Institute, Inc., September 2002); NREL, op. cit. note 11.

54. Information on EPA's Green Power Partnership available at <www.epa.gov/greenpower>.

55. Ibid.

56. DOE, Office of Energy and Renewable Energy, Green Power Network, "Summary of State Net Metering Programs," <www.eere.energy.gov/greenpower/netmetering/nmtable.shtml>, updated 9 August 2002; Lori Bird, Rolf Wüstenhagen, and Jørn Aabakken, *Green Power Marketing Abroad: Recent Experience and Trends* (Golden, CO: NREL, April 2002).

57. Tracey J. Woodruff et al., *America's Children and the Environment* (Washington, DC: U.S. Environmental Protection Agency, February 2003), pp. 94–95; Centers for Disease Con-

trol and Prevention, "Blood and Hair Mercury Levels in Young Children and Women of Childbearing Age—United States 1999," *Morbidity and Mortality Weekly Report*, 2 March 2001, pp. 140–43; Mercury Policy Project et al., "CDC Report Finds More U.S. Children and Pregnant Women at Risk from Mercury Exposure than Ever Before," press release (Washington, DC: 2 March 2001).

58. Charles O. Holliday, Jr., "Message from the Chief Executive," in Dupont, *Sustainable Growth 2002 Progress Report* (Wilmington, DE: 2002), pp. 2–3.

CHAPTER 10. RESPONDING TO THE SOCIAL CHALLENGE

1. Population estimates and projections from United Nations, *World Population Prospects: The 2002 Revision* (New York: February 2003); gap between rich and poor countries and individuals discussed in World Bank, *World Development Report 2000/2001* (New York: Oxford University Press, 2001), p. 51.

2. Population projections from United Nations, op. cit. note 1.

3. Population Reference Bureau (PRB), *2002 World Population Data Sheet*, wall chart (Washington, DC: August 2002).

4. Ibid.; unmet need from John A. Ross and William L. Winfrey, "Unmet Need for Contraception in the Developing World and the Former Soviet Union: An Updated Estimate," *International Family Planning Perspectives*, September 2002, pp. 138–43.

5. Janet Larsen, "Iran's Birth Rate Plummeting at Record Pace," in Lester R. Brown, Janet Larsen, and Bernie Fischlowitz-Roberts, *The Earth Policy Reader* (New York: W.W. Norton & Company, 2002), pp. 190–94; see also Homa Hoodfar and Samad Assadpour, "The Politics of Population Policy in the Islamic Republic of Iran," *Studies in Family Planning*, March 2000, pp. 19–34, and Farzaneh Roudi, "Iran's Family Planning Program: Responding to a Nation's Needs," *MENA Policy Brief*, June 2002.

6. Larsen, op. cit. note 5.

7. Ibid.

8. Ibid.

9. U.N. Population Fund (UNFPA), "Meeting the Goals of the ICPD: Consequences of Resource Shortfalls up to the Year 2000," paper presented to the Executive Board of the U.N. Development Programme and the UNFPA, New York, 12–23 May 1997; UNFPA, *Population Issues Briefing Kit* (New York: Prographics, Inc., 2001), p. 23.

10. UNFPA, "Meeting the Goals of the ICPD," op. cit. note 9.

11. Table 10–1 from Honduran Ministry of Health, *Encuesta Nacional de Epidemiología y Salud Familiar* (National Survey of Epidemiology and Family Health) (Tegucigalpa: 1996), cited in George Martine and Jose Miguel Guzman, "Population, Poverty, and Vulnerability: Mitigating the Effects of Natural Disasters," in *Environmental Change and Security Project Report* (Washington, DC: Woodrow Wilson International Center for Scholars, summer 2002), pp. 45–68.

12. "Bangladesh: National Family Planning Program," *Family Planning Programs: Diverse Solutions for a Global Challenge* (Washington, DC: PRB, February 1994).

13. Hilaire A. Mputu, *Literacy and Non-Formal Education in the E-9 Countries* (Paris: UNESCO, 2001), p. 5; Paul Blustein, "Global Education Plan Gains Backing," *Washington Post*, 22 April 2002; Gene Sperling, "Educate Them All," *Washington Post*, 20 April 2002.

14. United Nations General Assembly, "United Nations Millennium Declaration," resolution adopted by the General Assembly, 18 September 2000 (for more information on the Millennium Development Goals, see <www.un.org/millenniumgoals>); Blustein, op. cit. note 13; Sperling, op. cit. note 13.

15. See education chapter in World Bank, *Poverty Reduction Strategy Paper Sourcebook* (Washington, DC: 2001), pp. 2–4.

16. Gene B. Sperling, "Toward Universal Education," *Foreign Affairs*, September/October 2001, pp. 7–13.

17. World Bank, "World Bank Announces First Group of Countries for 'Education For All' Fast Track," press release (Washington, DC: 12 June 2002); World Bank, "Education for All the World's Children: Donors Have Agreed to Help First Group of Countries on Education Fast-Track," press release (Washington, DC: 27 November 2002); for more information

on the Bank's and the international community's involvement in the Education for All program, see <www1.worldbank.org/education/efa.asp>.

18. Sperling, op. cit. note 13.

19. Mputu, op. cit. note 13, p. 5; U.N. Commission on Population and Development, Thirty-sixth Session, *Population, Education, and Development*, press releases, 31 March–4 April 2003.

20. Blustein, op. cit. note 13.

21. Nita Bhalla, "Teaching Truck Drivers About AIDS," *BBC*, 25 June 2001; Hugh Ellis, "Truck Drivers Targeted in New AIDS Offensive," *The Nambian*, 17 March 2003; C. B. S. Venkataramana and P. V. Sarada, "Extent and Speed of Spread of HIV Infection in India Through the Commercial Sex Networks: A Perspective," *Tropical Medicine and International Health*, vol. 6, no. 12, pp. 1040–61, cited in "HIV Spread Via Female Sex Workers in India Set to Increase Significantly by 2005," *Reuters Health*, 26 December 2001.

22. Mark Covey, "Target Soldiers in Fight Against AIDS Says New Report," press release (London: Panos Institute, 8 July 2002); "Free Condoms for Soldiers," *South Africa Press Association*, 5 August 2001; HIV prevalence rate from Joint United Nations Programme on HIV/AIDS (UNAIDS), *Report on the Global HIV/AIDS Epidemic 2002* (Geneva: July 2002), pp. 189–202; UNAIDS, *AIDS Epidemic Update* (Geneva: December 2002), pp. 12–15.

23. Pledges received listed at The Global Fund to Fight AIDS, Tuberculosis and Malaria, "Contributions," at <www.globalfundatm.org/contribute.html>, updated 16 April 2003; minimum needed by 2005 for effective prevention programs in low- and middle-income countries estimated by the United Nations, cited in Lawrence K. Altman, "Women With H.I.V. Reach Half of Global Cases," *New York Times*, 27 November 2002.

24. Nada Chaya and Kai-Ahset Amen, with Michael Fox, *Condoms Count: Meeting the Need in the Era of HIV/AIDS* (Washington, DC: Population Action International, 2002); 2 billion condoms needed for contraception also based on estimates from Robert Gardner et al., *Closing the Condom Gap*,

Population Reports (Baltimore, MD: Johns Hopkins University School of Public Health, Population Information Program,
April 1999).

25. "Who Pays for Condoms," in Chaya, Amen, and Fox, op. cit.
note 24, pp. 29–36; Communications Consortium Media Center, "U.N. Special Session on Children Ends in Acrimony,"
PLANetWIRE.org, at <www.planetwire.org/details/2704>,
14 May 2002; Adam Clymer, "U.S. Revises Sex Information,
and a Fight Goes On," *New York Times*, 27 December 2002.

26. UNAIDS, July 2002, op. cit. note 22, pp. 22–26, 189–202;
UNAIDS, *Report on the Global HIV/AIDS Epidemic* (Geneva: June 2000), pp. 9–11.

27. UNAIDS, July 2002, op. cit. note 22, pp. 22–23.

28. Hunger as a risk factor for disease in World Health Organi-
zation (WHO), *World Health Report 2002* (Geneva: 2002),
and in Majid Ezzati et al., "Selected Major Risk Factors and
Global and Regional Burden of Disease," *The Lancet*, 30
October 2002, pp. 1–14; information on the toll of measles
and diarrhea in Jeffrey D. Sachs and the Commission on
Macroeconomics and Health, *Macroeconomics and Health:
Investing in Health for Economic Development* (Geneva:
WHO, 2001), pp. 43–44.

29. Tuberculosis from WHO, op. cit. note 28, p. 157; malaria
from WHO/UNICEF, *The Africa Malaria Report 2003* (New
York: 2003), p. 17; "Agency Puts Hunger No. 1 on List of
World's Top Health Risks," *Agence France-Presse*, 31 October
2002.

30. WHO/UNICEF, op. cit. note 29; Declan Butler, "Malaria Initiative Cries Out for Action in Africa," *Nature*, 20 November
2002, p. 351.

31. John Donnelly, "U.S. Seeks Cuts in Health Programs Abroad,"
Boston Globe, 5 February 2003.

32. WHO, "Air Pollution," fact sheet 187, revised September
2000, at <www.who.int/inf-fs/en/fact187.html>.

33. Automobile fatalities from World Bank, "Road Safety," at
<www.worldbank.org/html/fpd/transport/roads/safety.htm>,
viewed 5 May 2003.

34. WHO, op. cit. note 28, p. 10; "The Tobacco Epidemic: A Cri-

sis of Startling Dimensions," in *Message From the Director-General of the World Health Organization for World No-Tobacco Day 1998*, at <www.who.int/archives/ntday/ntday98/ad98e_1.htm>; air pollution from WHO, op. cit. note 32.

35. Alison Langley, "Anti-Smoking Treaty Is Adopted by 192 Nations," *New York Times*, 22 May 2003; information on WHO's Tobacco Free Initiative is at <www5.who.int/tobacco/index.cfm>.

36. Cigarette consumption from U.S. Department of Agriculture (USDA), *Production, Supply, and Distribution*, electronic database, Washington, DC, updated 13 May 2003; per capita estimates made using population from United Nations, op. cit. note 1.

37. USDA, op. cit. note 36.

38. Sachs and the Commission on Macroeconomics and Health, op. cit. note 28; WHO, "Fact Sheet on Smallpox," at <www.who.int/emc/diseases/smallpox/factsheet.html>, October 2001.

39. Sachs and the Commission on Macroeconomics and Health, op. cit. note 28.

40. Ibid.

41. George McGovern, "Yes We CAN Feed the World's Hungry," *Parade*, 16 December 2001; George McGovern, *The Third Freedom: Ending Hunger in Our Time* (New York: Simon & Schuster: 2001), chapter 1.

42. McGovern, *Parade*, op. cit. note 41.

43. Jeffrey Sachs, "A New Map of the World," *The Economist*, 22 June 2000; McGovern, *Parade*, op. cit. note 41.

44. McGovern, *Parade*, op. cit. note 41.

45. Ibid.

46. Ibid.

47. Numbers hungry from U.N. Food and Agriculture Organization, *The State of Food Insecurity in the World 2002* (Rome: 2002); less than $6 per person per year calculated from cost to battle hunger in McGovern, *Parade*, op. cit. note 41, and U.S. population from United Nations, op. cit. note 1; Roosevelt quoted in World Bank, *World Development Report 2003*

(New York: Oxford University Press, 2003), p. 59.

48. United Nations, op. cit. note 1; for a discussion of the "demographic bonus," see UNFPA, *The State of World Population 2002* (New York: 2002).

49. Costs of meeting social goals in Table 10–2 calculated by Earth Policy Institute, based on the following sources: universal primary education from World Bank, cited in Blustein, op. cit. note 13; adult literacy campaign is author's estimate; reproductive health and family planning based on the goals from and the progress since the 1994 International Conference on Population and Development (UNFPA, "Meeting the Goals of the ICPD," op. cit. note 9), combining the $5 billion shortfalls of the developing-country and industrial-country groups; closing the condom gap estimated from Chaya, Amen, and Fox, op. cit. note 24, and from Gardner et al., op. cit. note 24; school lunch program from McGovern, *Parade*, op. cit. note 41; assistance to preschool children and pregnant women is author's estimate of extending the U.S.'s Women, Infants, and Children program, based on McGovern, *Parade*, op. cit. note 41; universal basic health care from Sachs and the Commission on Macroeconomics and Health, op. cit. note 28, subtracting the $6 billion that is currently provided each year from the needed $27 billion.

CHAPTER 11. PLAN B: RISING TO THE CHALLENGE

1. See Chapter 5 and Population Reference Bureau, *2002 World Population Data Sheet*, wall chart (Washington, DC: August 2002) for more information.

2. "Iceland Launches New Hydrogen Economy," *Solar Access.com*, 7 February 2003.

3. Soren Krohn, "Wind Energy Policy in Denmark: Status 2002," Danish Wind Energy Association, at <www.windpower.org/articles/energypo.htm>, February 2002; Schleswig-Holstein in American Wind Energy Association, *Global Wind Energy Market Report* (Washington, DC: March 2002), p. 3.

4. European Photovoltaic Industry Association and Greenpeace, *The Solar Generation* (Brussels: September 2001).

5. Anthonie Gerard Welleman, project manager of the Bicycle Master Plan at the Dutch Ministry of Transport, Public

Works and Water Management, presentation at the Velo-City Conference '95 (Basel, Switzerland: 1995), at <www.communitybike.org/cache/autumn_bike_master_plan.html>.

6. Martin Mittelstaedt, "Putting Out the Fires," (Toronto) *Globe and Mail*, 15 March 2003.

7. World Commission on Dams, *Dams and Development* (London: Earthscan, 2000), p. 141; Sandra Postel, *Last Oasis* (New York: W.W. Norton & Company, 1997), pp. 103–07.

8. Author's observations while in the country, November 2000.

9. U.S. Department of Agriculture (USDA), Economic Research Service (ERS), *Agri-Environmental Policy at the Crossroads: Guideposts on a Changing Landscape*, Agricultural Economic Report No. 794 (Washington, DC: January 2001).

10. For information on mobilization, see Francis Walton, *Miracle of World War II: How American Industry Made Victory Possible* (Macmillan: New York, 1956).

11. Harold G. Vatter, *The US Economy in World War II* (New York: Columbia University Press, 1985).

12. Ibid.

13. Franklin Roosevelt, "State of the Union Address," 6 January 1942, at <www.ibiblio.org/pha/7-2-188/188-35.html>.

14. Vatter, op. cit. note 11, p. 13.

15. "War Production—The Job 'That Couldn't Be Done'," *Business Week*, 5 May 1945.

16. John B. Rae, *Climb to Greatness: The American Aircraft Industry, 1920–1960* (Cambridge: The MIT Press, 1968), p. 157.

17. Doris Kearns Goodwin, *No Ordinary Time—Franklin and Eleanor Roosevelt: The Home Front in World War II* (New York: Simon & Schuster, 1994), p. 316.

18. Ibid.

19. Car production from Rae, op. cit. note 16, p. 181; tank, armored cars, and aircraft production from "War Production," op. cit. note 15; Donald M. Nelsen, *Arsenal of Democracy: The Story of American War Production* (New York: Harcourt, Brace and Co., 1946), p. 243.

20. Sir Edward quoted in Walton, op. cit. note 10, p. 42.

21. "Point Rationing Comes of Age," *Business Week*, 19 February 1944.

22. Expansion in world economy from Erik Assadourian, "Economic Growth Inches Up," in Worldwatch Institute, *Vital Signs 2003* (New York: W.W. Norton & Company, 2003), p. 45.

23. Centers for Disease Control and Prevention (CDC), "Annual Smoking-Attributable Mortality, Years of Potential Life Lost, and Economic Costs—United States, 1995–1999," *Morbidity and Mortality Weekly Report*, 12 April 2002.

24. Effect of higher temperatures on crops from John E. Sheehy, International Rice Research Institute, Philippines, e-mail to Janet Larsen, Earth Policy Institute, 2 October 2002; ice melting and sea level rise from Intergovernmental Panel on Climate Change, *Climate Change 2001: The Scientific Basis. Contribution of Working Group I to the Third Assessment Report of the Intergovernmental Panel on Climate Change* (New York: Cambridge University Press, 2001).

25. John Holtzclaw, "America's Autos on Welfare: A Summary of Subsidies," at <www.prservenet.com/ATAutoWelfare.html>, October 1996.

26. Bangladesh status from World Bank, *World Development Report 1999/2000* (New York: Oxford University Press, 2000), p. 100; population from United Nations, *World Population Prospects: The 2002 Revision* (New York: February 2003); 40 million displaced is author's estimate based on the distribution of population in Bangladesh.

27. Cost of flooding from Munich Re, *Topics Annual Review: Natural Catastrophes 2001* (Munich, Germany: 2002), pp. 16–17; banning of tree cutting from "Forestry Cuts Down on Logging," *China Daily*, 26 May 1998; Erik Eckholm, "Chinese Leaders Vow to Mend Ecological Ways," *New York Times*, 30 August 1998; Erik Eckholm, "Stunned by Floods, China Hastens Logging Curbs," *New York Times*, 27 February 1998.

28. Eneas Salati and Peter B. Vose, "Amazon Basin: A System in Equilibrium," *Science*, 13 July 1984, pp. 129–38; Philip Fearnside from Barbara J. Fraser, "Putting a Price on the Forest," *LatinamericaPress.org*, on-line periodical at <www.lapress.org>, 10 November 2002.

29. Dahle from discussion with author at State of the World Conference, Aspen, CO, 22 July 2001.

30. Redefining Progress, *The Economists' Statement on Climate Change* (Oakland, CA: 1997).

31. David Malin Roodman, "Environmental Tax Shifts Multiplying," in Lester R. Brown et al., *Vital Signs 2000* (New York: W.W. Norton & Company, 2000), pp. 138–39.

32. Ibid.; second wave and Finland from European Environment Agency (EEA), *Environmental Taxes: Recent Developments in Tools for Integration*, Environmental Issues Series No. 18 (Copenhagen, November 2000); Germany from German Federal Environment Ministry, "Environmental Effects of the Ecological Tax Reform," at <www.bmu.de/english/topics/oekosteuer/oekosteuer_environment.php>, January 2002.

33. EEA, op. cit. note 32; U.S. chlorofluorocarbon tax from Elizabeth Cook, *Ozone Protection in the United States: Elements of Success* (Washington, DC: World Resources Institute, 1996); city of Victoria from David Malin Roodman, "Environmental Taxes Spread," in Lester R. Brown et al., *Vital Signs 1996* (New York: W.W. Norton & Company, 1996), p. 114–15.

34. Tom Miles, "London Drivers to Pay UK's First Congestion Tax," *Reuters*, 28 February 2002; Randy Kennedy, "The Day The Traffic Disappeared," *New York Times Magazine*, 20 April 2003, pp. 42–45.

35. Miles, op. cit. note 34.

36. USDA, ERS, "Cigarette Price Increase Follows Tobacco Pact," *Agricultural Outlook*, January–February 1999.

37. CDC, op. cit. note 23; Campaign for Tobacco-Free Kids et al., *Show Us the Money: A Report on the States' Allocation of the Tobacco Settlement Dollars* (Washington, DC: January 2003); New York from Jodi Wilgoren, "Facing New Costs, Some Smokers Say 'Enough'," *New York Times*, 17 July 2002.

38. Peter P. Wrany and Kai Schlegelmilch, "The Ecological Tax Reform in Germany," prepared for the UN/OECD Workshop on Enhancing the Environment by Reforming Energy Prices, Pruhonice, Czech Republic, 14–16 June 2000.

39. Organisation for Economic Co-operation and Development,

European Commission, and EEA, *Environmentally Related Taxes Database*, at <www.oecd.org/env/tax-database>, updated 13 May 2003.

40. "BTM Predicts Continued Growth for Wind Industry," op. cit. note 3, p. 8.

41. N. Gregory Mankiw, "Gas Tax Now!" *Fortune*, 24 May 1999, pp. 60–64.

42. "Addicted to Oil," *The Economist*, 15 December 2001; environmental tax support from David Malin Roodman, *The Natural Wealth of Nations* (New York: W.W. Norton & Company, 1998), p. 243.

43. André de Moor and Peter Calamai, *Subsidizing Unsustainable Development* (San José, Costa Rica: Earth Council, 1997); study quoted in Barbara Crossette, "Subsidies Hurt Environment, Critics Say Before Talks," *New York Times*, 23 June 1997.

44. World Bank, *World Development Report 2003* (New York: Oxford University Press, 2003), pp. 30, 142.

45. Belgium, France, and Japan from Seth Dunn, "King Coal's Weakening Grip on Power," *World Watch*, September/October 1999, pp. 10–19; coal subsidy reduction in Germany from Robin Pomeroy, "EU Ministers Clear German Coal Subsidies," *Reuters*, 10 June 2002; subsidy cut figures in China from Roodman, op. cit. note 42, p. 109; sulfur coals tax from U.S. Department of Energy (DOE), Energy Information Administration (EIA), *China: Environmental Issues* (Washington, DC: April 2001); coal use reduction from DOE, EIA, *International Energy Database*, Washington, DC, updated February 2003.

46. Internet's start from Barry M. Leiner et al., "A Brief History of the Internet," at <www.isoc.org/internet/history/brief.shtml>, 4 August 2000; wind power in California from Peter H. Asmus, *Wind Energy, Green Marketing, and Global Climate Change* (Sacramento, CA: California Regulatory Research Project, June 1999), and from California Energy Commission, "Wind Energy in California," at <www.energy.ca.gov/wind/overview.html>, 15 January 2003.

47. Tony Blair, "Concerted International Effort Necessary to Fight Climate Change," at <www.number-10.gov.uk/output/

Page3073.asp>, 24 February 2003.

48. Gordon Brown, "Marshall Plan for the Next 50 Years," *Washington Post*, 17 December 2001.

49. Gerard Bon, "France's Chirac Backs Tax to Fight World Poverty," *Reuters*, 4 September 2002.

50. Schrempp cited in Frank Swoboda, "Carmaker Shares Global Vision," *Washington Post*, 30 November 2001.

51. U.N. Development Programme, *Millennium Development Goals*, at <www.undp.org/mdg>.

52. Jeffrey Sachs, "One Tenth of 1 Percent to Make the World Safer," *Washington Post*, 21 November 2001.

53. Table 11–1 from Christopher Hellman, "Last of the Big Time Spenders: U.S. Military Budget Still the World's Largest and Growing," Center for Defense Information, at <www.cdi.org/issues/wme/spendersFY03.html>, 4 February 2002, based on data from the International Institute for Strategic Studies and the U.S. Department of Defense; U.S. defense budget includes monies for the Pentagon and for the defense functions of the U.S. Department of Energy, for more detail see "Fiscal Year 2002 Budget," at <www.cdi.org/issues/budget/fy'02/ index.html>.

54. See Table 10–2 and associated discussion for more information.

55. Ibid.

56. Stephan Richter, "The New Global Aid-Defense Standard," *The Globalist*, on-line magazine, 19 March 2002.

57. Japan for Sustainability, "Carbon Tax to be Introduced in FY2005," 14 February 2003, at <www.japanfs.org>.

Index

About the Author

Lester R. Brown is President of Earth Policy Institute, a nonprofit, interdisciplinary research organization based in Washington, D.C., which he founded in May 2001. The purpose of the Earth Policy Institute is to provide a vision of an environmentally sustainable economy, an eco-economy, along with a roadmap of how to get from here to there and an ongoing assessment of where we are moving ahead and where we are not.

Brown has been described as "one of the world's most influential thinkers" by the *Washington Post*. The *Telegraph* of Calcutta called him "the guru of the environmental movement." In 1986, the Library of Congress requested his papers for their archives, noting, "your writings and the work of the Worldwatch Institute under your direction have already strongly affected thinking about problems of world population and resources."

Some 30 years ago, he helped pioneer the concept of environmentally sustainable development, a concept he uses in his design of an eco-economy. He is widely known as the Founder of the Worldwatch Institute and as its President during its first 26 years.

During a career that started with tomato farming, Brown has been awarded over 20 honorary degrees and has written or coauthored some 30 books, including *Eco-Economy: Building an Economy for the Earth,* which E. O. Wilson called "an instant classic." He is also a MacArthur Fellow and the recipient of many prizes and awards, including the 1987 United Nations Environment Prize, the 1989 World Wide Fund for Nature Gold Medal, and the 1994 Blue Planet Prize for his "exceptional contributions to solving global environmental problems." In 1995, Marquis *Who's Who*, on the occasion of its fiftieth edition, selected Lester Brown as one of 50 Great Americans.